W9-CGN-999

THE BUDDHIST FEMININE IDEAL
Queen Śrīmālā and the Tathāgatagarbha

American Academy of Religion Dissertation Series

edited by
H. Ganse Little, Jr.

Number 30

THE BUDDHIST FEMININE IDEAL
Queen Śrīmālā and the Tathāgatagarbha
by
Diana Mary Paul

Diana Mary Paul

The Buddhist Feminine Ideal

Scholars Press

Distributed by
Scholars Press
PO Box 5207
Missoula, Montana 59806

THE BUDDHIST FEMININE IDEAL
Queen Śrīmālā and the Tathāgatagarbha

Diana Mary Paul
Ph.D., 1974, University of Wisconsin
Madison, Wisconsin

Library of Congress Cataloging in Publication Data

Paul, Diana Mary.
The Buddhist feminine ideal.

(Dissertation series - American Academy of Religion ; no. 30 ISSN 0145-272X)
Includes an annotated translation of the Srīmālā-devī-siṁhanāda-sūtra.
Originally published as the author's thesis, University of Wisconsin-Madison, 1974.
Bibliography: p.
1. Srīmālāsūtra—Criticism, interpretation, etc. 2. Tathāgatagarbha (Buddhism) I. Srīmālāsūtra. English. 1979. II. Title. III. Series: American Academy of Religion. Dissertation series - American Academy of Religion ; no. 30
BQ1797.P38 1979 294.3'82 79-12031
ISBN 0-89130-284-0
ISBN 0-89130-303-0 pbk.

Printed in the United States of America
1 2 3 4 5
Edwards Brothers, Inc.
Ann Arbor, MI 48104

INTRODUCTION

The *Śrīmālādevī simhanāda sūtra* (ŚDS) (*The Treatise on the Lion's Roar of Queen Śrīmālā*) is a Mahāyāna text no longer extant in Sanskrit but preserved in both the Chinese and Tibetan *Tripiṭakas*. This text is a unique development within the Buddhist tradition because of its egalitarian view concerning women, portraying, on the one hand, the dignity and wisdom of a laywoman and her concern for all beings, and on the other, the role of woman as a philosopher and teacher. Doctrinally, the major emphasis is upon the Tathāgatagarbha and Ekayāna.

Because of the number of citations and references which are retained in Sanskrit Buddhist texts, the *Śrīmālādevī sūtra* seems to have been widely circulated throughout India. This text is quoted in the *Ratnagotra-vibhāga-mahāyānottara-tantra śāstra* (*The Supreme Exposition of Mahāyāna: A Commentary on the Jewel Lineage*)[1] and the *Śikṣāsamuccaya* (*A Compendium on Instruction*)[2] with allusions made in the *Laṅkāvatāra sūtra* and the *Mahāyāna sūtrālaṃkāra* (*The Ornament of the Mahāyāna sūtras*).[4] The *Ch'eng wei-shih lun* (成唯識論) (*Vijñaptimātratāsiddhi*) by Hsüan-tsang also quotes from the *Śrīmālādevī sūtra* but does not identify the *sūtra* by name.[5]

According to the *Sung kao seng chuan* (宋高僧傳)[6] Bodhiruci used a Sanskrit text of the *Śrīmālādevī sūtra* for reference in translating the text into Chinese. From the above evidence, it may be concluded that a Sanskrit original of the *Śrīmālādevī sūtra* did exist and that this text was part of the Indian Buddhist tradition.

The classical Chinese text is extant in two recensions:

1. *Sheng-man shih-tzu-hou i-ch'eng ta-fang-pien fang-kuang ching* (勝鬘師子吼一乘大方便方廣経) (1 *ch.*) (T.v. 12, no. 353, pp. 217-223), translated by Guṇabhadra (394-468) in 435.
2. *Sheng-man-fu-jen hui* (勝鬘夫人會) which is the forty-eighth assembly in the *Ratnakūṭa* anthology (*Ta-pao chi ching*) (大宝積経) (T.v. 11, no. 310,

pp. 672-678), translated by Bodhiruci[7] (572-727) of T'ang between 706 and 713.

Because Guṇabhadra's translation is almost three hundred years older than Bodhiruci's, it has been chosen as the basic text in order to trace the development of Tathāgatagarbha thought in its original form. Bodhiruci's translation is used when Guṇabhadra's translation is ambiguous and when differences in interpretation are indicated.

The Tibetan recension, *Ḥphags-pa lha-mo dpal-phreṅ gi seṅ-geḥi sgra shes-bya-ba theg-pa chen-poḥi mdo* (Tōhoku no. 92, *Bkaḥ-ḥgyur*), which is part of the *Ratnakūṭa* anthology, will not be used. When significant differences between the Chinese and Tibetan recensions occur, the Tibetan text will be noted also.[8]

The commentaries which are extant are few and only in Chinese and Japanese. There are no Tibetan commentaries now extant, which discuss only the *Śrīmālādevī sūtra*.[9] According to the *Kao seng chuan* (高僧傳),[10] immediately after the translation of the *Śrīmālādevī sūtra* many commentaries were composed by monks who had studied and memorized the *Śrīmālādevī sūtra*. These texts, now lost, were dated between the fifth and sixth centuries A.D. According to Chi-tsang's *Sheng-man ching pao-k'u*, monks studied and composed commentaries on the *Śrīmālādevī sūtra* from the North-South dynastic periods through the Sui (i.e. from approximately 440-618 A.D.).

The major commentaries[11] extant in Chinese are:

1. *Hsieh-chu sheng-man ching* (挾注勝鬘経) (T.v. 85, no. 2763). Although the commentator is unknown, this text was probably the composition of a noble woman of Northern Wei, attested to by the calligraphy and literary style of the Tun-huang manuscript. Completed before 500 A.D., it is the oldest extant commentary on the *Śrīmālādevī sūtra*.[12] Only Chapter 5, "Ekayāna," is discussed.
2. *Sheng-man ching i-chi* (勝鬘経義記) (2 *ch.*) (*Dainihon zokuzōkyō*, v. 1, no. 30-1) by Hui-yüan (慧遠). (523-692) of Sui. Only the first half of the text is extant, corresponding to the first four chapters of the *Śrīmālādevī sūtra*.
3. *Sheng-man ching pao-k'u* (勝鬘経宝窟), (3 *ch.*)

(T.v. 37, no. 1744) by Chi-tsang (吉蔵) (549-623) of Sui.

4. *Sheng-man ching shu-chi* (勝鬘経述記), (2 *ch.*) (*Dainihon zokuzōkyō*, v. 1, no. 30-4) by K'uei-chi (窺基) (632-682) of T'ang.
5. *Sheng-man ching su-i ssu-ch'ao* (勝鬘経疏義私鈔), (6 *ch.*) (*Dainihon bukkyō zensho*, v. 4) by Ming-k'ung (明空)[13] of T'ang in 772.

The major commentaries extant by Japanese Buddhists are:

1. *Shōmangyō gisho* (勝鬘経義疏) (1 *ch.*) (T.v. 56, no. 2184) attributed to Prince Shōtoku (聖徳太子) (573-621) but probably the composition of a North Chinese Buddhist scholar.[14]
2. *Shōmangyō shoshō genki* (勝鬘経義詳玄記), (18 *ch.*) (*Dainihon bukkyō zensho*, v. 4) by Gyōnen (凝然) (1240-1321). First five *chüan* are missing. The extant text begins with the chapter "The Ten Ordination Vows."
3. *Shōman-shishikugyō kenshūshō* (勝鬘師子吼経顕宗鈔) (3 *ch.*) (*Nihon daizōkyō*, v. 5; *Dainihon bukkyō zensho*, v. 4) by Fūjaku (普寂) (1707-1781)

The *Sheng-man ching pao-k'u* and the *Shōmangyō gisho* are the two primary commentaries upon which the present study's interpretation of the *Śrīmālādevī sūtra* is based. These two commentaries have been selected because the former, written by a San-lun master, interprets Tathāgatagarbha from a Mādhyamikan perspective whereas the latter is representative of the North Chinese scholars' interpretation and frequently overshadows the sūtra itself in popularity, particularly in Japan. The *Sheng-man ching i-chi* and the *Hsieh-chu sheng-man ching* are used as references in analyzing Chapters 4 and 5, "The Acceptance of the true Dharma" and the "One Vehicle" respectively of the *Śrīmālādevī sūtra*.

In Chapter One, a historical analysis will be attempted, suggesting the place and time of composition on the basis of external and internal evidence now available. In Chapter Two, the evolution of the Tathāgatagarbha will be outlined, based upon the first two Tathāgatagarbhan texts, the *Tathāgatagarbha sūtra* and the *Pu tseng pu chien ching* (不増不減経), which predate the *Śrīmālādevī sūtra*.[15]

In Chapter Three the characteristic format of the *Śrīmālādevī sūtra* is summarized in relation to the *Tathāgatagarbha sūtra* and the *Pu tseng pu chien*. In Chapter Four the Tathāgatagarbha as presented in the *Śrīmālādevī-siṁhanāda sūtra* is analyzed with relation to the text as a whole, and in Chapter Five the annotated translation of the *Śrīmālādevī-siṁhanāda sūtra* is presented with notations of key differences between the two Chinese recensions and with references made to the two commentaries, *Sheng-man ching pao-k'u* and *Shōmangyō gisho*, and to the *Sanskrit* fragments noted above.

Appendix I is an attempt to lay the groundwork for a methodology of Buddhist studies which would provide a foundation for the skills needed for a critical analysis and interpretation of Buddhist phenomena. Appendix II is an annotated bibliography for studying the *Śrīmālādevī-siṁhanāda sūtra*. Appendix I is admittedly limited and will provide only the most general outline of the requisite methodological procedure in analyzing a Buddhist text.

INTRODUCTION

NOTES

[1]There are two English translations of the *Ratnagotravibhāga-mahāyānottara-tantra śāstra*: E. E. Obermiller, *The Sublime Science of the Great Vehicle to Salvation Being a Manual of Buddhist Monism* (Rome: *Acta Orientalia*, 1932), (Shanghai reprint: 1940) and Jikido Takasaki, *A Study on the Ratnagotravibhāga (Uttaratantra): Being a Treatise on the Tathāgatagarbha Theory of Mahāyāna Buddhism* (Rome: Series Orientale Rome XXIII, 1966). The Sanskrit text of the *Ratnagotra-vibhāga-mahāyānottara-tantra śāstra*, ed. by E. H. Johnston (Patna: Bihar Society, 1950) cites the *Śrīmālādevī sūtra* on pp. 3, 12, 15, 19, 20, 22, 30, 33, 34, 36, 37, 45, 50, 55, 56, 59, 72, 73, 74, 76 and 79. A portion of these Sanskrit fragments have been noted below in the translation, wherever differences or ambiguities in the Chinese recensions occur.

[2]Cf. *Çikshāsamuccaya* (*A Compendium on Buddhist Teaching*, ed. by Cecil Bendall (St. Petersburg: Imperial Academy of Sciences, (1897-1902), vol. I of *Bibliotheca Buddhica*, reprinted by *Indo-Iranian Journal* (The Hague: Mounton & Co., 1957), pp. 42 and 43.

[3]Cf. *Laṅkāvatāra sūtra*, ed. by Bunyiu Nanjio (Second edition, Kyoto: Otani University Press, 1956), p. 222 line 19 and p. 223 line 4.

[4]Cf. *Mahāyāna sūtrālaṁkāra*, ed. by Sylvain Lévi (Paris: 1907), (Shanghai reprint: 1940), Tome 1 (XI, 59), p. 70. The cited passage, attributed to the *Śrīmālādevī sūtra*, could not be found in either Chinese recension. Lévi also was unable to find the passage but does allude to the citation as being in the *Çikshāsamuccaya*, ed. by Cecil Bendall, *op. cit.*, but these two citations are not of the same passage.

[5]The following citations are quoted in the *Ch'eng wei-shih lun*, translated by Hsüan-tsang (T.v. 31, no. 1585, pp. 1-60):

a. 契経説心性浄者説心空理所顕真如
(2 *ch.*, p. 20) (Refers to ŚDS T.v. 12, no. 353, p. 222b)

b. 如契経説如取為縁有漏業因、続後有者而生三有. 如是無明習地為縁無漏業因、有阿羅漢独覚已得. 自在菩薩生三種意成身.
(8 *ch.*, p. 24) (ŚDS) p. 220a)

c. 若所知障有見疑等、如何此種契経説為無明住地.
(9 *ch.*, p. 7) (ŚDS p. 220a)

d. 若声聞等有無余依、如何有処説彼非有. 有処説彼都無涅槃. 豈有余依彼亦非有.
(10 *ch.*, pp. 10-11) (ŚDS p. 219a)

[6] 中宗神龍二年又住京北崇神寺譯大宝積経...其経旧新凡四十九會總一百二十巻. 先天二年四月八日進内此譯場中沙門思忠天竺大首領伊舍羅等譯梵文. 天竺沙門波若屈多沙門達摩證梵義.

> "In the second year of T'ang emperor Chung-tsung in the reign of Shen-lung (706) he (Bodhiruci) returned to the capital (Loyang) to Chao ch'ung-fu temple to translate the *Mahāratnakūta* anthology. This anthology had forty-nine old and new assemblies, totaling 120 *ch.*, which were finished in the fourth month, eighth day of the second year of Hsien-t'ien (713). In the translation hall, the monks Ssu-chung and the Indian director Iśara (?) translated the Sanskrit while the Indian monks Prajñāgupta (?) and Dharma were consulted concerning the Sanskrit meaning." (T.v. 50, no. 2061, p. 702b)

The *Sung kao seng chuan*, 30 *ch.*, was compiled by Chih-lun (智輪) and Tsan-ning (贊寧) of the Sung dynasty during the period from the beginning of the T'ang dynasty until 967 according to Ui Hakuju, *Bukkyō jiten* (*A Buddhist Dictionary*) (Tokyo: Daitō shuppansha, 1971), p. 654 and until 988 according to Nakamura Hajime, *Shin-bukkyō jiten* (*The New Buddhist Dictionary*), (Tokyo: Seishin shōbō, 1972), p. 329.

[7] According to the *Sung kao seng chuan*, *op. cit.*, (p. 720c) Bodhiruci died in the fifteenth year of K'ai-yüan (727) of T'ang at the age of 156.

[8] The differences noted between the Chinese and Tibetan recensions are based upon the *Shōmangyō hōgatsu dōji shomongyō* (Kyoto: Kōkyō shoin, 1940) by Tsukinowa Kenryū.

[9] Tibetan commentaries on the *Ratnagotravibhāga* do interpret the passages which cite the *Śrīmālādevī sūtra*. These are not discussed within the present study.

[10] *Kokyuaku-issaikyō hōshaku-bu shichi*, Ono Masao (gen. ed.) (Tokyo: Daitō shuppansha, 1958), p. 84 lists the monks who attempted to write commentaries now lost. The *Kao seng chuan*, compiled by Hui-chao (慧皎) of the Liang dynasty, is the record of approximately 253 eminent monks from 67 A.D. through 519 A.D. Cf. Ui, *Shin-bukkyō jiten*, *op. cit.*, p. 303.

[11] For a complete listing of all commentaries in both Chinese and Japanese, extant and no longer extant, see below--Appendix II, Annotated Bibliography.

[12] Fujieda Akira, "Hokucho ni okeru *Shōmangyō no tenshō*" in *Tōhō gakuhō*, v. XL, 1973, p. 334. (Journal of the Institute of Humanities) (Jimbun Kagaku kenkyūsho) (Kyoto University).

[13] According to the *Bussho kaisetsu daijiten*, Ono Masao (gen. ed.) (Tokyo: Daitō shuppansha, 1966), vol. V, p. 350, this text was composed by both Prince Shōtoku and Ming-k'ung.

[14]Prince Shōtoku most probably did not compose the *Shōmangyō gisho* since many of the texts which the *Gisho* cites were not known to Prince Shōtoku but were introduced to Japan at a much later date. For the transmission of the Chinese commentaries on the *Śrīmālādevī-siṁhanāda sūtra*, see "Hokucho ni okeru *Shōmangyō*," *op. cit.* For the "original" Gisho, composed by a Chinese scholar of the North-South dynastic period, residing in North China, see "Shōman gisho hongi" in *Shōtoku taishi kenkyū*, v. 5 (Osaka: Shitennoji Joshi Daigaku, 1973) by Koizumi Enjun in which the original Chinese commentary is edited and later almost entirely copied in the *Shōmangyō gisho*.

The research on these commenaries at the time of this writing has been undertaken by members of the Jimbun Kagaku kenkyusho who are affiliated with Kyoto University. From analyzing the Tun-huang manuscripts, two very similar hypotheses have been developed:

a. The Gisho itself was written by a Chinese scholar, or
b. The original for the *Shōmangyō gisho*, viz. *Shōman gisho hongi* (or, *Sheng-man i-su ben-i*), was composed by a Northern Chinese scholar and later almost entirely interpolated into the *Shōmangyō gisho* by Prince Shōtoku or one of his followers.

[15]The analysis of Tathāgatagarbha was undertaken in consultation with Professors Yuichi Kajiyama, Chairman of Buddhist Studies, Kyoto University, and Gadjin Nagao, Professor Emeritus in Buddhist Studies, Kyoto University.

CHAPTER I

HISTORICAL OVERVIEW

Place of Composition

The geographical location where Mahāyāna literature seems to have first emerged is southeast India, perhaps the Āndhra region. The majority view[1] is that, between 100 B.C. and 200 A.D., a profusion of Mahāyāna Buddhist literature developed in southeast India, centered in the Āndhra district which was an apparent Mahāsaṅghikan stronghold.

The Kharoṣṭī and Brahmī inscriptions as well as those at Nāgārjunakoṇḍa, c. 2nd-3rd C. A.D., demonstrate that the Mahāsaṅghikan sphere of influence was greatest in the southern districts of Guntur and Krishna where the Caityaka and Śaila, Mahāsaṅghikan offshoots, were popular.[2]

> Tout en gardant jusqu'à l'époque de Yi-tsing (fin du VIIe s.) le gros de leurs forces au Magadha, les Mahāsāṁghika, au cours de leur longue histoire, avaient dèjá essaimé à Mathurā en pays Śūrasena, à Wardak dans le Nord-Ouest, où ils détenaient le Varamaregra vihāra, et aussi à Karli sur la côte occidentale, où ils voisinaient avec des Dharmottarīya. Mais aux premiers siècles de l'ère, le fief principal des Mahāsāṁghika fut le pays Āndhra et plus spécialement le district de Guntur: la secte y prend souvent le titre d'Ayirahamgha "Sainte commaunauté." Elle s'y fractionna en nombreuses écoles, notamment Bahuśrutīya, Caitika ou Śaila.[3]

The Caityakans' date of appearance remains unknown. According to Paramārtha, a new Mahādeva caused trouble in the Saṅgha by falsely ordaining monks. From inscriptions at Amarāvatī, it appears that this Mahādeva and his disciples were forced to retreat to the mountains of Āndhra, after having been expelled from the Ganges' valley. The Pūrva Śailas and Apara Śailas, Caityakan offshoots, are equally obscure as to date of appearance. Because the difference between the Caiytakans and the Śailans is virtually ignored, it can be concluded that their tenets were almost identical.[4]

Paramārtha also states that two hundred years after the Mahāsaṅghika developed (second century B.C.), the Mahāsaṅghika divided into three sects, Ekavyavahārika, Lokottaravāda, and

Kukkuṭika. They quoted the *Avataṁsaka*, *Mahāparinirvāṇa*, *Śrīmālādevī*, *Vimalakīrti*, *Suvarnaprabhāsa*, *Prajñāpāramitā*, and other Mahāyāna sūtras in the course of their development. Some believed in these sūtras while others did not.[5] No dates are given for the acceptance of these sūtras, nor the locality at the time of acceptance.

The Caityakans, or one of their offshoots, the Pūrva (or Uttara) and Apara Śailas, may have developed the very first *Prajñāpāramitā* text upon which the *Aṣṭasāhasrikā-prajñāparamitā sūtra* was based:

> Near Amarāvatī ("The sojourn of the immortals") and Dhānyakaṭaka (the modern Dharanikot), the Mahāsaṅghika had two famous monasteries which gave their names to the sects of the Pūrvaśailas and of the Aparaśailas. These sects 1) had a Prajñāpāramitā in Prakrit; they 2) spoke of the dharmadhātu in the same sense as the Prajñāpāramitā, and 3) their Buddhology prepared that of the Prajñāpāramitā. The doctrines which the *Kathāvatthu* attributes to the Andhakas are so much akin to the Mahāyāna doctrines that the latter may well have developed from them.[6]

However, according to Bareau, only a brief description of the Apara Śaila's canon is given in an inscription at Nāgārjunakoṇḍa, omitting any mention of a Prajñā literature. The Uttara Śaila are placed among the later Mahāsaṅghika, along with the Apara Śailas and little distinction is made between the two Śailan sects and the Mahāsaṅghika.

We can hypothesize, however, that the *Aṣṭa-sāhasrikā-prajñāpāramitā sūtra* developed in the southeastern region of India because the text itself describes the direction of transmission as beginning in the South, then East, and then towards the North.[8] The relationship between the Mahāsaṅghikan sects and the *Prajñāpāramitā*, however, is still unknown today.

Nāgārjuna (c. 150-250 A.D.), through whom the *Prajñāpāramitā* was disseminated throughout the South, was born near Śrī Parvata or Śrī Śailam[9] where he spent the majority of his life. Because he is associated with the Āndhra district, the *Prajñāpāramitā* may have been composed in this region, being favorably received by the Mahāsaṅghikan who were amenable to the ideas exemplified in the *Aṣṭasāhasrikā*, having themselves developed theories of intrinsically pure mind,[10] a transcendental Buddha, and Bodhisattva stages.[11] Moreover, the deification of Wisdom as a female goddess would be conducive to the southeastern regions of India where matriarchal societies were present:

> In this area (Dhānyakaṭaka) both Dravidian and Greek influences made themselves felt, and Grousset has rightly called the Stūpa of Amarāvatī a "Dravido-Alexandrian synthesis." In view of the close analogies which exist between the Prajñāpāramitā and the Mediterranean literature on Sophia, this seems to me significant. Also, the Āndhras were a non-Aryan people who spoke a Telugu language, and the matriarchal traditions of the Dravidians may well have something to do with the introduction of the worship of the "Mother of the Buddhas" into Buddhism.[12]

The *Śrīmālādevī sūtra* is related to the *Prajñāpāramitā* literature in the following manner:

1. In the *Aṣṭasāhasrikā-prajñāpāramitā* (Gaṅgādevībhāginī) (XIX, 11.365-9, p. 53), there is the prediction of the future Buddhahood of the Ganges goddess, after transforming into the body of a man. In the *Śrīmālādevī sūtra*, the Buddha predicts that Queen Śrīmālā will become the Buddha Samantaprabhā, without specifying the transformation of sex. Moreover, the Buddha Samantaprabhā (P'u-kuang) (普光) is portrayed in the Chinese pantheon as the "Mother of the Buddhas" (fo-mu) (佛母).[13]

2. Doctrinally, the *Śrīmālādevī sūtra* is an exegesis on Emptiness which attributes positive qualities to this concept, considered to be the ultimate and final cycle of the Buddha's teaching on Emptiness.[14] Consequently, it is considered a text which completely explains the concept of Emptiness embodied in the *Prajñāpāramitā*.

3. The ideas of intrinsically pure mind, Dharma-nature (*dharmadhātu*) and the Acceptance of the true Dharma (*Saddharma-parigraha*)[15] which are doctrinal tenets in the *Prajñāpāramitā* literature are maintained in the Tathāgatagarbhan literature, particularly in the *Śrīmālādevī sūtra* and the *Ratnagotravibhāga*.

4. Like the *Prajñāpāramitā*, the *Śrīmālādevī sūtra* addresses the members of the assembly as "good sons" (*kula putrāḥ*) and "good daughters" (*kula duhitāraḥ*), thus including women in the audience.

Other evidence which links the *Śrīmālādevī sūtra* to the *Prajñāpāramitā* is found in the *Ratnakūṭa* (*The Collection of*

Jewels) anthology (T.v. 11, no. 310) (100 *ch.*), now extant in forty-nine assemblies, in which the *Śrīmālādevī sūtra* is incorporated as the forty-eighth assembly and *Wen-chu shuo po-ju* (文殊說般若) (*Mañjuśri Explains the Prajñāpāramitā*) is incorporated as the forty-sixth assembly.

The *Ratnakūṭa* was originally the name of the *Kāśyapa parivarta*, now incorporated as the forty-third assembly. According to the Theravāda,[16] in the *Nikāyasaṅgraha*, the *Ratnakūṭa* (as a sūtra) was composed by the Āndhra schools, most probably by the Caityaka. Consequently the Āndhra Mahāsaṅghika may have composed both a *Prajñāpāramitā* and the *Kāśyapa parivarta*, one of the oldest discourses on Emptiness accepted as Mahāyānist.

The anthology of forty-nine assemblies, now collectively designated the *Ratnakūṭa*, was translated by Bodhiruci of T'ang between 706 and 713, approximately six hundred years after the composition of the *Kāśyapa parivarta*, incorporating fourteen sūtras which are independently listed in the *Mahāvyutpatti*. Bodhiruci re-translated some old recensions and retained others. According to the catalogue for the Derge edition of the Tibetan *Tripitaka*, the *Ratnakūṭa* is claimed to be a compilation of forty-nine sūtras from India, Khotan, and China,[17] suggesting the collation of the anthology may have taken place in either China or Central Asia. Moreover, some of the assemblies in the Tibetan recension of the *Ratnakūṭa* were based on the Chinese rather than the Sanskrit, but the *Śrīmālādevī sūtra* was not one of these. Consequently, there can be no single place of composition for this anthology, due to the diversity of the texts incorporated.

Because the *Śrīmālādevī sūtra* is the only one of the forty-nine assemblies which discusses Tathāgatagarbha, its incorporation into the *Ratnakūṭa* must be due to its analysis of Emptiness and to its association with *Prajñāpāramitā* literature. The fact that both the *Prajñāpāramitā* and *Ratnakūṭa* are associated with the Āndhra district suggests that the *Śrīmālādevī sūtra* may also have originated in that area, later being incorporated along with other Āndhran texts, into the *Ratnakūṭa* in the eighth century. The prototypic models for Tathāgatagarbha literature in general, viz.

intrinsically pure mind and Dharma-nature, also indicate that the Āndhra region was a suitable place for the fermentation of these ideas embodied in both the concepts of Prajñāpāramitā and Tathāgatagarbha.[18]

A particularly differentiating characteristic found in both the *Śrīmālādevī sūtra* and the *Mahāvibhāṣa*, concerns the scheme of defilement and its disassociation from the intrinsically pure mind. It will be demonstrated below[19] that the analysis of defilement presented in the *Śrīmālādevī sūtra* must be related to the defilement schema developed by the Mahāsaṅghika of either Āndhra or of one of the other subsects, the Ekavyavahārika, Lokottaravāda, or Kukkuṭika. The *Śrīmālādevī-siṁhanāda sūtra* may also have been influenced by the Mahāsanghika with reference to the levels (*bhūmi*) which are attained only by the Tathāgata. These levels are identical to those in the *Mahāvastu*, the first book of the *Vinayapiṭaka* of the Lokottaravädin sect of Mahāsaṅghika.[20]

In addition, the introduction to the Chinese recension of the *Ekottarikāgama*, in which the term "Tathāgatagarbha" first appears, may also be the composition of a Mahāsaṅghikan sect.

> De plus, les indications contenues dans la préface de la traduction chinoise de l'*Ekottarāgama* montrent que, selon toutes probabilitiés, la recension de celui-ci ainsi traduite appartenait à une secte Mahāsaṅghika.[21]

The passage in which "Tathāgatagarbha" appears will be discussed in the next chapter.

The above evidence which suggests that the *Śrīmālādevī sūtra* may have originated in the Āndhra district of southeast India, retaining certain Mahāsaṅghikan characteristics, centers on three major factors:

1. The relationship with *Prajñāpāramitā*: The female symbolism, the inclusion of women in the assembly, and the illustration of a woman who becomes a Buddha are distinctive features in both the Prajñāpāramitā and Tathāgatagarbhan literatures, characteristics appropriate to matriarchal societies such as those found in Āndhra. The affinity of ideas, viz. intrinsically pure mind, Dharma-nature, and the Acceptance of the true Dharma reinforces the hypothesis that these two literatures are closely related. Moreover, the *Śrīmālādevī*

sūtra is considered within the third and ultimate teaching of the Dharma wheel, completely understanding the meaning of Emptiness.

2. The relationship with the *Ratnakūṭa*: Like the *Kāśyapa parivarta*, the *Śrīmālādevī sūtra* is associated with the *Prajñāpāramitā* vis-à-vis the teaching of Emptiness. The Mahāsaṅghika of Āndhra, who may have composed the *Kāśyapa parivarta*, perhaps had access to the more recent text, the *Śrīmālādevī sūtra*, both being collated into the anthology *Ratnakūṭa* at a much later date. Further evidence which suggests that the *Śrīmālādevī sūtra* was known and accepted by the Mahāsaṅghika is provided by Paramārtha in his history of Buddhism.

3. The relationship to the Mahāsaṅghikan interpretation of defilement and Tathāgata-bhūmi: The *Śrīmālādevī sūtra* borrows the Tathāgata-bhūmi from the *Mahāvastu*. It also analyzes adventitious defilement and its disassociation from the intrinsically pure mind concordant with the Mahāsaṅghikan tradition. The preface to the *Ekottarikāgama*, in which "Tathāgatagarbha" is first mentioned, indicates the Mahāsaṅghika had attributed some significance to this term.

All three factors indicate Mahāsaṅghikan influence over the *Śrīmālādevī sūtra*. The Mahāsaṅghika themselves, however, divided into eight recorded sects whose literature and traditions have been almost totally lost, obfuscating any identification of tenets with a particular subsect.

From the Chinese records it is possible to indicate the general routes of the first translators who introduced Tathāgatagarbha texts, including the *Śrīmālādevī sūtra*, to China, viz. Dharmakṣema, Buddhabhadra, Guṇabhadra and Bodhiruci of Northern Wei. By retracing their routes from available evidence, in certain cases one may postulate the point of disembarkment from Indian soil.

The oldest Tathāgatagarbhan text, the *Mahāvaipulya Tathāgatagarbha sūtra*,[22] was first translated by Fa-li (法立) and Fa-chü (法炬) in the late third century, prior to the fall of Loyang in 311 and Ch'ang-an in 316. Almost nothing is known of these two monks with regard to their personal history. Both were from Western Tsin and collaborated in the translation of the *Ekottarikāgama* which is also no longer extant.[23] Fa-chü also translated the *Aṅgulimala sūtra* (T.v. 2, no. 119) which is now considered a Tathāgatagarbhan text but has been erroneously incorporated in the Āgama division of the Chinese *Tripiṭaka* along with Guṇabhadra'a translation (T.v.2, no. 120).[24]

After the fall of Loyang and Ch'ang-an, non-Chinese clans of Turkic and Tibetan origin gained the hegemony over north China. Some of these clansmen were to become devout Buddhists, particularly during the reign of Yao-hsing (393-415), when Kumārajīva (344-413) established his translation center at Ch'ang-an in 401 and Fa-hsien first journeyed to India two years prior to its establishment. At that time, Central Asian influences on Chinese culture were to be at their zenith for three hundred years, with a continual flow of Buddhist texts into north China.

A Central Indian scholar who rose to prominence at this time was Dharmakṣema (385-433) who arrived in Liang-chou, capital of the Pei Liang dynasty, in 413. He was soon appointed royal advisor by the Turkic ruler Chü-ch'ü Meng-hsün[25] because of his reputed powers of the occult. Soon he became invaluable as a military advisor, coveted by other clans. Of the translations credited to Dharmakṣema, the most noteworthy for subsequent Chinese Buddhism was the first Chinese translation of the *Mahāparinirvāṇa sūtra* (大般涅槃經) (T. v. 12, no. 356), a Mahāyāna text explicating Buddha-nature and Tathāgatagarbha, translated between 416 and 423.[26] When Dharmakṣema left for Central Asia to appropriate other Sanskrit editions of the *Mahāparinirvāṇa sūtra*, Chü-ch'ü Meng-hsün suspected him of treason and had him assassinated. Other translations attributed to him are the *Laṅkāvatāra* and the *Śrīmālādevī* but these are doubtful since no earlier catalogues record them.[27]

At approximately the same time that Dharmakṣema was translating at Liang-chou, Buddhabhadra (359-429), a North Indian from Kapilavastu, was translating the *Mahāvaipulya Tathāgatagarbha sūtra* (T.v. 16, no. 666) at Kumārajīva's translation center, having been persuaded to go to China by Chih-yen, companion to Fa-hsien, while they were in Kashmir.

After arriving in Ch'ang-an in 406, Buddhabhadra worked with Kumārajīva for several years, until a dispute over the meaning of Emptiness forced him to move south in 410 or 411, where he translated meditational texts with Hui-yüan (344-416), the Pure Land patriarch, at Tung-lin temple in Lu-shan of Kiangsi province. He also translated the *Mo-ho-seng-ch'i lü* (摩訶僧祇律) (*Mahāsaṅghika Vinaya*) (T.v. 22, no. 1425) at the request of Fa-hsien.[28] Saṅghadeva, the Kashmirian Mahāsaṅghika master who may have written the preface to the *Ekottarikāgama*, was also residing there at that time.

Guṇabhadra (394-468), a Central Indian scholar who departed for Canton in 435 via Ceylon, brought the first Vijñānavādin literature with him, only to be virtually neglected until late Wei, when Ratnamati, Bodhiruci and Buddhaśanta would come to China to translate Vijñānavādin texts. In the seventy year interim, Gunabhadra's *Hsiang-hsü chieh-t'o ti po-lo-mi liao-i ching* (相続解脱地波羅密了義経 (*The Treatise on the Complete Meaning of the Pāramitās and the Liberation from Saṁsāra*), later incorporated as chapters four and five of the *Saṅdhinirmocana*, was ignored by Chinese scholars.

Working closely with Hui-yen (慧厳) and Hui-kuan (慧観), Guṇabhadra corrected Dharmakṣema's translation of the *Mahāparinirvāṇa sūtra* in the capital of the Liu Sung kingdom, Chien-k'ang, near present Nanking. He then left for Ch'i-heng (祇桓) temple in Nan-king to translate the *Samyuktāgama*. At Tung-an (東安) temple he translated the *Mahābherihāraka parivarta* (*Ta-fa ku ching*) (大法鼓経), a Tathāgatagarbhan text, and at Tan-yang (丹陽) temple he translated the above-mentioned segment of the *Saṅdhinirmocana*, *Śrīmālādevī sūtra*, and *Laṅkāvatāra*. The translation of the *Śrīmālādevī sūtra* was in collaboration with Pao-yün, disciple of Kumārajīva and companion to Fa-hsien, who translated the Sanskrit text into Chinese, discussing the meaning with Guṇabhadra.[29]

In the northern capital, Loyang, Bodhiruci of Northern Wei, formerly a North Indian, was also translating the *Laṅkāvatāra* (T.v. 6, no. 480) and the complete translation of the

Saṁdhinirmocana as well as the *Daśabhūmikasūtraśāstra* by Vasubandhu, translated in collaboration with Ratnamati. His other translations include the *Pu tseng pu chien ching* which is a Tathāgatagarbhan text predating the *Śrīmālādevī sūtra*, the *Ch'eng wei-shih lun* (*Vijñaptimātratā siddhi*), the *Vajracchedika-prajñāpāramitā śāstra*, the *Saddharmapuṇḍarīka* and the *Smaller Sukhāvatīvyūha*, now lost. Bodhiruci was also founder of the Ti-lun school,[30] the forerunner of the Hua-yen school, as well as a Pure Land follower responsible for the converstion in 530 of T'an-luan (476-542) who was the great disseminator of Pure Land in North China.[31]

Of the four principal early translators of Tathāgatagarbhan texts, three are associated with north China for at least part of their careers as translators, viz. Dharmakṣema, Buddhabhadra, and Bodhiruci. Two of the three, Buddhabhadra and Bodhiruci, are from North India, and all three went to China via Central Asia. None of the four translators were from South India, although Guṇabhadra most likely travelled southeast along the Indian coast, before departing by sea for Canton.

The Central Asian countries were an important source for the Sanskrit recensions of the *Mahāparinirvāṇa sūtra*, as evidenced by Dharmakṣema's ill-fated trip. Central Asia may also have been the location for the collation of the *Ratnakūṭa* anthology. In addition, the overwhelming majority of early commentaries on the *Śrīmālādevī-siṁhanāda sūtra* during the North-South dynastic periods[32] were first composed in North China, based upon available manuscripts, all exclusively from Tun-huang. If Tun-huang were one of the centers for the distribution of Tathāgatagarbhan texts, then Central Asia was certainly one very important source for China's appropriation of not only the *Mahāparinirvāṇa sūtra* but also for the early Tathāgatagarbhan texts such as the *Mahāvaipulya Tathāgatagarbha sūtra* and the *Pu tseng pu chien ching*.

Since the earliest commentary on the *Śrīmālādevī sūtra*, viz. *Hsieh-chu sheng-man ching*, dated no later than 500 A.D., was written in north China, Guṇabhadra's translation of the *Śrīmālādevī sūtra* in the southern city of Nanking must have been rapidly disseminated to the north. The frequent interaction between monks of north and south China verifies that regionalization of Buddhist texts had terminated, resulting in rapid dissemination throughout China. However, the catalogues record two translations prior to Guṇabhadra's, the above-mentioned one attributed to Dharmakṣema which is doubtful and the other, also questionable, by an obscure monk named Seng Fa-ni (僧法尼) of Ch'i, said to have translated the *Śrīmālādevī sūtra* in 320.[33] Both monks resided in north China.

In addition, scholars associated with Guṇabhadra had contact with north China, although Guṇabhadra himself never went to the north. Hui-kuan, one of the principal commentators on the *Śrīmālādevī sūtra* who had assisted Guṇabhadra in revising Dharmakṣema's translation of the *Mahāparinirvāṇa*, must have had either direct access to this northern text or had appropriated it from a northern scholar. Pao-yün, co-translator of the *Śrīmālādevī* recension bearing Guṇabhadra's name, had developed proficiency in Sanskrit during his apprenticeship under Kumārajīva. Because of his age and scholastic reputation, Pao-yun's interpretation of the text was not contested by Guṇabhadra. He may have acquired the Sanskrit text while in north China, transporting it to the south to translate together with Guṇabhadra.

The prior two translations, attributed to Seng Fa-ni and Dharmakṣema, mentioned in the Chinese catalogues as emerging in north China, are perhaps an indication that the Sanskrit text was first imported to north China through Central Asia, even though the circumstances remain obscure. If no translation prior to Guṇabhadra's ever existed, the two prior translations recorded in the catalogues may have been due to the availability of a Sanskrit text which had been circulated with abortive attempts at translation. If one rejects the hypothesis that the Sanskrit text was first accessible in the northern regions of China, then the dissemination of Guṇabhadra's translation must be regarded as remarkably rapid, having been translated in 435, first read by southern scholars and then transported to north China to be studied and disseminated within a period of approximately sixty years when the commentary *Hsieh-chu sheng-man ching* was completed.[34]

From the lack of concrete evidence concerning the importation of the Sanskrit text of the *Śrīmālādevī sūtra*, one may only definitely claim that intense translation activity and composition of commentaries were taking place throughout China during the North-South dynastic periods, facilitating the transportation of Sanskrit texts from both the north and south through the cooperation between monks. Because Tun-huang was one particularly popular center for the analysis and composition of treatises on the *Śrīmālādevī sūtra*, it is valid to postulate that the *Śrīmālādevī sūtra* was first imported through this area for the following reasons:

1. Related Tathāgatagarbhan literature now extant first came to north China through Central Asia.
2. The three principal translators of these texts, with the exception of Guṇabhadra, came to China via Central Asia.
3. All four translators had means of communicating with northeast China where many Sanskrit texts were being translated. In addition, during Northern Wei, Central Asia had close diplomatic relations with northeast China, particularly with flourishing Buddhist countries such as Khotan, Kashgar, Karashar, and Kucha, all located west of Tun-huang.
4. One source of texts later collected in the *Mahāratnakūṭa* was Central Asia, particularly Khotan.
5. The overwhelming majority of early commentaries on the *Śrīmālādevī sūtra* were excavated at Tun-huang, the earliest composed no more than sixty years after Guṇabhadra's translation, perhaps even earlier since the manuscript may not have been the first printed. The earliest excavated manuscripts of the *Śrīmālādevī sūtra*, however, are dated sixth century (c. 511-514)[35] and are of the Northern Dynastic style, suggesting that there were earlier manuscripts in order to have composed commentaries prior to 500 A.D. but these are now lost.
6. Dharmakṣema's name is associated with both the *Śrīmālādevī* and *Laṅkāvatāra* sūtras. Although this is probably a false attribution, the fact that Dharmakṣema

was the first translator of the *Mahāparinirvāṇa sūtra* (which later was closely associated with the *Śrīmālādevī sūtra* in the *Pao-k'u*) suggests that a tradition developed which related the incipience of Tathāgatagarbha literature with Dharmakṣema who resided in Liang-chou in Chü-ch'ü Meng-hsün's kingdom (which included Tun-huang). As a royal advisor to Meng-hsün, Dharmakṣema most likely had access to all the Tun-huang materials available after his initial accumulation of texts at Tun-huang on his way to Liang-chou, upon first arriving in China.

7. Dharmakṣema, in leaving to obtain other Sanskrit editions of the *Mahāparinirvāṇa sūtra*, chose Central Asia as the source for his material.
8. The proximity in time of the two translations, the *Mahāparinirvāṇa sūtra* (416-423) and the *Śrīmālādevī sūtra* (435) suggests that both are cotemporaneous in composition the former perhaps slightly earlier in formation.
9. The translation of the *Śrīmālādevī sūtra* attributed to Seng Fa-ni suggests that the Sanskrit text may have existed in north China during his time.
10. Pao-yün, co-translator with Guṇabhadra of the earliest extant translation, had resided in north China for many years, easily having access to all Sanskrit manuscripts available at Kumārajīva's center.
11. Sanskrit texts of Tathāgatagarbha literature were available at Kumārajīva's center, attested to by Buddhabhadra's translation of the *Mahāvaipulya Tathāgatagarbha sūtra* at this center.

From the above evidence based upon Chinese sources, we may postulate that the first most likely place for the introduction of Tathāgatagarbhan literature was Tun-huang, and that the Sanskrit texts were transported from there to north China.

Because Central Asia is the intermediary for the importation of Tathāgatagarbhan texts, it is difficult to place the locality for the composition of the *Śrīmālādevī sūtra* within the Indian peninsula. The frequency of travel to Central Asia from all regions of India renders impossible the task of localizing the route to Central Asia from any given locality.

Since no explicit relationship between the Mahāsaṅghika and the four principal translators is attested to in the Chinese records, except perhaps in the case of Buddhabhadra, there is a chasm between the exportation of the Tathāgatagarbhan texts from India and their importation to north China through Tun-huang. Based solely upon the evolution of ideas alluded to above, to be discussed in more detail in the next chapter, the two general localities in India where the *Śrīmālādevī sūtra* must have extended its influence, are Mathura and Āndhra, regions where the Mahāsaṅghika were in the majority. Due to the initial importation of Tathāgatagarbhan literature to north China via Tun-huang, the frequency of travel through the northern regions of India, the land route, was greater than through the southern regions, the sea route, via Ceylon. However, the foundation for the Tathāgatagarbhan doctrine of intrinsically pure mind disassociated from defilement is more intimately related to the southern Mahāsaṅghika rather than to their counterparts in the north. Consequently, the fermentation of ideas embodied in the *Śrīmālādevī sūtra* most likely occurred in southeastern India, in the proximity of Āndhra, strongly influenced by the Āndhran Mahāsaṅghika, to be transported northward and disseminated to the Mathuran Mahāsaṅghika before exportation to north China via Tun-hunag.

Date of Composition

1. Internal Evidence:

There are three principal characters in the *Śrīmālādevī sūtra*: King Prasenajit and his wife Mallikā, rulers of the state of Kośala, and Queen Śrīmālā, their daughter and wife of King Mitrayaśas, the queen of the state of Ayodhyā. The setting is in the Jeta grove in Śrāvastī, shifting to the state of Ayodhyā, both common locations for a number of Buddhist texts, used as a literary device to lend authenticity to the text as a composition during the Buddha's lifetime.

The person Queen Śrīmālā remains obscure. In other Buddhist literature, she is sometimes identified with King Prasenajit's wife instead of his daughter. In the *Sarvāstivādin Vinaya* (有部毘那耶雜事)[36] (Chapter 7),

Śrīmālā is the daughter of a village administrator in Kapilavastu but raised by the king of that state, Mahānāma. Because she went out daily to pick flowers for her hair she was known as Śrīmālā, "Beautiful Flower-Garlands." One day King Prasenajit visited King Mahānāma on returning from a hunting trip. Śrīmālā greeted him, bathed his feet and offered him food and drink. After King Prasenajit announced to King Mahānāma that he would spend the night, Śrīmālā ordered the palace gates closed during his stay. The following morning King Prasenajit discovered his enemies had tried to seize the castle but had failed because of Śrīmālā's foresight. He immediately asked her to be his first wife, and having accepted his proposal, Queen Śrīmālā ruled over the citizens of Kośala alongside her husband with great compassion.

A similar story is described in the *Four-Division Vinaya* (四分事) (chapter 18) but Śrīmālā is referred to as Mallikā, "One wearing flowers." In the *Five-Division Vinaya* (五分事) (chapter 22) King Prasenajit is portrayed as a powerful ruler who sends a messenger to the king of the Śākyas, compelling him to send a princess to be his queen. The royal family refused to relinquish a princess to such a fate, sending the very beautiful daughter of a commoner, identified as Śrīmālā, instead. In all three of these Vinaya texts one fact remains identical. Śrīmālā (or Mallikā) is not the daughter of King Prasenajit, as claimed in the *Śrīmālādevī sūtra*, but is his queen.

The account given of Śrīmālā in the commentaries on the *Śrīmālādevī sūtra* vary. All of these early commentaries, available only in Chinese, have now been tentatively dated between the fifth and seventh centuries, based upon the analysis of the Tun-huang manuscripts. The oldest extant commentary, the *Hsieh-chu sheng-man ching*, gives no historical account of the person Śrīmālā. According to the *Sheng-man i-chi*[37] (T.v. 85, no. 2761) women, being inferior and weak beings, are incapable of practicing the ten Bodhisattva vows although they profess them.[38] Queen Śrīmālā is an exception to her sex, however, since she is said to practice according to her vows, attested to by the miraculous sounds and heavenly flowers which appear from heaven.

In the *Sheng-man ching i-chi*, composed in 613, Hui-yüan records only information concerning Queen Śrīmālā's name. Because she wears the most exquisite garlands of flowers, she is known as "Śrīmālā." After she cultivates virtue she no longer wears earthly flowers but "garlands" of virtue.[39] In the *Shōmangyō gisho* the implication is that Queen Śrīmālā is not really a human being but the Buddha transformed into a woman's body, appearing as the wife of King Mitrayaśas.[40]

The Honan monk Tao-k'ung (道空), in his introduction to the *Sheng-man pao-k'u*, describes Queen Śrīmālā as of a gentle and compassionate nature, born in Kapilavastu. Adding details to the narration given in the sūtra, Tao-k'ung states that at daybreak, having received a letter from her parents, Queen Śrīmālā sees an image in the sky which causes her to study the Dharma, promising to vanquish the evil of Māra. Within the *Pao-k'u* itself, however, Queen Śrīmālā is not considered historical but a Dharma-Body Bodhisattva who assumes the form of a woman and hides in the palace, dimming the illumination of his body for the sake of the common people.[41] Chi-tsang adds that women, being vulgar due to the five obstacles and three limitations,[42] are suited for explaining the universal vehicle, assisting all those seven years of age and older to reach Buddhahood.

King Prasenajit, according to the Pao-k'u, prayed for the well-being of his child before its birth and subsequently became the father of a daughter. All the country's nobility rejoiced and paid tribute to the child, offering jewel-flowers. This is contrary to the Pāli Canon, however, in which King Prasenajit was very displeased at having a daughter but the Buddha consoled him, saying that daughters may be a blessing.[43]

In contrast to the earlier *Hsieh-chu sheng-man ching* in which Śrīmālā's sex is disregarded and the *Sheng-man i-chi* in which Queen Śrīmālā's capabilities are acknowledged, the tone of Chi-tsang's commentary is apologetic towards the Chinese audience for the attribution of superior spiritual attainment to Queen Śrīmālā, in a similar manner to the *Shōmangyō gisho* and the *Sheng-man ching i-chi*. In all three of these later commentaries Queen Śrīmālā is a male Bodhisattva of the eighth *bhūmi* who is capable of transforming himself into a woman for the benefit of converting living beings. Chi-tsang explains that the purity of this Bodhisattva, disguised as a woman named Śrīmālā, is denoted by *devī*--"goddess" or "queen"--to disassociate this woman from the more mundane bodies of mortals.[44] Her purity of senses is stressed although she appears in physical form.[45]

Based upon the spiritual name "garland of virtue" attributed to Śrīmālā in the *Sheng-man ching i-chi* and the *Shōmangyō gisho*, Chi-tsang identifies Śrīmālā with Te-man (德鬘) ("garland of virtue") (Bhadramālā?), a laywoman in the *Mahāparinirvāṇa sūtra* who also wears virtue as her garland. According to the *Mahāparinirvāṇa sūtra* Te-man is a tenth stage Bodhisattva abiding in non-action (*acala*) and appearing as the laywoman Te-man on behalf of all living beings.[46] If these two laywomen were later assimilated in Buddhist tradition, it may explain the differences with regard to Queen Śrīmālā's name as the future Buddha, either Samantaprabhā or Samantabhadra, corresponding to the Chinese and Tibetan recensions respectively.[48]

The above-mentioned commentaries therefore provide little evidence which would avail the historian in positioning Queen Śrīmālā in Indian history. There was a King Prasenajit of Kośala who reigned in the fourth century B.C. Little is known concerning his chief queen. Śrīmālā may have been either his wife or daughter historically but with regard to the *Śrīmālādevī sūtra* itself, she remains a symbol, interpreted variously as the model for all Buddhists or as a skillful means utilized by a Bodhisattva in order to convert living beings.

Although Queen Śrīmālā may be a symbolic figure for propagating the Dharma, it may be said that from the time of the *Saddharmapuṇḍarīka* in which a young girl becomes a Buddha, there is a gradual elevation of the woman's role in Buddhism. Before the *Śrīmālādevī-siṁhanāda sūtra* there was no symbolization attributed solely to a woman as a key figure in propagating the Dharma, devoting an entire scriptural text to her exposition on the Dharma.

2. External Evidence

Because the *Śrīmālādevī-siṁhanāda sūtra* is no longer extant in Sanskrit, there can be no analysis of the literary style of the original text. The Sanskrit fragments which remain (as cited in the texts mentioned above)[49] are written in classical Sanskrit and appear in texts composed within one hundred years after the composition of the *Śrīmālādevī-siṁhanāda sūtra*.

The Chinese recension *Sheng-man shih-tzu-hou i-ch'eng ta-fang-pien fang-kuang ching* was translated in 435 by Guṇabhadra (394-468).[50] The *Sheng-man fu-jen hui* was translated as part of the *Ratnakūṭa* anthology between 706 and 713 by Bodhiruci (572-727).[51] Two other alleged translations are recorded in the Chinese catalogues which would have been earlier. The older of the two, attributed to Seng Fa-ni of Ch'i, was translated in 320 according to the *K'ai-yüan* catalogue.[52] The other, by Dharmakṣema (385-433) is recorded in both the *K'ai-yüan* and the *Li tai san-pao chi* (歷代三宝紀) but no earlier catalogues cite either of these two translations.[53]

In the preface to the *Śrīmālādevī sūtra* by Hui-kuan (慧觀), recorded in the *Chu san-tsang chi-chi*, the king of P'eng-ch'eng (彭城) asks Guṇabhadra to translate this text in consultation with Pao-yün (宝雲) on behalf of his people. This preface does not mention the Pei-liang translation by Dharmakṣema nor the Fa-ni translation. If Hui-kuan, a person of great esteem and scholarship, did compose this preface, then he certainly would have listed any previous translations. Consequently, it is extremely doubtful that there ever was a translation by Dharmakṣema or Seng Fa-ni. Although there is insufficient evidence to conclude whether a translation existed prior to Guṇabhadra's, the rapidity with which Guṇabhadra's text would have had to be transported to north China, if circumstances were otherwise, does suggest the existence of a more ancient text.

From the two extant Chinese translations by Guṇabhadra and Bodhiruci a lower limit for the *Śrīmālādevī sūtra* may be fixed at approximately 350 A.D., allowing a seventy-five year span for the development and composition of this text in India before its translation into Chinese in 435 A.D. by Guṇabhadra.

The upper limit for the *Śrīmālādevī sūtra* is more difficult to establish since the relationship between Tathāgatagarbha and the two great Buddhist schools, Mādhyamika and Yogācāra, has not as yet been determined.

Because the evolution of the Tathāgatagarbha theory is not yet known, dating the Tathāgatagarbha-oriented treatises is extremely difficult. There is no master having the stature of Nāgārjuna, Asaṅga, or Vasubandhu associated with these treatises. The only commentary in Sanskrit now extant which is solely an exposition on Tathāgatagarbha and is greatly influenced by the *Śrīmālādevī sūtra* is the *Ratnagotravibhāga*.

According to Tibetan tradition, the *Ratnagotravibhāga* is believed to be one of the five major treatises by Maitreya and is therefore considered Mādhyamikan. The auto-commentary is attributed to Asaṅga. The Chinese tradition agrees with reference to the authorship of the auto-commentary but attributes the treatise to Saramati. Consequently, the date of composition ranges between 300 A.D. and 450 A.D., depending upon authorship.[54] In addition, the *Tathāgatagarbha sūtra* and the *Śrīmālādevī sūtra* are connected with the third and last cycle of the Buddha's sermons according to Indo-Tibetan tradition, thus interpreting the Tathāgatagarbha theory as Mādhyamikan.[55]

The analysis of Emptiness presented in the *Śrīmālādevī sūtra*[56] is more substantialist than in the treatises of Nāgārjuna, composed as an alternative exposition on Emptiness and re-interpreting the *Prajñāpāramitā*.[57] According to Tibetan exegesis,[58] the *Ratnagotravibhāga* represents the Mādhyamikan views of its author, Asaṅga. However, the authorship of this text remains a subject of controversy. The text itself does not expound on only Mādhyamikan tenets but also those of Vijñānavāda. Consequently, the *Ratnagotra* and its authority, the *Śrīmālādevī sūtra*, are an intermediary development between the two great schools of Buddhism.[59]

Since no mention of the *Śrīmālādevī sūtra* occurs in either the treatises of Nāgārjuna or Āryadeva, it can be postulated that 1) the *Śrīmālādevī sūtra* was not considered important to their Mādhyamikan position, if the sūtra were composed at that time or 2) the *Śrīmālādevī sūtra* was not mentioned because it was either unknown to them or was composed after their period.

Because the first known Tathāgatagarbhan text was translated in the late third century,[60] Tathāgatagarbha thought may be considered a Buddhist phenomena of the third century, thus hypothetically placing the emergence of Tathāgatagarbha thought, as a systemized body of literature, in the beginning of the third century A.D. at the earliest, approximately during the last half of Nāgārjuna and Āryadeva's lifespan.

Since the earliest extant translation of the *Śrīmālādevī sūtra* is dated 435 A.D. in contrast to the *Tathāgatagarbha sūtra*, the latter being translated one hundred years prior, perhaps the *Śrīmālādevī sūtra* represents an evolution in Tathāgatagarbha thought occurring over a period of between fifty to one hundred years after the composition of the *Tathāgatagarbha sūtra*.[61] Therefore, if the Tathāgatagarbha theory is hypothetically a third century phenomenon, the *Śrīmālādevī sūtra*, as a leading canonical authority on this doctrine, may be considered as emerging in its rudimentary form approximately mid-third to early fourth century A.D. The extreme upper limit woudl then be approximated as 250 A.D., in the post-Nāgārjuna period.

In contrast to relating Tathāgatagarbha with Mādhyamika, Ui Hakuju attempts to classify Tathāgatagarbha literature as an outcome of the *Avataṁsaka* and *Mahāparinirvāṇa* sūtras.[62] Therefore, all Tathāgatagarbha literature, beginning with the (*Mahāvaipulya*) *Tathāgagarbha sūtra* would be placed chronologically after the *Avataṁsaka* and *Mahāparinirvāṇa* sūtras. Tathāgatagarbha literature would then be influenced by *citta-mātra* more markedly than by *śunyavāda*, which were the two trends that developed into Yogācāra or Vijñānavāda and Mādhyamika respectively.

Lamotte also considers the *Śrīmālādevī sūtra* idealistic in tendency, distinctly separating it from the *Prajñāpāramitā*, *Avataṁsaka*, and *Ratnakūṭa* sūtras:

> Par sa date relativement ancienne, par ses sources d'inspiration autant que par les théories qu'il développe, le Vkn (*Vimalakīrtinirdeśa sūtra*) se range parmi les plus anciens Mahāyānasūtra. Comme la Prajñāpāramitā, l'Avataṁsaka, le Ratnakūṭa et le Mahāsaṁnipāta, il représente ce Madhyamaka à l'état brut qui servit de base à l'école de Nāgārjuna. Il se sépare nettement des Sūtra de tendance idéaliste, Saṁdhinirmocana, Laṅkāvatāra, Śrīmālādevī siṁhanāda, etc., qui furent seulement traduits en chinois au milieu du Ve siècle, et qui firent autorité dans l'école épistémologique des Vijñānavādin.[63]

However, the *Śrīmālādevī sūtra*, which appears to have been composed after the formative period in the evolution of Tathāgatagarbha, has no relationship with the *ālaya-vijñāna*, one of the major tenets in Vijñānavāda. In contrast to the *Śrīmālādevī sūtra* and prior Tathāgatagarbha literature, the *Laṅkāvatāra* and the *Awakening of Mahāyāna Faith* (*Ta-ch'eng ch'i hsin lun*) (大乘起信論, which emerge in the late fourth centuries, synthesize the theory of Tathāgatagarbha and *ālaya-vijñāna*. It is reasonable to hypothesize, therefore, that the Tathāgatagarbha theory evolved prior to the systematization of Vijñānavāda by the masters Asaṅga (310-390) and Vasubandhu (400-480)[64] though not necessarily composed prior to texts such as the *Sandhinirmocana* and *Mahāyānābhidharma* which were later accepted as Vijñānavādin scriptural authority. Consequently, some of these scriptures may have been studied by Tathāgatagarbhan adherents and interpreted in terms compatible with Tathāgatagarbhan principles, later to be re-interpreted by the Vijñānavāda.

Tathāgatagarbha literature resides between the Mādhyamikan position and the Vijñānavādin position not only vis-à-vis its interpretation of Emptiness and consciousness but also with reference to the theory of Buddha-Body. For the Mādhyamikan adherents there are two bodies and for the Vijñānavāda there are three, corresponding to the levels of truth in each respective school. In the *Ratnagotravibhāga*, however, both a two-body theory and a three-body theory occur, perhaps illustrating the earlier and later portions of the *Ratnagotra* as well as the midway position of Tathāgatagarbha literature with relation to Mādhyamika and Vijñānavāda. It will be demonstrated below[65] that the Tathāgatagarbhan adherents initiated a third element in the Buddha-Body theory, which functioned as a basis for the other two bodies of the Buddha.

In summary, the *Śrīmālādevī-siṁhanāda sūtra* was composed between approximately 250 A.D. and 350 A.D. for the following reasons:

1. The earliest extant Chinese recension was translated in 435, rendering the date of development and composition approximately seventy-five years prior, i.e. circa 340-350 A.D. Several earlier translations are recorded in the catalogues but these are doubtful.

A Sanskrit text may have been exported to north China earlier than Guṇabhadra's arrival, as mentioned above, with several earlier unsuccessful translations attempted.

2. Because the *Śrīmālādevī sūtra* does not refer to the *ālaya-vijñāna* in its interpretation of consciousness, it must be prior to the systemization of Vijñānavāda under the teachers Asaṅga and Vasubandhu, thus placing the text prior to 350 A.D.
3. The Tathāgatagarbha theory reinterprets Emptiness more positively than does Nāgārjuna. Although the Tibetan exegetical tradition considers the *Śrīmālādevī sūtra* a Mādhyamikan text, the *Ratnagotravibhāga*, which cites it as an authority, is not strictly Mādhyamikan in teaching due to its interpretation of Emptiness and consciousness as well as its theory of Buddha-Body. Because certain idealistic tendencies are evidenced, Tathāgatagarbha literature must be a link between the Mādhyamika treatises of Nāgārjuna and the Vijñānavādin works of Asaṅga and Vasubandhu.
4. The *Tathāgatagarbha sūtra*, the oldest known text concerning the Tathāgatagarbha theory, was developed within the first half of the third century A.D. The *Śrīmālādevī sūtra*, a text of greater complexity in doctrine, cannot therefore have been composed prior to 250 A.D., allowing a fifty-year period for development of more complex concepts.

The suggested position of the *Śrīmālādevī sūtra* within the chronology of Buddhist literature, based upon the above evidence, is illustrated in Figure 1.[66]

The Socio-Economic Context of Southeast India

On the basis of the above evidence it was hypothesized that the *Śrīmālādevī siṁhanāda sūtra* was composed in the mid-third to early fourth centuries A.D. in southeast India. A general overview of the socio-economic conditions of that area at that time will be attempted, based upon the archaeological and literary evidence available, which admittedly is scanty.

	Beginning of Common Era to 270 A.D.	c. 270 - 400 A.D.	c. 400 - 500 A.D.
Principal Teachers:	Nāgārjuna (c. 150-250)	Maitreyanatha (c. 270-350)	Vasubandhu (c. 400-480)[77]
	Āryadeva (c. 170-270)	Asaṅga (c. 300-390)	Dignāga (480-540)
Principal Texts	*Aṣṭasāhasrikā*[67] (100 B.C.-100 A.D.)	*Sandhinirmocana*	*Laṅkāvatāra*
	Larger Sukhāvatīvyūha[68] (c. 50-100 A.D.)	*Nirvāṇa sūtra/ Tathāgatagarbha sūtra*	*Awakening of Mahāyāna Faith*
	Saddharmapuṇḍarīka[69] (c. 100 A.D.)	*Pu tseng pu chien ching*[75]	
	Avataṁsaka[70]	*Śrīmālādevī*	
	Aṣṭadaśasāhasrikā[71] (100 A.D. - 300 A.D.)	*Mahāyāna sūtrālaṅkāra*	
	Pañcaviṁśatisāhasrikā (100-300)	*Ratnagotra*[76]	
	Śatasāhasrikā (100-300)		
	portions of the *Ratnakūṭa*[72]		
	Vimalakīrtinirdeśa[73]		

Figure 1 Suggested Chronology of Major Mahāyāna Sūtras[78]

The commencement of this text's composition may have been during the eclipse of the Sātavāhana empire (c. 235 B.C. - 225 A.D.),[79] one of the longest dynasties in Indian history. Centered in Āndhra and Mahārāṣṭra, the Sātavāhana dynasty included most of south India, demarcated by the area south of the Krishna and Tungabhadrā rivers, except for the Coḷa, Pandya, and Chera kingdoms. At one time its suzerainty may have extended as far north as Magadha. Founded by King Simuka, the Sātavāhanas were to be the principal conveyors of Āryan civilization to the South,[80] a civilization which would be faithfully maintained while the Greeks, Kushans, Parthians, and Śakas were competing for the northwest frontier. Both Brahmanism and Buddhism flourished during this period[81] with the latter constructing many stūpas and sculptures at Amarāvatī and Nāgārjunakoṇḍa in tribute to their religion. Because of South India's coastline, studded with porttowns, commerce and trade were extremely successful, ensuring generous patronage of Buddhist institutions.[82] City-life attracted many guilds of prosperous merchants and craftsmen who became a faithful Buddhist constituency. Local administration was relatively autonomous[83] with feudal overlords supervising city-life.

The prosperity of the Sātavāhana empire was to rapidly decline however. At the beginning of the third century the Vākāṭakas emerged in the northern Vindhya regions as a formidable power with the subsequent dominance in the northwest by the Ābhīras, and in the south by the Chutus and Pallavas.[84] The eventual downfall of the Sātavāhana dynasty in the mid-third century resulted in the Vākāṭakas retaining sovereignty throughout the Deccan from the mid-third through the mid-sixth centuries A.D. The Coḷa, Pandya, and Cheras maintained their kingdoms in the far south while the Ikṣvākus[85] gained the hegemony in Āndhradeśa,[86] between the mouths of the Krishna and Godāvarī rivers. Although these were the principal kingdoms, many tiny independent ones retained their suzerainty during this period.[87]

Throughout the third century, with the dissolution of the Sātavāhana dynasty, feudalism continued to penetrate South India with warring factions and chaos commonplace, and tensions escalating among kingdoms.[88] Until the rise of the illustrious

Gupta empire under Chandragupta I in c. 324 A.D., religions were to contend for the patronage of the overlord. Decentralization and economic recession had caused a steady decline in the cities and a concomitant ascendancy in village autonomy.[89] The economic power structure had shifted from the mercantile guilds to the feudal overlords with an impending Brahmanical Hindu renaissance to be actualized during the Guptan Age.[90] However, the Guptan Age cannot be considered the period of Buddhist decline since not only the zenith of Buddhist art is evident at this time but also some of the greatest philosophers in Mādhyamika and Yogācāra appear in the fourth and fifth centuries, engaging in voluminous exegeses concerning the Dharma.[91]

Migration, which was rapid and continual between the north and south appears to have included many diversified sects of Buddhism which co-existed rather successfully.

> Le Bouddhisme est donc représenté à peu près partout dans l'Inde et en Asie centrale. Hsüan-tsang compte en tout plus de 200,000 moines, vivant dans quelque 7,000 monastères, dont untiers est en ruines. Certaines régions, où il est prospère, semblent caractérisées par le fait que des sectes très diverses et les deux véhicules y vivent côte à côte.92

Māhāyanists were travelling throughout India with the Theravādins also maintaining centers in the south, particularly along the Mahāraṣṭran coastline, as well as in Ceylon. According to I-tsing, the Therāvadins comprised nearly the entire community in South India.[93] Southwest India appears to have been predominantly Theravādin, particularly Dharmottarīyan (a Vātsīputrīyan offshoot), in Aparānta and Bhadrayānīyan in Nāsikā.[94] However, information concerning the prosperity of the Saṅgha in this southwest region is scarce. Inferring from the inscriptions of the caves at Kanheri and Ajanta which illustrate the popularity of both Theravāda and Mahāyāna in the fifth through eighth centuries,[95] Theravāda most certainly but also perhaps some Mahāyānists were inhabiting this area at this time. The Buddhist caves at Karle reveal Theravādin influence c. 1st-2nd C.A.D. and Mahāyāna influence in later centuries.[96]

In the north, the transmission of both Mahāyānist and Theravādin teachings was also at its height. The Theravādins continued to establish new communities in the northeast around Magadha and on the eastern coast in Kaliṅga. Magadha became the center of interaction for all sects because it was the holy land of Buddhism where daily pilgrimages from distant regions were undertaken.[97]

The northwest was Sarvāstivādin and Mūlasarvāstivādin territory, particularly in Kashmir, although they maintained centers in Mathura and Gandhara.[98] Little is known about the state of Buddhism in Sindhu at this time. The Vātṣīpūtrīyans and the Sammatiyans became very powerful in Central India, extending to other areas as well. From the records of Fa-hsien, Hsüan-tsang, and I-tsing it is evident that Theravāda and its sects were far more extensive than Mahāyāna and were not overthrown by the ascendancy of the latter.[99]

It can be said, then, with relative certainty, that in the period encompassing the hundred years before the Common Era through the third century afterwards, literature was proliferating to a heretofore unknown extent, in both Theravādin and Mahāyāna schools. Interaction and confrontation between schools must have initiated new developments, borrowing from each other and yet claiming their orthodoxy over all others. There is no definitive way of mapping each school's conveyance of their particular interpretation of the Dharma throughout the Indian peninsula. However, certain simple but plausible routes may be traced according to archaeological and literary-historical references.

> Rares sont les régions où ils ne signalent la présence que des adeptes d'une seule secte. Très généralement, si une secte a une prédominance plus ou moins marquée dans un région donnée, d'autres sectes y résident également. Il semble bien, d'après certain indices, que l'ordre de ces prédominances ait varié au cours des siècles, certaines écoles déclinant ou même disparaissant alors que d'autres prenaient leur essor. Des circonstances très diverses, et variables au cours de l'histoire, ont joué leur rôle dans cette répartition; circonstances géographiques, comme l'isolement insulaire ou montagneux préservant certaines écoles di'influences extérieures trop sensibles ou au contraire comme le grand brassage d'idées qui se faisait au long des grandes routes de transit....
>
> Mais, de ce que plusieurs sectes aient été représentées conjiontement à peu près dans toutes les régions de l'immense Inde, il ne s'ensuit pas que toutes les écoles aient été présentes partout.100

The two central districts where interaction was at its greatest are in the Āndhra and Magadha kingdoms with the coastal regions of Aparānta and Tamralipti serving as conveyors to Central Asia and Canton respectively. The transmission of the Dharma from southwestern India to the north would most likely be along the Mahāraṣṭran coast with Aparānta, or cities in between, as the point of departure. From the northwest regions, near Kasmir or Gandhara, the transmission route would be through Afghanistan across the Hindukush Mountains. After having left the Indo-Iranian borders to embark across the vast plains of Central Asia, one of the two caravan or "silk" routes would be travelled, crossing the Taklamakan desert and the Pamir highlands to north China. All travellers to north China via Central Asia would have to travel either across the regions of Kashmir or Gandhara or further west, then over the plains of Central Asia. However, the Kasmir and Gandharan schools of Sarvāstivāda and Mūlasarvāstivāda did not influence Tathāgatagarbhan literature, as evidenced by the latter's interpretation of the dharmas which is far different from the *Adhidharmakośa* schema.

From southeast India the transmission route to Canton in south China would probably be by sea from Ceylon. From north-east India, the two ports of Kaveripattanam in the Bay of Bengal and Tamralipti at the mouth of the Ganges would serve as ports of embarkation to Canton. Either the eastern or western coastline of the Indian peninsula could be utilized by travelling east or west along the Godāvarī and Krishna rivers which were navigable throughout the year.

In summary, third and fourth century southeast India was the locus of fermentation for both Brahman and Buddhist innovations. These two religions expectedly enhanced and antagonized each other as they vied for royal patronage which was regional. Hence, multifarious doctrines had to appeal to diversified interests. In one such regional frontier, in Āndhra most probably, the *Śrīmālādevī sūtra* was to attract the interest and devotion of Buddhists, appealing almost certainly to royal women similar to those of the Ikṣvāku dynasty, who generously financed the sculptures at Nāgārjunakoṇḍa.

In conclusion, the interaction between north and south India, and the trade with Central Asia provided diverse influences on the Buddhist literature developing at this time, representing not only Indian influences but Central Asian contributions as well. The paucity of available literature which belongs to the eighteen sects provides little information concerning the sectarian beliefs which contributed to the subsequent evolution of Buddhist thought. In addition, the Tathāgatagarbha concept may be related to the concurrent Brahmanic thought which was developing at that time.[101] Consequently, all of the possible influences upon Tathāgatagarbha thought are an immense and complex problem. In the next chapter some of the major influences within the Buddhist tradition which nurtured the development of the concept Tathāgatagarbha and its body of literature will be discussed.

CHAPTER I

NOTES

[1]Cf. Edward Conze, *Buddhism: Its Essence and Development* (New York: Harper Torchbooks, 1959) (reprinted from Bruno Cassirer Ltd. edition, 1951), pp. 119-124; Edward Conze, *The Prajñāpāramitā Literature* (The Hague: Mouton & Co., 1960) (Indo-Iranian Monographs), p. 9; Nalinaksha Dutt, *Aspects of Mahayana Buddhism and Its Relation to Hīnayāna* (London: Luzac and Co., 1930), pp. 28-43; Sarvepalli Radhakrishnan (gen. ed.), *The Cultural Heritage of India*, vol. I: *The Early Phases: Prehistoric, Vedic, and Upanishadic, Jaina, and Buddhist* (Calcutta: Ramakrishna Mission of the Institute of Culture, 1937), p. 517; Kajiyama Yuichi, "Hannya-gyō" (Prajñā literature") in *Nihon no buten (Buddhist Literature of Japan)*, ed. by Toshinori Takeuchi and Takeshi Umehara (Tokyo: Chueiko ronsha, 1969), (Chūkō shinsho No. 179 in a series), p. 25; and A. K. Warder, *Indian Buddhism* (Delhi: Motilal Banarsidass, 1970), pp. 352-353.

[2]Etienne Lamotte, *Histoire du Bouddhisme Indien* (Louvain: Institut Orientaliste, Université de Louvaine, 1958), pp. 580-581.

[3]Lamotte, *Histoire du Bouddhisme, ibid.*, p. 582.

[4]André Bareau, *Les Sectes Bouddhiques du Petit Véhicule* (Saigon: École Française D'Extrême-Orient, 1955), pp. 32-33.

[5]Chūkan (or, Chūzen), Japanese Mādhyamikan and Tantric master (1227-1307) cites Paramārtha in *Sanron gengi kennyū shō* (三論玄義檢幽鈔) (T.v. 70, no. 2300, p. 459b).

[6]Conze, *The Prajñāpāramitā Literature, op. cit.*, p. 9.

[7]Bareau, *Les Sectes Boddhiques, op. cit.*, pp. 99 and 105.

[8]*Ime khalu punah Śāriputra ṣaṭ-pāramitā-pratisaṁyuktāh sūtrāntās tathāgatasyātyayena Dakṣiṇāpathe pracariṣyanti. Dakṣiṇāpathāt punar eva Vartanyāṁ pracariṣyanti. Vartanyāḥ punar uttarapathe pracariṣyanti. ...Śāriputra āha, iyam api Bhagavan Prajñāpāramitā evam gambhīrā paścime kale paścime samaye vaistārikī bhaviṣyaty uttarasyām diśy uttare digbhāge.* Quoted in *Abhisamayālaṁkārāloka prajñāpāramitāvyakhā* by Haribhadra, ed. by U. Wogihara (Tokyo: Bunka, 1934), p. 487.

"Moreover, these Sūtras associated with the six perfections will, after the passing away of the Tathāgata, appear in the South. From the South they will spread to the East, and from there to the North. Śāriputra: 'Will even this so deep perfection of wisdom in the last time, in the last period, be wide-spread in the Northern direction, in the Northern part of the world?'" - *The Perfection of Wisdom in Eight Thousand Slokas*, trans. by Edward Conze (Calcutta: Asiatic Society, 1958), pp. 79-80.

The translation of the *Aṣṭasāhasrikā* into Chinese by Chih Ch'ien is the only Chinese translation which differs in its route of transmission. See Etienne Lamotte, *La traitê de la grande vertu de sagesse* (*Mahāprajñāpāramitāśāstra*) (Louvain: Institute Orientaliste Bibliothèque de l'Université, 1966-67), v. I, p. 26. The direction in Chih-Ch'ien's translation is first, the country of the Śākya clan, then East, and then North. (T.v. 3, no. 225, p. 490a).

[9]Nāgārjuna's birthplace was in South India according to his biography translated by Kumārajīva and in South Kośala or the province of Vidarbha (modern Berar) according to Hsüan-tsang. Because Kumārajīva lived one hundred years after Nāgārjuna, his biography is more credible than Hsüan-tsang's. Cf. Bhikshu Sangharakshita, *A Survey of Buddhism* (Bangalore: Indian Institute of World Culture, 1957), p. 332; E. Obermiller, *History of Buddhism (Chos-hbyung) by Bu-ston* (Heidelberg, 1931) (Reprinted by Suzuki Research Foundation, 1965), pp. 110 and 120; *Shinbutten kaidai jiten*, ed. by Nakamura Hajime and Hirakawa Akira (Tokyo: Shunjūsha, 1966), p. 15.

[10]The notion of an originally pure mind can be considered a Mahāsaṅghikan innovation since the Sthaviravādins did not adapt it to their dharma schema.

> The idea of an absolute thought which is perfectly pure and translucent (*prabhāsvara*) in its own nature, its own being, its own substance, and which remains so forever, does not fit in very well with the dharma-theory of the Sthaviras. They accordingly did not quite know what to do with it, whereas the Mahāsaṅghikas and the Māhāyana gave it a central place in their scheme of things.... Deliverance is then conceived as the gradual purification of this consciousness which finally attains to the summit of the 'Realm of the Dharma' (*dharmadhātu*).." Edward Conze, *Buddhist Thought in India* (London: George Allen and Unwin Ltd., 1961), p. 196.

[11]Cf. J. J. Jones, *The Mahāvastu*, vol. I (London: Luzac & Co., 1949), p. 1, pp. 53-124, in which the four stages in the Bodhisattva career and the ten Bodhisattva-bhūmi are discussed. Also see Lamotte, *Histoire du Bouddhisme*, *op. cit.*, pp. 695-696. According to Lamotte, the bhūmis presented in the *Mahāvastu* are exemplary qualities of past Buddhas in contrast with the *bhūmi* of Māhāyana which are a progression of practice in relation to the pāramitās. To claim that the *Mahāvastu bhūmi* system influenced the emergence of the Mahāyānist *bhūmi* system is tenuous at best.

[12]Conze, *The Prajñāpāramitā Literature*, *op. cit.*, p. 10.

[13]See Walter Eugene Clark, *Two Lamaistic Pantheons* (New York: Paragon Book Reprint, 1965) for a representation of the Buddha Samantaprabhā, "Mother of the Buddhas" (Plate 4 A 5, 435, p. 118).

[14]David Seyfort Ruegg, *La Théorie du Tathāgatagarbha et du Gotra: Études sur la Sotériologie et al Gnoséologie du Bouddhisme* (Paris: École Française D'Extreme-Orient, 1969), p. 4.

[15]These concepts will be expalined below, see Chapter IV: "Tathāgatagarbha thought in the *Śrīmāladevī sūtra* - Part II."

[16]E. W. Adikaram, *Early History of Buddhism in Ceylon* (Ceylon: D. S. Puswella, 1946), p. 100.

[17]Kajiyama Yuichi, "Bhāvaviveka, Sthiramati, and Dharmapāla" in *Beiträge zur Geistesgeschichte Indiens Festschrift für Erich Frauwallner*, v. XII-XIII, 1968-69, p. 196.

[18]"Intrinsically pure mind" and "Dharma-nature" will be discussed below, see Chapter II: "Tathāgatagarbha."

[19]See Chapter II: "Tathāgatagarbha" for the analysis of defilement according to the Mahāsaṅghika and Chapter IV: "Tathāgatagarbha thought in the *Śrīmālādevī sūtra* - Part II" for the influence of the Mahāsaṅghikan schema on the ŚDS.

[20]See J. Rahder, *Daśabhūmikasūtra et Bodhisattvabhūmi* (Paris: Paul Guethner, 1926), p. xxviii in which he states that *jñeya-bhūmi, sarva-dharmavaśita-bhūmi, apunaḥ-kāryānupalabhita-bhūmi, abhayabhūmi, āśvasta-sthāna-nirvāṇa-bhūmi, sopadhiśeṣa-bhūmi,* the four *kleśa-bhūmi* and *avidyā-bhūmi* enumerated in the ŚDS are references to the *bhūmi* in the *Mahāvastu*. Although he does not cite the corresponding passages in either the *Mahāvastu* or the *Śrīmālādevī sūtra*, the latter text's Chinese equivalents for the above *bhūmi* may be found on p. 220c (T.v. 12, no. 353) (with the omission of the *jñeya-bhūmi*) viz. *i-chieh fa tzu-tsai chih ti* (一切法自在之地), *wu-so-tso wu-so-te ti* (無所作無所得地), yu-yü ti (有餘地), and on p. 220a, the *ssu chu-ti* (四住地) and *wu-ming chu-ti* (無明住地). No interpretation is given by Rahder.

[21]Bareau, *Les Sectes Bouddhiques, op. cit.*, p. 57.

[22]Takasaki Jikidō, "Nyoraizō shisō ni okeru *Shōmangyō* no chii," p. 187 in *Shōmangyō gisho rombun, Nihon bukkyō genryū kenkyū kiyō*, No. 2, 1965.

[23]*K'ai-yüan shih chiao mo-lu*, cited in Tokiwa Daijō, *Gokan yori Sō Sei ni itaru yakkyō sōroku* (Tokyo: Tōhō bunka gakuin tōkyō kenkyūsho, 1938), pp. 683, 768-769.

[24]See Katsumata Shunkyō, *Bukkyō ni okeru shinshikisetsu no kenkyū* (Tokyo: Sankibō busshorin, 1969), (3rd ed.), pp. 601-606 for an analysis of the *Angulimala sūtra* of Tathāgatagarbhan literature, not to be confused with the tales of Aṅgulimala in the Nikāyas.

[25]Under Chü-ch'ü Meng-hsün's sovereignty was Tun-huang, the hub of mercantilism in northwest China due to its central location where the north and south routes across Central Asia converge. It is at Tun-huang that a majority of manuscripts of the *Śrīmālādevī sūtra* and its commentaries have been discovered.

[26]The first six chapters of the *Mahāparinirvāṇa sūtra* have been discovered at Tunhuang. Cf. Tokiwa, *Gokan yori Sō Sei, op. cit.*, p. 903.

[27]Cf. *Kao seng chuan* (T. v. 50, no. 2059, pp. 102c-103b) and the *Ch'u san-tsang chi chi* (T. v. 55, no. 2145, pp. 335c-337b). Dharmakṣema's alleged translation of the *Śrīmālādevī sūtra* is described in detail below, under date of composition.

[28]Cf. *Kao seng chuan* (T. v. 50, no. 2059, pp. 334b-335c) and Tokiwa, *Gokan yori Sō Sei, op. cit.*, pp. 762-769.

[29]Cf. *Kao seng chuan* (pp. 344-345a) and the *Ch'u san-tsang chi chi* (pp. 105b-106b).

[30]The Ti-lun school (地論宗) was considered the "northern" school of Consciousness-Only (*citta-mātra*) in contrast to the She-lun school (攝論宗) led by Ratnamati in the south. There is a possibility that the two schools developed because of a disagreement between Ratnamati and Bodhiruci, the former's translation of the *Ratnagotravibhāga* being the only one now extant although Bodhiruci also is alleged to have translated that text. (Cf. Hattori Masaaki, "Busshoron no ichikōsatsu" in *Bukkyōshigaku*, v. IV, 1955, p. 30).

The Ti-lun school, based upon the *Daśabhūmika*, envisioned the *ālaya-vijñāna* as pure, thus being compatible with the intrinsically pure nature of mind, the perspective maintained in Tathāgatagarbha treatises. Consequently, the evolution from the Ti-lun school to Hua-yen was a logical outcome since the Hua-yen school of Fa-tsang placed considerable emphasis on Tathāgatagarbha. In contrast to Ti-lun, the She-lun school, based upon the *Mahāyānasaṃgraha*, considered the *ālaya-vijnāna* as the source of impurity, i.e. discriminative thinking, and therefore was incompatible with Tathāgatagarbha. The evolution from the She-lun school was Fa-hsiang, the major Chinese school of Vijñānavāda, founded by Hsüan-tsang.

[31]Cf. Tokiwa, *Gokan yori Sō Sei, op. cit.*, p. 363 and Katsumata, *Bukkyō ni okeru shinshikisetsu, op. cit.*, p. 642.

[32]See Fujieda, "Hokucho ni okeru *Shōmangyō*" in *Tōhō gakuhō, op. cit.*, pp. 325, 327.

[33]*Chu san-tsang chi chi* (T. v. 55, no. 2145, p. 40a-b):
今依安旧録附之末... 僧法尼所誦出経入疑録
時年十六 勝鬘経一巻、永元元年....

[34]If earlier manuscripts once existed, the date of composition would be even earlier, shortening the period between Gunabhadra's translation and this commentary to less than sixty years. Fujieda considers the production of a commentary in north China within sixty years of Guṇabhadra'a recension an impossibility given such a severe time restraint. Cf. Fujieda, "Hokucho ni okeru Shomangyo," *op. cit.*, pp. 347-348.

[35]Fujieda, *ibid.*, p. 329.

[36]Citations from the different recensions of the Vinaya are based upon the *Kokuyaku issaikyō, op. cit.*, pp. 86-87.

[37]The *Sheng-man i-chi* (勝鬘義記) (T. v. 85, no. 2761), the second oldest commentary, author unknown, was completed in 504 A.D. Cf. Fujieda, "Hokucho ni okeru *Shomangyo*," *op. cit.*, p. 334.

[38]現為我證者名雖有十統攝萬善、女人卑弱謂不能行。 (T. v. 85, no. 2761, p. 253c).

[39]勝鬘父母借彼世間殊勝之鬘以名其人故號勝鬘...如世華鬘故號為鬘、德慧為鬘。 (*Dainihon zokuzōkyō*, v. 4, p. 276d) *The Sheng-man ching pao-k'u* repeats this explanation verbatim. (T. v. 37, no. 1744, p. 2c).

[40]夫勝鬘者本是不可思議。何知如来分身...以女質為化....則生於舍衛國王...則為阿踰闍友稱夫人 (p. 1 from Hōryūji edition)

[41]和光同俗 : This passage can be found in Lao Tzu and evidently has influenced Chi-tsang in his commentary on the *Śrīmālādevī sūtra*. Cf. *Shinbukkyō jiten*, *op. cit.*, p. 554.

[42]The three limitations which were the destiny of all women during their lifetime were: 1) subjection to parents, 2) subjection to husband and 3) subjection to children.

The five obstacles which the female sex must endure with regard to rebirth are the incapability of being born in 1) Mahābrahman's heaven, 2) Śakra (or Indra's) heaven, 3) the Paranirmitavaśavartin heaven and the incapability of becoming either 4) a Cakravartin king, or 5) a Buddha. Although these five obstacles are enumerated in the *Saddharmapuṇḍarīka sūtra*, the chapter on the Nāga princess describes the Buddahood of this young girl within her female body. As Ekayāna, the "Universal Vehicle of Salvation," became more influential and popular, the woman's position within Buddhism was also elevated.

[43]Cf. *Saṁyutta-Nikāya*, I. 83.

[44]七地已前為色身。八地已上為法身則勝鬘應是八地已上法身。又如淨名天女辯屈身子。 (T. v. 37, no. 1744, p. 3a).

[45]又釈六根清淨中地前菩薩是受於肉身。 (T. v. 37, no. 1744, p. 3a).

[46]若依涅槃経其名日德鬘優婆夷。位階十地安住不動。為衆生故現受女身。 (T. v. 37, no. 1744, p. 3a).

[47]*Bussho kaisetsu daijiten*, v. 7, p. 414.

[48]Cf. Tsukinowa, *Shōmangyō hōgatsu dōji shomongyō*, *op. cit.*, p. 3, in which both the Chinese and Tibetan reconstruction of the name of the Buddha, Samantaprabhā and Samantabhadra, are given.

[49]See Introduction.

[50]*Ch'u san-tsang chi chi*, T. v. 55, no. 2145, p. 105b.

[51]*Sung kao seng chuan*, T. v. 50, no. 2061, p. 720b.

[52] See footnote 33.

[53] Tokiwa, *Gokan yori Sō Sei*, *op. cit.*, p. 911.

[54] For a discussion concerning the authorship of the *Ratnagotravibhāga*, see Takasaki, the *Ratnagotravibhāga*, *op. cit.*; Obermiller, *The Sublime Science*, *op. cit.*; Nakamura, *Kukyō ichijō hōshōron no kenkyū* (Tokyo: Sankibō busshorin, 1972); Ruegg, *La Théorie du Tathāgatagarbha*, *op. cit.*; and Katsumata, *Bukkyō ni okeru shinshikisetsu*, *op. cit.*

[55] Reugg, *La Théorie du Tathāgatagarbha*, *op. cit.*, p. 4.

[56] See below, Chapter IV for the analysis of Emptiness in the *Śrīmālādevī sūtra*.

[57] Ruegg postulates that the substantialist interpretation of Emptiness was a reaction against Nāgārjuna who was considered nihilistic. *La Théorie du Tathāgatagarbha*, *op. cit.*, pp. 345-346.

[58] E. H. Johnston, *Ratnagotra*, *op. cit.*, p. v.

[59] Johnston, *ibid.*, p. xiv.

[60] The *Tathāgatagarbha sūtra* was first translated into Chinese by Fa-chü and Fa-li during the reign of Emperor Hui (290-306). For a discussion of this sūtra, see Chapter II: "Tathāgatagarbha" below. Also see Katsumata Shunkyō, *Bukkyō ni okeru shinshikisetsu no kenkyū*, *op. cit.*, pp. 594-597.

[61] In Chapters II and III the complex, and thus, more developed, analysis of Tathāgatagarbha in the *Śrīmālādevī sūtra* is presented, precluding the cotemporaneous composition of the *Tathāgatagarbha* and *Śrīmālādevī sūtras*.

[62] Ui Kakuju, *Bukkyō kyōtenshi* (Tokyo: Tosie shuppansha, 1957), p. 137. Also see Ruegg, *La Théorie du Tathāgatagarbha*, *op. cit.*, pp. 111-112) for the relationship between the Tathāgatagarbha and the *Daśabhūmika-sūtra* (which is part of the *Avataṁsaka*).

[63] Etienne Lamotte, *L'Enseignement de Vimalakīrti* (Louvain: Institut Orientaliste, 1962), p. 40.

[64] According to the biography of Vasubandhu (婆藪槃豆法師傳) (T. v. 50, no. 2049) written by Paramārtha, Vasubandhu wrote a commentary on the *Śrīmālādevī sūtra* among others, after Asaṅga's death. 阿僧伽法師殂歿後、天親方造大乘論、解釋諸大乘經、華嚴 涅槃 法華 維摩 勝鬘等諸大乘経論、悉是法師所造。 Cited in Tsukinowa, *Shōmangyō hōgatsu*, *op. cit.*, p. 14.

[65] See below, Chapter II.

[66] Figure 1 is adapted from Ui Hakuju. *Bukkyō kyōtenshi*, *op. cit.*, pp. 93-95.

[67]The oldest of the Prajñā literature is the *Aṣṭasāhasrikā*, composed perhaps over a two hundred year span, the oldest portions dating c. 100 B.C. Cf. Conze, *The Prajñāpāramitā Literature*, *op. cit.*, p. 9.

[68]The larger *Sukhāvativyūha* was first translated into Chinese between 147 and 186 A.D. Cf. Maurice Winternitz, *A History of Indian Literature*, vol. II: *Buddhist and Jaina Literature* (Calcutta: University of Calcutta, 1933), p. 311.

[69]The kernel of the *Saddharmapuṇḍarīka* is probably c. 100 A.D. Ui, *Bukkyō kyōtenshi*, pp. 113-115. Also see Winternitz, *A History of Indian Literature*, *op. cit.*, p. 304. Har Dayal, *Bodhisattva Doctrine*, *op. cit.*, p. 382 dates the oldest portion as c. 100 B.C. Warder, *Indian Buddhism*, *op. cit.*, pp. 395 ff. discusses the *Saddharmapuṇḍarīka*, *Vimalakīrtinirdeśa*, *Suvarṇaprabhāsa* and portions of the *Ratnakūṭa* anthology in what seems to be a post-Nāgārjuna period of development. His reference to their dates of composition is extremely vague. Conze, *Buddhism: Its Essence and Development*, *op. cit.*, pp. 123-124, groups the *Saddharmapuṇḍarīka* and the *Vimalakirtinirdeśa* in the period 100 B.C. to 200 A.D.

[70]Portions of the *Avataṁsaka sūtra* are very old, having been translated into Chinese as independent sūtras in the early 3rd. C. A. D. by Dharmarakṣa. See Takasaki, *The Ratnagotravibhāga*, *op. cit.*, p. 35 and Winternitz, *A History of Indian Literature*, *op. cit.*, vol. II, p. 328.

[71]The *Aṣṭadaśasāhasrikā*, *Pañcaviṁśatisāhasrikā*, and *Śatasāhasrikā* are expansions of the same root text with varying degrees of repetition, developed at the beginning of the Common Era over a period of three hundred years. Conze, *Prajñāpāramitā Literature*, pp. 17-18.

[72]There is a divergence of opinion concerning the date of compilation, ranging from the time of Nāgārjuna to the fifth century. Bodhiruci used the old translations of assemblies 3, 4, 8, 9, 12, 14, 15, 16, 17, 18, 19, 23, 26, 32, 33, 36, 38, 39, 41, 43, 44, 46, 47), made new translation of assemblies 1, 5, 6, 10, 13, 21, 24, 25, 27, 28, 29, 30, 37, 42, 48, 49) and added assemblies 2, 7, 11, 20, 22, 31, 34, 35, 40 and 45. The Tibetan *Ratnakūṭa* also has the same number of assemblies but had translated assemblies 7, 11, 13, 14, 17, 20 and 40 from the Chinese rather than from the Sanskrit. Perhaps the *Kāśyapa parivarta*, the forty-third assembly, is the oldest since it was often referred to as the *Ratnakūṭa sūtra*. The anthology as it exists today may have gradually developed over several centuries, expanding upon some of the tenets in the *Kāśyapa parivarta*. *Shinbutten kaidaijiten*, *op. cit.*, p. 93.

[73]The *Vimalakīrtinirdeśa sūtra* was first translated into Chinese between 222 and 280 A.D. by Chih Ch'ien (支謙) of the Wu dynasty from Yüeh-chih. Nanjio Bunyiu, *A Catalogue of the Chinese Translation of the Buddhist Tripiṭaka* (Oxford: Clarendon Press, 1883) (Tokyo reprint 1930), p. 47, no. 147.

[74]It is still unresolved as to which text is earlier, the *Mahāparinirvāṇa sūtra* or the *Tathāgatagarbha sūtra*. For different hypotheses concerning their chronological positions, see Takasaki Jikido, "Nyoraizō shisō ni okeru *Shōmangyō*," *op. cit.*, in which Takasaki places the *Mahāparinirvāṇa sūtra* immediately after the *Tathāgatagarbha sūtra*, and hypothesizes it may be later than the *Pu tseng pu chien ching*. Ui Hakuju, *Bukkyō kyōtenshi*, *op. cit.*, places the *Mahāparinirvāṇa* before the *Śrīmāladevī*. Katsumata Shunkyō, *Bukkyō ni okeru shinshikisetsu*, *op. cit.*, p. 593, places the *Mahāparinirvāṇa sūtra* immediately after the *Śrīmāladevī*.

Since Dharmakṣema, translator of the *Mahāparinirvāṇa sūtra*, is also alleged to have translated the *Śrīmālādevī*, evidence is inadequate for determining the relation between the two texts. The evolution of Tathāgatagarbhan thought in these two texts has not yet been established.

[75]The doctrinal development among the *Tathāgatagarbha sūtra*, *Pu tseng pu chien*, and *Śrīmālādevī sūtra* are discussed below in Chapters II and III.

[76]Depending upon whether Maitreya (270-350) or Saramati (350-450) is the author, the *Ratnagotra* may be dated between 300 and 450 A.D.

[77]Vasubandhu's dates are given according to Erich Frauwallner, "Landmarks in the History of Indian Logic," *Wiener Zeitschrift für die Kunde Süd-und Ostaseins*, V, 1961, pp. 129-131.

[78]The time periods are not rigid with considerable overlapping due to the fact that the dating of these texts remains tentative at this time.

[79]The Sātavāhana chronology is still uncertain. The dates given above are based upon the Puranic regnal periods although there are discrepancies within the *Purāṇas* with reference to the entire duration of the Sātavāhana period. See K. Gopalachari, Chapter X: "The Sātavāhana Empire" in *A Comprehensive History of India*, ed. by K. A. Nilakanta Śastri, vol. II: *The Mauryas and Sātavāhanas* (Bombay: Orient Longmans, 1957), p. 295 and K. Gopalachari, *Early History of the Āndhra Country* (Madras: University of Madras, 1941), pp. 28-29.

[80]Warder, *Indian Buddhism*, *op. cit.*, pp. 326-327 and K. M. Panikkar, *A Survey of Indian History* (Bombay: Asia Publishing House, 1957) (Reprinted from the 3rd ed.), pp. 62-63.

[81]K. A. Nilakanta Śastri, *A History of South India From Prehistoric Times to the Fall of Vijayanagar* (London: Oxford University Press, 1955), pp. 94-95.

[82]Copalachari in *A Comprehensive History of India*, *op. cit.*, p. 293.

[83]For a delineation of the hierarchical power structure of the Sātavāhana administration, see Gopalachari, *Early History of the Āndhra Country*, *op. cit.*, pp. 73-85.

[84]Nilakanti Śastri, *A History of South India, op. cit.*, p. 95.

[85]Information is scarce concerning the Ikṣvāku dynasty of the Krishna-Guntur region, founded by Śāntamūla. Their capital was apparently in Vijayapurī (Śrīparvata), in the valley of Nāgārjunakoṇḍa. The Ikṣvākus were eventually overthrown by the Pallavas at the end of the 3rd C. A.D. The majority of the generous patrons of Buddhism were women of the royal family, indicating their prominent social position and the possession of their own property. See Dines Chandra Sircar, Chapter IV, "Eastern Deccan" in the *Vākāṭaka-Gupta Age*, Ramesha Chandra Majumdar and Anant Sadashiv Altekar (gen. ed.) (Delhi: Motilal Banarsidass, 1960), pp. 64-68; D. C. Sircar, Chapter XI: "The Deccan after the Sātavāhanas" in *A Comprehensive History of India, op. cit.*, pp. 333-334; and Nilakanta Śastri, *A History of South India, op. cit.*, p. 96.

[86]Warder, *Indian Buddhism, op. cit.*, p. 394 and R. C. Majumdar, *Ancient India* (Delhi: Motilal Banarsidass, 1964), p. 135.

[87]Majumdar, *Ancient India, op. cit.*, p. 268.

[88]Charles Drekmeier, *Kingship and Community in Early India* (Stanford: Stanford University Press, 1962), p. 180 and Majumdar, *Ancient India, op. cit.*, p. 230.

[89]Drekmeier, *Kingship and Community, op. cit.*, p. 181.

[90]Majumdar, *Ancient India, op. cit.*, p. 426.

[91]A. S. Altekar, Chapter XIX: "Religion and Philosophy" in *Vākāṭaka-Gupta Age, op. cit.*, pp. 386-395.

[92]Bareau, *Les Sectes Boudhiques, op. cit.*, p. 38.

[93]Bareau, *Ibid.*, p. 39.

[94]Warder, *Indian Buddhism, op. cit.*, pp. 292-293. Also see Binayendra Nath Chaudhury, *Buddhist Centres in Ancient India* (Calcutta: Sanskrit College, 1969), p. 181.

[95]Chaudhury, *Buddhist Centres in Ancient India, op. cit.*, pp. 170-171.

[96]Chaudhury, *Buddhist Centres, op. cit.*, pp. 178-179.

[97]Bareau, *Les Sectes Bouddhiques, op. cit.*, p. 47.

[98]Chaudhury, *Buddhist Centres, op. cit.*, pp. 128-129.

[99]*Shinbutten kaidai jiten, op. cit.*, p. 11.

[100]Bareau, *Les Sectes Bouddhiques, op. cit.*, p. 40.

[101]Ruegg, *La Théorie du Tathāgatagarbha, op. cit.*, p. 392.

CHAPTER II

TATHĀGATAGARBHA

What Is "Tathāgatagarbha"?

The compound *tathāgata-garbha* has two constituents, *tathāgata* signifying "thus come" or "thus gone," designating a Buddha and *garbha* signifying "womb, inside, middle, interior of anything...a foetus or embryo, child, brood."[1] *Tathāgatagarbha*, as a genitive *tatpuruṣa* compound, would then signify an interior container or womb of the Tathāgata or a Tathāgata-in-embryo. The hidden passive nature of the Tathāgata is represented by the "container" or "interior" nature of *garbha* while the potentiality of becoming a Tathāgata is represented by the foetus or "embryo" nature of *garbha*. If *garbha* is interpreted as womb, the "container" dimension in which the Tathāgata resides is implied; if interpreted as embryo, the seed and eventual birth of the Tathāgata is implied.

From the two definitions of *garbha* then, a passive and an active interpretation can be derived. *Garbha* as Tathāgata-in-utero refers to the passive relationship of a receptacle in which the Tathāgata resides. *Garbha* as Tathāgata-in-embryo refers to the active faculty by which the process of growth and birth will occur, initiating the emission of the Tathāgata within oneself. The question then arises: Is the Tathāgatagarbha an active process in which the production of the Tathāgata nature is realized as a seed which eventually grows and is born or is the Tathāgatagarbha a receptacle of the Tathāgata nature, a container in which the Tathāgata resides? Or, is the Tathāgatagarbha best explained as both container and seed?

If one analyzes the compound *Tathāgatagarbha* as a *bahuvrīhi*, i.e. as "the one who holds the Tathāgata-in-embryo" (or the Womb of the Tathāgata), who is the one who holds the Tathāgatagarbha? Is it the Tathāgata himself or living beings who have within themselves this *Tathāgatagarbha*? On which level does one apprehend Tathāgatagarbha--from the level of Complete Enlightenment or from within the human condition?

Analyses of the compound *Tathāgatagarbha* are bifurcated between *tatpuruṣa* vs. *bahuvrīhi* on the grammatical level, and between active vs. passive on the soteriological level. Suzuki, in his study on the *Laṅkāvatāra sūtra*, interprets Tathāgatagarbha as a passive receptacle soteriologically and as a *tatpuruṣa* grammatically. The Tathāgatagarbha then, is "the womb wherein the Tathāgata is conceived and nourished and matured"[2] which Suzuki identifies with the purified Ālayavijñāna for the Ālayavijñāna is considered the source of delusion and impure in nature.

Richard Robinson synthesizes both the active and passive faculties of Tathāgatagarbha and analyzes the compound as a *tatpuruṣa*: "the purified store-consciousness is the womb where the Tathāgata is conceived and nourished and matured,"[3] which is the "container" dimension of Tathāgatagarbha, agreeing with Suzuki. Robinson adds to this, the seed and growth dimension: [the Tathāgatagarbha is] "the embryonic Buddha consisting of the pure dharmas in a person's *ālaya-vijñāna*."[4] Both Suzuki and Robinson are interpreting Tathāgatagarbha based upon the *Laṅkāvatāra sūtra*, which is a late development within the Tathāgatagarbha theory, becoming assimilated with Vijñānavāda.

Nakamura Hajime appears to analyze Tathāgatagarbha as a *bahuvrīhi*, viz. as the "potentiality to become a Tathāgata which exists within the mind of the ordinary man,"[5] suggestive of the receptacle dimension which is associated with the mind. Ui Hakuju suggests that the Tathāgatagarbha is another name for Suchness (*tathatā*) and Buddha-nature, interpreting *garbha* as essence or nature. Ui also associates Tathāgatagarbha with the "inherently pure mind hidden within the defilements of all living beings,"[6] suggestive of an analysis of the compound as a *bahuvrīhi*.

Takasaki Jikido, who has investigated the Tathāgatagarbha theory in considerable detail, considers the term Tathāgatagarbha as "probably a name given to the inherently pure mind contaminated by defilement, a problem dating from primitive Buddhism."[7] The association of the mind as a container for the Tathāgata is reiterated, grammatically analyzing the compound as a *tatpuruṣa*, and equating the *garbha* with the inherently pure mind but not with a living being's ordinary mind.

David Ruegg also analyzes the compound as a *tatpuruṣa*, based upon citations from Tathāgatagarbha literature which employ the compound, in the majority of cases, as a *tatpuruṣa*.[8] Moreover, when the term Tathāgatagarbha is used as a *bahuvrīhi*, a strict identity between living beings and the Tathāgata is not intended. Rather, the Tathāgatagarbha refers to the nature of mind, hidden *within* defiled living beings. For example, "...*tathāgatasyeme garbhah sarvasattvā iti*" (*Rathnagotravibhāga*, p. 70) refers to the living being's having the Tathāgatagarbha as his true nature but not as identical with his present state. According to Ruegg, a *tatpuruṣa* analysis of the compound is the more prevalent because information derived from the Tathāgatagarbha literature now extant interprets the compound in such a way, not necessarily indicating a representative sample of the Tathāgatagarbha literature which once existed however. From the sources now available, among which the *Śrīmālādevī sūtra* is represented, we may assert that the *tathāgatagarbha*, in the majority of cases, is correctly analyzed as a genitive *tatpuruṣa*.

In analyzing the head noun *garbha*, Ruegg distinguishes between the Tibetan translation and the Chinese. The Tibetan term for *garbha* (in the compound *Tathāgatagarbha*) is *sñiṅ po*, which connotes "essence," "seed," or "heart." The Sanskrit word *garbha* also may assume secondary meanings of "interior," "essence," and "heart" as attested to in the *Laṅkāvatāra* which employs the term *Tathāgatagarbhahṛdayam*.[9] This citation in the *Laṅkāvatāra-sūtra* supports the relationship between heart or essence (*hṛdayam*) and *Tathāgatagarbha*.

The Chinese term for *garbha* is *tsang* (藏) denoting "storehouse," "container," or hidden place (often used to translate the Sanskrit *kośa*). No reference is made to embryo (児), essence (体), or womb (胎). The relationship between *Tathāgatagarbha* and mind is explicitly demonstrated when *Tathāgatagarbha* literature is assimilated to the concept of *ālayavijñāna*, employing the same word, *tsang*, for both *Tathāgatagarbha* (如来藏) and *ālayavijñana* (藏識).

From the above translators' interpretations it is evident that the connotation of seed or embryo, essence or germ, predominates among translators relying on the Tibetan translation while the connotation of matrix receptacle, or womb appears to be preferred by translators relying on the Chinese translation. Figure 2 summarizes alternative translations for *Tathāgatagarbha*.[10]

Translation	Translators
"Embryo"	Conze, Lamotte, La Vallee Poussin Tucci
"Essence"	Guenther, Obermiller, Ruegg
"Germ"	Jacobi
"Seed"	T. R. V. Murti
"Keim"	Frauwallner
"Matrix" or "Womb"	R. Robinson, D. T. Suzuki, Takasaki

Figure 2. Different Translations of *garbha* in the term *Tathāgatagarbha*

The Incipience of the Tathāgatagarbha Concept

Before an hypothesis is postulated concerning the function of *Tathāgatagarbha* within its generic literature, an historical survey of literature prefiguring this theory is a prerequisite for investigating the rise and evolution of this concept within Buddhist thought. The problem of the origin of *Tathāgatagarbha* and the environment within which it evolved is an immense one, for no great teacher associated solely with *Tathāgatagarbha* has been transmitted through literature now extant. A summary of Buddhologists' hypotheses concerning the development of *Tathāgatagarbha* will aid the reader in understanding the complexity involved in investigating *Tathāgatagarbha* thought.

1. David Seyfort Ruegg:

In his vast and monumental work, *La Théorie du Tathāgatagarbha et du Gotra*, David Ruegg reviews major sūtras and śāstras prefiguring and contributing to the systemization of *Tathāgatagarbha*, within the Tibetan historical context. He delineates common traits shared with primitive Buddhism and yet, concomitantly, demonstrates that peculiarities within

Tathāgatagarbha as a system of thought are a missing link between the two great schools, Mādhyamika and Vijñānavāda.

One of the characteristics of *Tathāgatagarbha*, traceable to primitive Buddhism, is that of the luminous, inherently pure mind tainted by defilements,[11] attested to in the *Aṅguttara-nikāya*. It has been noted previously[12] that the Mahāsaṅghika also incorporated into their schema a theory of pure mind contaminated by defilements. Based upon the criticism of the impeccability of the Arhat, the direct cause of the schism between the Sthaviravāda and Mahāsaṅghika, the non-defiled ignorance (*akliṣṭājñāna*) associated with the Arhat, was to become an important factor in the theory of Ekayāna, and in the theory of "the latent stage of ignorance" (*avidyāvāsabhūmi*), first developed in the *Śrīmālādevī-sūtra*. The relationship between the pure mind and defilements, appears to have been wholly adopted by the Mahāsaṅghika, and later by the Mahāyāna.

While the luminous mind can be claimed to be accepted by Nikāya Buddhism, Ruegg's historical analysis emphasizes the relationship between the theory of *garbha* and *gotra*, a much later development. The development of the "essence of Tathāgata" is compared and contrasted with the "lineage of the Buddha" (*Buddhagotra*), a theme of great importance in Vijñānavādin treatises, some of which claim the identity between the lineage of the Buddha existing by nature (*prakṛtisthagotra*) and t-at of the "essence of Tathāgata" (*Tathāgatagarbha*).[13] Ruegg investigates the most important sūtras from which Vijñānavāda developed, viz. the *Sandhinirmocana* and the *Laṅkāvatāra*, the former sūtra expounding a three-*gotra* theory corresponding to each of the three vehicles, while the latter expounds on a five-*gotra* theory distinguishing not only three *gotra* corresponding to the three vehicles, but also an indeterminate *gotra* and no-*gotra* (*agotra*), the last *gotra* being associated with the Icchantika.[14]

Moreover, Ruegg's comparison between the development of *Tathāgatagarbha* and Mādhyamika also focuses on the concept of *gotra* and *garbha*. As contrasted with the Vijñānavādin treatises however, the Mādhyamikan śāstras do not appear to give importance to the notion of *gotra*,[15] having few references in the major treatises of this school. However, in the *Kāśyapa parivarta*, the *āryagotra* is mentioned as unconditioned, immaculate, permanent, and real (perhaps pre-figuring the four *guṇa-pāramitā* in the *Śrīmālādevī-sūtra* to be discussed below). The *Daśabhūmika-sūtra*, part of the *Avataṁsaka*, also comments on the *Buddha-gotra* as being present from the eighth *Bodhisattva-bhūmi* and above, brilliant like a jewel with the qualities of the Buddha.[16] This metaphor of the jewel is reiterated in the arising of the thought of omniscience (*sarvajñatā-ratna-cittotpāda*) described in a *Tathāgatagarbha* text, the *Dharāṇīśvararāja-sūtra*, quoted in the *Ratnagotra-vibhāga*, in which the "element of the Tathāgata" (*Tathāgata-dhātu* or *Buddha-dhātu*) is compared to a precious jewel.[17] However, Ruegg concludes, the majority of the classical treatises of the Mādhyamikan school do not explicate either *Tathāgatagarbha* or the *gotra* existing by nature (*prakṛṭistha-gotra*). The literary allusions refer, rather, to the family of the Tathāgata, fixed at the eighth *Bodhisattva-bhūmi*. A distinction between the *gotra* theory of the Mādhyamika and the *Tathāgatagarbha* theory must be made, the former being expounded principally in the śāstras while the *Tathāgatagarbha* theory is embodied in a distinctive group of sūtras. Moreover, in the *Ratnagotravibhāga* itself, there is no explicit identification between *gotra* and *Tathāgata-garbha*.[18]

With reference to the relationship between *gotra* and *Tathāgatagarbha* then, one must exercise caution in identifying them. Their relationship will again by the subject of study when the literature which foreshadowed *Tathāgatagarbha* is discussed below.

2. Takasaki Jikido

In numerous articles and in his translation and analysis, *A Study on the Ratnagotravibhāga (Uttaratantra): Being a Treatise on the Tathāgatagarbha Theory of Mahāyāna Buddhism*, Takasaki recognizes the difficulty in investigating the origin of the *Tathāgatagarbha* as a system. "The transmitters and methods of transmission of the *Tathāgatagarbha* system is still not known."[19] He bases his investigation of the evolution of the *Tathāgathagarbha* theory upon the *Ratnagotravibhāga* because that text appears to be the first systematic commentary on Tathāgatagarbha.[20] In the volume of quotations within the

Ratnagotra-vibhāga, two passages appear to contribute the necessary key for his thesis. These two quotes, from the *Mahāyāna Abhidharma sūtra* and from the *Mahāyānasutralaṅkāra*, both Vijñānavādin texts, are suggestive of a relationship between *Tathāgatagarbha* and Vijñānavāda. Moreover, since none of the *Tathāgatagarbha* literature appears to be known to Nāgārjuna, Takasaki places the Tathāgatagarbha theory as a later Mahāyānist innovation and post-Nāgārjuna. Takasaki, like Ruegg, traces the first appearance of the notion of pure mind (*cittaprakṛti*) to the Pāli canon. Four sects are known to have accepted the concept of pure mind, viz. the Therāvada of Ceylon, the Vaibhāṣika, the Vātsīputrīya, and the Mahāsaṅghika.[21]

The concept of "extraneous" defilements (*āgantukaklēsa*), however, is not found among the oldest portions of the Pāli Canon. The controversy among the Therāvadin sects apparently did not arise in Mahāyāna Buddhism since the concepts of pure mind and foreign defilements were accepted in all Mahāyāna literature. Because the *Ratnagotravibhāga* is called the *Mahāyānottaratantra*, the "highest exposition of Mahāyāna," for Takasaki this suggests not the preemption of the *Prajñā-pāramitā* tradition but its natural culmination in the thought exemplified in the *Ratnagotravibhāga*.[22]

Moreover, according to Takasaki, the *Sandhinirmocana* is a synthesis of both the positive and negative aspects of Emptiness, or the ultimate exposition of *śūnyavāda*. The distinction between the "highest teaching" in the *Ratnagotravibhāga's* criticism of *Prajñāpāramitā* and that in the *Sandhinirmocana* is tenuous in Takasaki's study, for both treatises are criticisms of *Prajñāpāramitā* and both describe *śunyatā* in positive attributions yet they are claimed to be different systems with different origins, without stating the points of difference. The distinction is made between the *Tathāgatagarbha* as a description of reality from the reference of Supreme Enlightenment, and the Vijñānavāda as a description from the reference of the phenomenal world. However, such differences in standpoint do not preclude either the hypothesis that Vijñānavāda and Tathāgatagarbha have the same source from which they diverged or that, while developing synchronically, with different origins, they mutually influenced each other.

With reference to the relationship between *Buddhagotra* and *Tathāgatagarbha*, Takasaki compares different texts, hypothesizing that the relationship between the two is not one of identity but rather alternative interpretations of one problem, viz. of an inherently pure mind contaminated by defilements.[23] According to his survey of the literature expounding *Buddhagotra* or *Buddhadhātu* (佛性), the substitution of *Buddhagotra* for *Tathāgatagarbha* appears to have been used for the first time in the *Mahāparinirvāṇa-sūtra* (the Mahāyāna *Nirvāṇa-sūtra*). Because of other differences between the *Mahāparinirvāṇa-sūtra* and the *Śrīmālādevī-sūtra*, Takasaki postulates that these two sūtras are different interpretations of the same problem, viz. inherently pure mind tainted by defilements, both based upon the *Pu tseng pu chien ching* (不增不減經).[24] Therefore, one cannot conclude that the *gotra* and the *Tathāgatagarbha* are identical.

3. Katsumata Shunkyō[25]

Again Katsumata, like Ruegg and Takasaki, recognizes the difficulty in hypothesizing the period when Tathāgatagarbha literature first appeared. The first appearance is traced to the *Ekottarikāgama* (T. v. II, n. 125, p. 550c):

"If someone devotes himself to the *Ekottarikāgama*,
其有專心持增一
Then he has the Tathāgatagarbha.
便為總持如来藏。
Even if his body cannot exhaust defilement in this life,
正便今身不尽結
In his next life he will attain supreme wisdom.
後生便得高才智。

However, one cannot be absolutely certain as to the meaning of *Tathāgatagarbha* in this passage with relation to *Nikāya* doctrine. Moreover, because the *Ekottarikāgama* is one of the later additions to the Canon, this could be closely approximating Mahāyāna ideas.

Again, in the *Daśabhūmika-sūtra*, eight kinds of liberation are enumerated in the tenth *Bodhisattva-bhūmi*, employing the words *ju-lai-tsang fa-chieh tsang* (如来藏法界藏) (T. vol. 10, no. 286, p. 569c). However, the Sanskrit equivalent is *Tathāgatakośa, dharmatāgarbha*[26] signifying that *ju-lai-tsang* in this instance is not *Tathāgatagarbha* as "essence" (or "embryo," "womb") of the Buddha but as "storehouse of the Buddha," "the container" of the dharma-nature. Katsumata interprets this phrase as reflecting the identical meaning between *garbha* and *kośa*.[27]

4. Ui Hakuju

In analyzing the compound "*Tathāgatagarbha*," Ui considers the original meaning of this compound as "the Womb of the Tathāgata," because "sentient beings are the womb from which the Tathāgata is born," and simultaneously as the "Embryo of the Tathāgata," because they "are an Embryo which will become the Tathāgata."[28] Therefore, *Tathāgatagarbha* is identical with Buddha-nature. (Ui distinguishes the concept of Buddha nature from *Tathāgatagarbha* historically, stating that Buddha-nature (佛性 : Buddhatā, Budhagotra) is fundamentally the notion of *Tathāgatagarbha* without anticipating its existence among defilements as contrasted to the concept Tathāgatagarbha (as a system) which necessarily is concerned with its existence among defilements.) When the inherently pure mind is liberated from such defilements it becomes the Dharma-Body itself. The fundamental difference between Buddha-nature and Tathāgatagarbha is that the latter emphasizes the human condition in the defiled state whereas the former emphasizes the pure, enlightened condition.[29]

According to Ui, the fundamental idea that all must work for enlightenment is present from the very earliest period of Buddhism but the technical term *Tathāgatagarbha* does not appear in ancient Buddhism.[30]

The Concept of Luminous Mind

1. *In Abhidharmist Literature:*

Several references to a luminous mind (*pabhassaram cittam*) are incorporated in the *Aṅguttara Nikāya*, a late addition to the Canon. The Theravādins who had rejected a theory of pure mind, considered the mind defiled, necessitating its severance and the subsequent birth of the mind of the Arhat. The Mahāsaṅghika and certain Vaibhāṣika, on the other hand, accepted the notion of a pure, luminous mind.

a. *Ekottarikāgama*

In the introduction (序品) to the *Ekottarikāgama* (*Aṅguttara Nikāya*), in the Chinese recension (T. V. II, n. 125, p. 550c), the attainment of *ju-lai-tsang* (如來藏= Tathāgata-garbha?) is correlated with studying the *Ekottarikāgama*.[31] However, the introduction is a comparatively late addition to the main body of the text. The original has been lost, resulting in the addition of many chapters not evidenced in the Pāli.[32] Among them is the introduction which appears to have been completed after the formation of Mahāyāna[33] and translated in 384 by Saṅghadeva, a Mahāsaṅghika. This introduction could have been added by Saṅghadeva himself or its prototype may have existed in the 2nd to 3rd C. A.D.

Because the Chinese recension of the *Pañca Nikāya* (五部四阿含) is not the Canon of the only one sect, as in the case of the Pāli Canon, the recension includes the traditions of at least three sects.[34] There are now available texts of seven Abhidharmist sects--the Siṁhalese Theravāda, Sarvāstivāda, Mahīśāsaka, Dharmaguptika, Mahāsaṅghika, Kāśyapīya, and Sautrāntika--upon which the differentiation between parts of the Canon may be hypothesized. The *Ekottarikāgama* appears to be the transmission of the Mahāsaṅghika, but of a different subsect than that of the Mahāsaṅghikan Vinaya now extant (perhaps paralleling the Northern vs. Southern Mahāsaṅghika, i.e. the Kashmirian Mahāsaṅghika as contrasted with the Andhran Mahāsaṅghika). In the *Chü-she lun chi-ku* (俱舍論稽古) Fa-ch'uang (法幢) also claims that the *Ekottarikāgama* belongs to the Mahāsaṅghikan tradition.[35] Portions of the *Ekottarikāgama*, in which the *ālaya-vijñāna* appears (e.g. T. v. 2, no. 127-130) are most probably extractions from the Sarvāstivādin Canon.

Since the introduction to the *Ekottarikāgama* adds a Mahāyāna element in its depiction of *bodhi-citta, dharma-kāya* (*Vajra-kāya*), and in its affirmation of the *Prajñāpāramitā*, it is reasonable to postulate that the present introduction to the *Ekottarikāgama* is Mahāsaṅghika, reflecting the gradual transition in doctrine to that of Mahāyāna.[36]

Nothing can be hypothesized, however, with regard to the interpretation of *ju-lai-tsang* in the introduction to the

Ekottarikāgama, a term which was to be employed as the Chinese equivalent for Tathāgatagarbha. Due to the absence of any exposition of *ju-lai-tsang* in this one instantiation, no interpretation is possible.

b. *Aṅguttara-Nikāya* in Pāli Canon:

The luminous mind is referred to in the following passage (I., p. 10):

> pabhassaram idam bhikkave cittaṁ/ tañ ca kho āgantukehi upakkilesehi upakkiliṭṭhaṁ/ taṁ assutavā puthujjano yathābhūtam nappajānāti/ tasmā assutavato puthujjanassa cittabhāvanā natthī ti vadāmī ti/ pabhassaram idam bhikkave cittaṁ/ taṁ ca kho āgantukehi upakkilesehi vippamuttaṁ/ taṁ sutvā ariyasāvako yathābhūtaṁ pajānāti/ tasmā sutavato ariyasāvakassa cittabhāvanā atthī ti vadāmī ti/

"O Bhikṣu, cette Pensée est lumineuse (*pabhassaram*). Tantôt elle est affectée par les Affects adventices, et le profane qui l'ignore ne la connaît pas telle qu'elle est; par conséquent, je dis que le profane qui l'ignore n'a pas la cultivation de la Pensée. Et tantôt elle est libre des Affects adventices, et l'Auditeur Saint qui en a eu communication la connaît telle qu'elle est; par conséquent, je dis que l'Auditeur Saint qui en a eu communication a la cultivation de la Pensée."[37]

The luminous mind here is equivalent to the substratum of consciousness for the Theravādins, perhaps a parallel to the Sarvāstivādin *ālaya-vijñāna*.[38] The relationship between luminous mind untouched by defilement (*āgantukakleśa*) however, is absent from the Theravādin literature and generally attributed to the Mahāsaṅghika and certain Vaibhāṣika.[39]

c. *Mahāvibhāṣa-śāstra*[40]

The Vaibhāṣaikan passage, referred to as expounding luminous mind untouched by defilements, is found in the *Mahāvibhāṣaśastra* (T. v. 27, no. 1545, p. 140b-c), translated by Hsüan-tsang and rejected by the Sarvāstivāda-Vaibhāṣika:

"Q: Why was this śāstra composed?

"A: Because I wished to explain the meaning of the sūtra, viz. the sūtra which discusses the mind liberated from (the three poisons of) greed, hate, and delusion. Although the sūtra was composed to discuss this, it does not explain extensively. What kind of mind is liberated? Is the mind liberated since it has greed, hate, and delusion? Or, is the mind liberated when it is separated from greed, hate, and delusion? In this śāstra which is based upon that sūtra, I will explain what was not explained in that text.

"As the Vaibhāṣika (or, as the Vaibhāṣikan text) explains: the intrinsically pure mind which is contaminated by extraneous defilement (*āgantukakleśa*) is marked by impurity. In order to prevent such a bias, I will demonstrate the fact that there is no intrinsically pure mind which is marked by impurity due to its contamination by extraneous defilement. If the intrinsically pure mind is marked by impurity because it is contaminated by defilement why is there no intrinsically contaminated defilement which, interacting with an intrinsically pure mind, becomes marked by purity? Or, why not an intrinsically contaminated (mind of) defilement, interacting with an inherently pure mind, which becomes marked by impurity? Consequently it would be similar in principle to the intrinsically pure mind which is not based upon extraneous defilement but is marked by impurity.

"(Another alternative argument would be:) Is this intrinsically pure mind born before the extraneous defilement or is it born at the same time (as the defilement)? If the mind is born and then assumes a defiled nature, then the mind still continues for two seconds in duration, and the argument contradicts (Buddhist) doctrine and you lose (the argument). If the mind is born at the same time as defilement, why does one say it is intrinsically pure? Your school does not explain that the future state of mind can be called intrinsically pure. In order to prevent other doctrines' biases of a similar nature and to demonstrate that my doctrine has no contradictory ideas, I have composed this śāstra. When one has not eliminated defilements within oneself, the mind cannot continue to function automatically in the world. If the mind cannot automatically function continually in the world, it is not called 'liberated.' If defilements are eliminated within oneself, at that time one realizes liberation because the mind automatically functions continually in the world.

"The Vaibhāṣika (or the Vaibhāṣikan text) speaks of the mind which is contaminated and that which is not contaminated, as not different (in essence). If the interaction with defilement is not eliminated, then the mind is called 'contaminated.' When the interaction with defilement is eliminated, the mind is not called contaminated, as in the case of a copper vessel. When the defilement is not yet eliminated, it is like a dirty vessel. Having removed the defilement it is not called a dirty vessel. The mind is also like this."

In this passage from the *Mahāvibhāṣaśāstra*, the relationship between the intrinsically pure mind and extraneous defilement is explicitly discussed in order to disprove some misinterpretations of certain unspecified Vaibhāṣika sūtras which adhere to the intrinsically pure, but extraneously defiled, mind. The innovation developed here, between luminous mind and extrinsic defilement, will be identified with one dimension of Tathāgatagarbha in Tathāgatagarbha literature, e.g. in the *Śrīmālādevī*, *Laṅkāvatāra*, and *Ratnagotra*, but is rarely mentioned in Vijñānavāda literature.

Because both the intrinsically pure mind and the neutral mind (which can be either pure or impure) are mentioned in the Nikāyas, the eighteen sectarian schools debated both alternative trends. The Abhidharmists scathingly criticized the theory of extraneous defilement disassociated from mind while the Mahāsaṅghika and certain Vaibhāṣika of the southern sects emphasized intrinsically pure mind.[41] These Vaibhāṣika, who are criticized in the *Mahāvibhāṣa śāstra* for their views concerning intrinsically pure mind, remain unidentified because the name "Vaibhāṣika" refers to different sects, depending upon the text cited. In the *Mahāvibhāṣa śāstra* the "Vaibhāṣika" are most probably a subsect of Mahāsaṅghika because the tenets ascribed to the Vaibhāṣika are ascribed to the Mahāṣaṅghikan sects in both the *Sui-hsiang lun* (隨相論) (*Lakṣaṇānusāra śāstra*) (T. v. 32, no. 1641) and the *I bu tsung lun lun* (異部宗輪論) composed by Vasumitra (T. v. 49, no. 2031).[42]

Interaction between mind and mentals (defilement) was first seen in the southern schools and later developed by the Sarvāstivāda,[43] mind and mentals being separate but interacting entities. In contrast to the Sarvāstivāda, certain Vaibhāṣika considered fundamental defilement (*anuśaya*) mind-disassociated and the seed for active defilement (*paryavasthāna*) which were mind-associated.[44] The Mahāsaṅghika, in the *I bu tsung lun lun*, agree with this Vaibhāṣikan interpretation.[45] The fundamental defilement, eliminated only by the Buddha, is also acknowledged in the *Mahāvibhāṣa śāstra*, later to be acknowledged by the author of the *Śrīmālādevī sūtra*. Therefore, the relationship between the intrinsic and extrinsic nature of mind, together with the analysis of defilement delineated in the *Śrīmālādevī sūtra*, have been borrowed from the "Vaibhāṣika" who are most likely southern Mahāsaṅghika in the Āndhra region.

2. *In Mahāyāna Literature:*

Although the luminous mind has been traced to the *Aṅguttara Nikāya* and to other paracanonical literature, it is among the Mahāyāna that we find a wholehearted endorsement of the theory of an intrinsically pure mind which nevertheless is obfuscated by "adventitious" or "extraneous" defilements (*āgantukakleśa*). In both Mādhyamika and Vijñānavāda, the intrinsically pure mind is expounded but the relationship between the inherently pure mind and Buddha-gotra or Tathāgatagarbha is more direct in the Vijñānavādin tradition.

> Il y a des relations étroites entre la "Pensée lumineuse" des sectes hīnayānistes et le Tathāgatagarbha "Embryon du Tathāgata" tel que le décrivent certains Sūtra et Śāstra de l'école idealiste des Yogācāra.
>
> Pour ces Sūtra, qui ne comptent pas parmi les plus anciennes productions du Mahāyāna, le Tathāgatagarbha est en principe lumineux, pur, éternal, immanent à tous les êtres, mais accidentellement souillé par les passions adventices.[46]

It is not possible, within the present study, to delineate all the sūtras which discuss the intrinsically pure mind.[47] However, for the purposes of differentiating the Mādhyamikan expositions from that of the Tathāgatagarbha literature and the subsequent Vijñānavādin treatises, key passages contributing to the development of Tathāgatagarbha thought, are discussed below.

a. *Aṣṭasāhasrikā-prajñāpāramitā*, p. 3, Vaidya edition:

> punar aparaṁ bhagavan bodhisattvena mahāsattvena prajñāpāramitāyāṁ caratā prajñāpāramitāyāṁ bhāvayatā evam śikṣitavyaṁ yathāsau śikṣyamāṇas tenāpi bodhicittena na manyeta/ tat kasya hetoḥ/ tathā hi tac cittam acittam, prakṛtiś cittasya prabhāsvarā// atha khalvāyuṣman śāriputra

āyuṣmantaṁ subhūtim etad avocat/ kiṁ punar āyuṣman subhūte asti tac cittam yac cittam acittam// evam ukte āyuṣmān subhūtir āyuṣmantaṁ śāriputram etad avocat/ kiṁ punar āyuṣman śāriputra yācittatā tatrācittatāyām astitā va nāstitā vā vidyate vā upalabhyate vā// śāriputra āha/ na hy etad āyuṣman subhūte// subhūtir āha/ saced āyuṣman śāriputra tatrācittatāyām astitā vā nastitā vā na vidyate vā nopalabhyate vā, api nu te yukta eṣa paryanuyogo bhavati yad āyuṣman śāriputra evam āha: asti tac cittam yac cittam acittam iti// evam ukte śāriputra āyuṣmantaṁ subhūtim etad avocat/ kā punar eṣāyuṣman subhūte acittatā// subhūtir āha/ avikārāyuṣman śāriputrāvikalpācittatā//

"Moreover, O Lord, when the Bodhisattva-Mahāsattvas practice and meditate on the Prajñāpāramitā they should learn so that what is learned is not thought of even by the bodhicitta. Why? Because the mind is no-mind; the inherent nature of mind is luminous." Then the venerable Śāriputra spoke to the venerable Subhūti: "Venerable Subhūti, is there a mind which, being a mind, is (yet) no-mind?"/ Then the venerable Subhūti spoke to the venerable Śāriputra:/ "Venerable Śāriputra, does one apprehend or know that what is 'no-mindedness' (*acittatā*), in being no-mindedness, neither has existence or non-existence (*nāstitā*)." Śāriputra spoke: "Not so, Venerable Subhūti."

Subhūti spoke: "Venerable Śāriputra, if one does not apprehend or know either existence or non-existence in no-mindedness, then is this refutation that you advocated when you said: 'Is there a mind which, being a mind, and (yet) no-mind' coherent?" Then Śāriputra spoke to the venerable Subhūti: "But what is this no-mindedness (*acittatā*), O Subhūti?" Subhūti spoke: "No-mindedness, Śāriputra, is immutable and non-discriminative."

The intrinsically luminous mind in the above passage is associated with neither existence nor non-existence (*qua* Emptiness) and is expressed in the *prajñā-pāramitā* and in the manifestation of *bodhicitta*. The understanding of the nature of mind is *prajñā* and conversely, *prajñā* is identical with the intuition of the mind as pure, immutable, and non-discriminative. This same exposition of pure mind as identical with no-mentation (*acittatā*) is reiterated in the *Vimalakīrtinirdeśa*, but is also not an assimilation of pure mind and Tathāgatagarbha.

Chronologiquement parlant, le Vkn (*Vimalakīrtinirdeśa*), se situe entre les Sectes hīnayānistes parlant d'une

> Pensée lumineuse, et les Mahāyānasūtra, relativement recents, assimilant cette Pensée lumineuse au Tathāgatagarbha, la Nature de Buddha presente en tous les êtres. ....Ainsi donc, pour la Prajñāpāramitā et le Mādhyamaka, la pensée lumineuse (*cittam prabhasvaram*) est, purement et simplement, l'inexistence de la pensée (*cittābhāvamātra*). Et pour le Vkn qui denie toute base (*pratiṣṭhāna*) au monde phenomenal, la Pensée lumineuse, dont il parle au ch. III s. 34, se reduit a l'absence de toute pensée (*acittatā*).[48]

In the *Prajñāpāramitā* and the *Vimalakīrtinirdeśa*, pure mind is equated with Emptiness, with absence of self-nature, denying any ground to the phenomenal world, a theme to be evaluated and systematized by Nāgārjuna. The significance of Prajñā literature and its proponents to the evolution of Tathāgatagarbha then, rests in the continuation of the transmission of intrinsically pure mind, but is radically different from Tathāgatagarbha because of the Śūnyavāda interpretation of the nature of mind as groundless (*apratiṣṭhāna*) and as absent of self-nature (*asvabhāva*). Pure mind reflects the nature of all things (*dharmatā*) precisely because it is Empty, lacking self-nature, and groundless.

b. *Vijñānavāda:*

Mahāyānasūtrālaṅkāra

1. matam ca cittam prakṛtiprabhāsvaram sadā tad āgantukadoṣadūṣitam/

   na dharmatācittamṛte 'nyacetasaḥ prabhāsvaratvam prakṛtau vidhīyate. //19
   (Lévi ed., p. 88, ch. 13)

   "And the mind--thought--has a luminous nature which is defiled by extraneous defilement.

   Except for the mind which is the dharma-nature (*dharmatā*) there is no other mind whose nature is luminous."//

2. sarveṣām aviśiṣṭāpi tathatā śuddhim āgatā/

   tathāgatvam tasmācca tadgarbhāh sarvadehinaḥ//37
   (Lévi ed., p. 40, ch. 9)

   "Suchness, which is characteristic of all things, is purity and has the nature of the Tathāgata./

Therefore that essence (*garbhah*) belongs to all beings."/ In case 1, the luminous nature of mind is equated with the dharma-nature, not unlike the equation of luminous nature with Emptiness, cited in the *Aṣṭasāhasrikā-prajñāpāramitā* and the *Vimalakīrti-nirdeśa* sūtras. However, in case 2, this luminous mind as suchness, i.e., the dharma-nature, is presented as the nature or essence belonging to all beings in *garbha*-form. Moreover, in commenting on this latter verse, Sthiramati, in the *Trimśika*, v. 17, cites the *Māhāyānabhidharma sūtra*:

> *Anādikāliko dhātuḥ sarvadharmasamāśrayaḥ*
> *Tasmin sati gatiḥ sarvā nirvāṇādhigamo 'pi vā.//*
>
> "The causal element (*dhātuḥ*) which continues from beginningless time is the basis for all phenomena.
> Because of its existence, there are all levels of existence as well as the attainment of Nirvaṇa."

In the Vijñāvāda framework, the *āśraya*, the *dhātu* of all phenomenal existence, is equated with the *ālaya-vijñāna*. This *āśraya* and *dhātu* are equated with the cause for the attainment of Nirvāṇa and concomitantly with the cause for conditioned phenomena (*saṁskṛta-dharma*) as well. Consequently, the above verse is a restatement of the identity of Nirvāṇa and Samsāra since there is one beginningless basis for both. The Tathāgatagarbha theorists will interpret this basis for all phenomena, both conditioned and unconditioned, as the Tathāgatagarbha instead of the Ālaya-vijñāna. Both systems of thought are proximate in that both see only one basis for all conditioned and unconditioned phenomena, and that basis is mental. It is the perspective maintained with regard to the nature and functioning of that mind which will be shown to be radically different.

As contrasted with the Mādhyamikan treatises, the Vijñānavāda also regard the nature of mind as a basis as do the Tathāgatagarbha advocates. Whereas the Śūnyavāda texts consider the mind as baseless, thus reflecting the nature of phenomena, the Vijñānavāda and Tathāgatagarbha proponents consider some dimension of the mind as both the true nature of all phenomena and as the basis for both the conditioned and unconditioned.

The Concept of Gotra

As mentioned previously, the development of Tathāgatagarbha thought is often investigated in relation to the development of the *gotra* theory, the latter being a later development in Buddhist history. The word "gotra" used in the technical sense of *Tathāgatagotra*, *Buddha-gotra*, or *ārya-gotra*, does not appear in the Pāli Canon.[49] *Gotra-bhū*, signifying "becoming a disciple (of the Buddha)," does occur in the Canon and is continued in Mahāyāna literature as the first of the technical meanings of *Buddha-gotra*.

The notion of a pure lineage or family to which all knowledgeable beings belong is prefigured in many Mahāyānist sūtras but it is not the purpose of this study to exhaust the development of the theory of *gotra* per se but only with relation to its contribution to Tathāgatagarbha thought. Certain distinct features of *gotra*, representative of pre-Tathāgatagarbha literature are delineated below as possibly affecting the evolution of Tathāgatagarbha doctrine within Buddhist thought.

The concept of Tathāgatagarbha as the "essence" or "embryo" of the Buddha proximates the concept of *Buddha-gotra* or "nature," "lineage" of the Buddha, the latter being a theme of considerable importance in Vijñānavādin treatises, some of which equate Tathāgatagarbha with *Buddha-gotra*.

1) *Kāśyapa parivarta*, forty-third assembly of the *Mahāratnakūṭa* anthology

In this sūtra, *ārya-gotra*, "the noble lineage," is discussed as the lineage in which one realizes the equality of all dharmas, without particularization, being free from both body and thought (*kayacitta-vivekatā*), pure (*vimala*), true (*satya*), and conforming (*anuloma*) to Nirvāṇa, yet egoless (*anātam*) and unapprehended (*anupalambha*).[50]

> yad āryānāṁ gotra / tatra rna śikṣā na niśrayo nāniśrayaḥ yatra na śikṣā na niḥśrayo nāniśra-(53a3) yaḥ tatra na śikṣāvyatikramaḥ yatra na śikṣāvyatikramaḥ tatra na saṁvaro nāsaṁvaraḥ yatra na saṁvaro nāsaṁ-(53a4) vara / tatra na cāro nācāraḥ na pracāraḥ yatra na cāro nācāra na pracāraḥ tatra na cittaṁ na cetasikā dharmāḥ (53a5) yatra na cittaṁ na cetasikā dharmāḥ tatra na mano na vijñānaḥ yatra na mano na vijñāna / tatra na karmo na vipākaḥ yatra na (53bl) karmo na vipākaḥ tatra na sukhaṁ na duḥkhaṁ yatra na sukhaṁ na duhkhaṁ tad āryāṇāṁ gotraṁ yad āryāṇāṁ gotraṁ / tatra na karmo (53b2) na karmābhisaṁskāro nāpi tatra gotre kāyena karma kṛyate na vācā na manasā / nāpi tatra gotre hīno-(53b3) t-kṛṣṭamadhyamavyavasthānaṁ samaṁ tad gotram ākāśasamatayā / nirviśeṣaṁ tad gotraṁ sarvadharmaikarasatayā /[51]

"Where there is the lineage of the holy (*āryānāṁ gotra*) there are no instructions (in the moral percepts) nor resources nor non-resources. Where there are no instructions, no resources, nor non-resources, there is no transcending instructions. Where there is no transcending instructions, there is neither restraint nor rules. Where there is neither restraint nor rules, there is neither practice nor the practice which is no practice. Where there is neither practice nor the practice which is no practice, there is neither mind nor mentals. Where there is neither mind nor mentals, there is no mentation (*manas*) nor sensation (*vijñāna*). Where there is no mentation nor sensation, there is no action (*karma*) nor consequence (*vipākaḥ*). Where there is neither action nor consequence, there is neither happiness nor suffering. Where there is neither happiness nor suffering, there is the lineage of the holy. Where there is the lineage of the holy, there is no action nor performance of action. In this lineage, there also is no action performed by the body, nor the voice, nor the mind. In this lineage there also is no distinction of inferior, mediocre, or superior. That gotra is equal to space in its nature. That gotra is without distinctions due to the same quality of all phenomena."

The interpretation of *ārya-gotra* in this sūtra, accepted by the Mādhyamikan transmission, again suggests the non-discriminative (*acitta*) dimension of mind, equated with luminosity of mind in the *Aṣṭasāhasrikā* and in the *Vimalakīrtinirdeśa*.[52]

2) *Avataṁsaka-sūtra*

a) *Daśabhūmika-sūtra*, chapter 22 in *Avataṁsaka*

The Buddha-gotra, in pre-Tathāgatagarbha and pre-Vijñānavāda literature, is associated with being a member of the Tathāgata's family, particularly emphasizing the eighth and ninth stage Bodhisattvas, the stages in which retrogression from the path to Buddhahood is precluded. At these stages of spiritual attainment, the Bodhisattva is welcomed into the Tathāgata's family without fear of losing his purity in mind.

> yo 'yam bhavanto jinaputrā bodhisatva evam apramāṇajñeyavicāritayā buddhyā bhūyas cottarān chāntān vimokṣān adhyavasyann adhyālambamānah/ bhūyaś cottaraṁ tathāgatajñānaṁ susamāptaṁ vicārayan/ *tathāgataguhyā*nupraveśaṁ cāvataran/ ...navamīṁ bodhisatvabhūmim ākramati/ (Rahder, Bhumi, ix A, p. 73)

"He who is a Bodhisattva, sons of the Buddha, desiring the tranquil, most excellent liberation through the practice of the immeasurable knowledge of the Buddha, attains it. Practicing the most excellent knowledge of the Tathāgata in which he is proficient, and practicing to enter the *mysteries* of the Tathāgata, ...he enters the ninth Bodhisattva stage."

佛子菩薩摩訶薩以如是無量智慧善觀佛道。欲求轉勝寂滅解脱、欲轉勝思性如来智慧、欲入如来深密法藏.... 得入第九地。

(T.v. 9, 278, 567c-68a)

The Sanskrit *Tathāgataguhya* is translated into Chinese by *ju-lai shen-mi fa-tsang* (如来深密法藏, the last character also being employed as *garbha* in Tathāgatagarbha literature.

> Sa khalu punar bho jinaputrā bodhisatva evam imām bodhisatvabhūmim anugato 'cintyaṁ ca nāma bodhisatvavimokṣaṁ pratilabhate/ anāvaraṇaṁ viśuddhivicayaṁ samantamukhāvabhāsaṁ tathāgatakośam apratihatacakrānugatam tryadhvānugataṁ dharmadhātugarbhaṁ vimuktimaṇḍalaprabhāsam aśeṣaviṣayagamaṁ bodhisatvavimokṣaṁ pratilabhate/
> (Rahder, Bhumi x G, p. 88)

是菩薩摩訶薩隨是地行、得菩薩不可思議解脱。無礙解脱、浄行解脱、普門明解脱、如来藏解脱、隨無礙論解脱、入三世解脱、法性藏解脱、明解脱、勝進解脱。

(T. v. 9, no. 278, 573a)

"Moreover, the Bodhisattva, sons of the Tathāgata, having attained this Bodhisattva stage, attains the unthinkable, viz. the Bodhisattva liberation. He attains the Bodhisattva liberation which is the way without remainder, the light of the sphere of liberation, the Womb (*garbha*) of the dharma-nature (or, dharma-realm), the accomplishments of the triple world, the accomplishments of the indestructible wheel, the storehouse (*kośa*) of the Tathāgata, the universal appearance, the accumulation (*vicaya*) of purity, the unobstructed."

The notion of *gotra* in both the *Kaśyapaparivarta* and the *Daśabhūmika-sūtra* focuses on the Bodhisattva stages and membership in the Tathāgata's family as a son (*jinaputra*), in the eighth and ninth stages (and above). The focus remains on the level of spiritual attainment personified by these particular Bodhisattvas and not on a concept of Buddha-nature as intrinsic to all living beings. The relationship between dharma-nature and *gotra*, viz. between dharma-nature and Buddha-nature, is only to be expounded in the Tathāgatagarbha and Vijñānavāda treatises.

b) *Pao wang ju-lai hsing-ch'i p'in* (宝王如来性起品) (=*Tathāgatotpattisaṁbhava parivarta*), chapter 33 in *Avataṁsaka-sūtra*

According to Takasaki Jikido, the concept of *hsin hsing-ch'i* (心生起) (*cittotpatti*) in the *Pao wang* refers to the *Tathāgata-citta*, the emanation being Tathāgatajñāna (如来智).[53] On the phenomenal level, the *Tathāgata-citta* (or, *Tathāgata-jñāna*) is first manifested in "the awakening of the thought of enlightenment" (*bodhicittotpatti*). On the absolute level, *Tathāgata-citta* is identical with *Tathāgata-jñāna*. For living beings who are seeking enlightenment, viz. *Tathāgata-jñāna*, "the thought of enlightenment" (*bodhicitta*) is the incipience of this enlightenment.

Although the "thought of enlightenment" is a concept dating back to ancient Buddhism, its relationship to and redefinition by the Tathāgatagarbha theory seems to be presented for the first time in the *Avataṁsaka*, with qualities attributed to *Tathāgatajnāna* (or, *Tathagata-citta*) re-appearing as qualities either attributed to the Tathāgatagarbha itself or to the *Tathāgata-jñāna* as a result of the Tathāgatagarbha, the latter being presented in the *Ratnagotravibhāga*.[54]

The relationship, then, between Tathāgata-garbha, *bodhicitta*, and *Tathāgata-jñāna* are most clearly interrelated in the systemization of Tathāgatagarbha literature[55] but the *Pao wang ju-lai hsing-ch'i p'in* contributed the idea of a relationship between *bodhicitta* and *Tathāgata-citta*, attributes of both being identical and manifested, at least latently, in the minds of living beings.

Closely aligned with the concepts of *bodhicitta* and *Tathāgata-gotra*, is the triple-body theory of the Buddha. Since the emergence of Māhayāna sūtras such as the *Avataṁsaka* and t-e *Sukhāvatīvyūha*, all the elements necessary for a triple body theory of the Buddha were available for future synthesis by the Vijñānavādins Asaṅga and Vasubandhu.[56] In the triple-body theory thus synthesized, the *svabhāvika-kāya* or

Essence-body is equivalent to the Dharma (-Essence) Body (*dharma-kāya*),[57] the Buddha-nature being equivalent to the Dharma-nature. If, as in the Tathāgatagarbha treatises, one understands the Essence of the Tathagata, the Essence of the Dharma, to be the Tathāgatagarbha, then the Tathāgatagarbha is identical with the Dharma-kāya, the conclusion which some Tathāgatagarbha treatises, including the *Śrīmālādevī-sūtra*, are later to maintain.

Among the meanings of *kāya* are substance (體), dependence (依), essential nature (體性), and basis (依止).[58] Thus, the "basis for the Dharma," "the essential nature of the Dharma," may be equated with Dharma-kāya and/or Tathāgatagarbha. If one is to hypothesize the identification of *Dharma-kāya* and Tathāgatagarbha, it also must be admitted that a tension remains logically between their identity and the prior existence epistemologically (and soteriologically) of the Tathāgatagarbha as the cause, explicitly manifested by *bodhicitta*, for the Dharma-kāya itself. The latter causal relationship between Tathāgatagarbha and Dharma-kāya, attained through *bodhicitta*, is more clearly defined in terms of *gotra*, delineated in some Tathāgatagarbha treatises.

> Selon le RGV (*Ratnagotravibhāga*) c'est du gotra existant par nature (*prakṛtistha*) que procède le *svabhāvikakāya* du buddha alors que les deux autres Corps constituant le *rūpakāya* de ce dernier naissent du *gotra* acquis (*samudānīta*). Et c'est en vertu de l'indifférenciation du *dharmadhātu* auquel est assimile le *prakṛtisthagotra* et dont l'objectivation mène à la réalisation spirituelle que le suprême et parfait Eveil est en dernier analyse universel et le même pour tous, et aussi que le Chemin qui relie pour ainsi dire la cause et le Fruit est lui-même ultimement unique (*ekayāna*).[59]

Because the world (as *dharma-dhātu*) reflects the nature of the Dharma, beings within the world must also reflect this nature. And it is through the intrinsically pure mind of living beings (viewed as *prakṛtisthagotra* or as Tathāgatagarbha), manifested explicitly by the "thought of enlightenment," that the attainment of the Dharma-Body is realized. The ineluctable conclusion is all beings, included in the *dharma-dhātu*, must reflect the Dharma-nature, Dharma-Body, i.e. the enlightenment of living beings to their own true nature is immanent.

Tathāgatagarbha Literature

In Tathāgatagarbha literature, the theme of luminous mind is considerably expanded, becoming a basis for both conditioned and unconditioned phenomena, inextricably related to the first awakening to the thought of enlightenment, and non-interacting with defilements. Buddha-nature, on the other hand, is explained as Tathāgatagarbha, the world or nature of the Dharma. The gradual evolution of the notion of Tathāgatagarbha then, will culminate in the merging of luminous mind both as the basis of the phenomenal, linking it with the world of living beings, and as the basis of the unconditioned, linking it with the world of the Tathāgata, viz. the nature of the Dharma. Concomitantly, the trikāya theory will be explained causally as the chain of events triggered by the pure luminous mind itself manifested first as the awakening to the thought of enlightenment, and culminating in the realization of Dharmakāya. Such a realization is essentially the realization of the meaning of Tathāgatagarbha.

1. *Tathāgatagarbha sūtra*

Regarded by most scholars[60] as the initial text of the Tathāgatagarbha transmission, the *Tathāgatagarbha sūtra*, a text quoted in the *Ratnagotravibhāga*, is considered to be in the third and last Cycle of the Buddha's teaching,[61] according to the Indo-Tibetan exegetical tradition, thus signifying the ultimate or complete doctrine (*uttara-tantra*). This text is the point of departure for investigating the incipience of Tathāgatagarbha thought as embodied in a specific collection of literature.

The *Tathāgatagarbha sūtra* is now extant in two Chinese recensions, *Ta-fang-teng ju-lai-tsang ching* (大方等如来藏経) (*Mahāvaipulya Tathāgatagarbha sūtra*) (T. v. 16, no. 666) translated by Buddhabhadra (佛陀跋陀羅) (358-429) of Eastern Tsin and the *Ta-fang-huang ju-lai-tsang ching* (大方廣如来藏経) (T. v. 16, no. 667) translated by Amogha (or, Amoghavajra) (不空) (705-774) of T'ang. There is also one Tibetan recension now extant in the *bKa' 'gyur*.

According to Chih-sheng's *K'ai-yüan shih chiao mo-lü*[62] there was another translation called the *Ta-fang-teng ju-lai-tsang ching*, identical in name with Buddhabhadra's recension, and translated by Fa-li (法立) and Fa-chü (法炬) of Western Tsin, during the reign of Emperor Hui (290-306). This recension was also known as the *Fo-tsang fang-teng ching* (佛藏方等經) in older catalogues in order to distinguish from the recension by their contemporary Pai-yüan (白遠) who also translated this text under the same title. Still another Western Tsin text, considered to be the first recension, is recorded in the *K'ai-yüan* catalogue and known as the *Nai-tsang fang-teng ching* (內藏方等經) which is not identified with the *Fo-tsang ta-fang-teng ching* but with the Fa-li/Fa-chü recension. Because the *Fo-tsang ta-fang-teng ching* is another name for Fa-li/Fa-chü's translation, the *K'ai-yüan* must be in error here.

The summary of the *Tathāgatagarbha sūtra*[63] presented below is based upon the older of the two extant recensions, the *Ta-fang-teng ju-lai-tsang ching* by Buddhabhadra, a North Indian, who went to Ch'angan in 406. There he discussed Vijñānavāda (*fa-hsiang*) with Kumārajīva and lectured on meditational texts at the request of Hui-yüan.[64] Among the other texts Buddhabhadra translated are the *Kuan fo san-wei hai ching* (觀佛三味海經 10 ch. (T. V. 15, no. 645), a meditational text; *Fo chieh wu-liang men wei mi ch'ih ching* (佛說無量門微密持經) (T. v. 19, no. 1012, p. 682) also known as the *Chu sheng wu-liang men ch'ih ching* (出生無量門持經), considered a Tantric text (*mi-chiao*) and also translated by Amogha, the translator of the other recension of the *Tathāgatagarbha sūtra* as well as by Guṇabhadra, the translator of the *Śrīmālādevī sūtra*, among others. There appears to have been a special interest in meditational, tantric, and *citta-mātra* texts among the translators of Tathāgatagarbha literature but the mutual reciprocity between devotionalism and tantricism on the one hand, and Tathāgatagarbha literature on the other are not within the purpose of this study.

Other translations by Buddhabhadra, now extant, are the *Mo-ho-seng-chieh lü* (摩訶僧祇律) (Mahāsaṅghikan Vinaya) (T. v. 22, no. 1425, p. 227) translated at the request of Fa-hsien, according to the *Chu-san-tsang chi* and the *Kao seng chuan*; the *Ta-fang-huang fo hua-yen ching* (大方廣佛華嚴經) in 6 *ch.*, incorporated in the *Avataṁsaka sūtra*, and based upon a Sanskrit text from Khotan obtained by Chih Fa-ling (支法領)

according to *Chu-san-tsang chi*; and the *Wen-shu-shih-li fa yüan* (文殊師利發願経) (*The Text on Mañjuśrī's Profession of Vows*) in 1 *ch.*, (T. 10, no. 296, p. 878). Among his translations no longer extant are the *Ching liou po-lo-mi ching* (淨六波羅密経) (*The Six Pure Pāramitās*) in 1 *ch.*, and *Hsin-wei mi ch'ih ching* (新微密持経), a Tantric text.

In the *Tathāgatagarbha sūtra* the claim is made that all living beings, though they are defiled, possess the Tathāgatagarbha within themselves:

> "I, with my Buddha-vision, see all living beings who, within a state of defilement such as (the three poisons of) hate, greed, and delusion,
> 我以佛眼観一切衆生貪欲恚癡諸煩悩中
> Have the Tathāgata's wisdom, the Tathāgata's vision, and the Tathāgata's body.
> 有如来智、如来眼、如来身。
> Sitting majestically in the lotus position, they do not move.
> 結加趺坐儼然不動。
> Good sons, all living beings, although they reside in the various levels of existence,
> 善男子、一切衆生雖在諸趣、
> Have the Tathāgatagarbha within their defiled selves, which is never impure, being complete with virtues and not different from myself."
> 煩悩身中有如来蔵常無染汚徳相備足我無異。
> (T. v. 16, no. 666, p. 457b-c)

The most fundamental concept of Tathāgatagarbha thought is delineated here, viz. that within every defiled living being there is the nature and wisdom of the Tathāgata, i.e. the Tathāgatagarbha (457c). Nine metaphors are used to express this relationship between the Tathāgata nature and the defiled living being, metaphors which will be retained in the *Ratnagotravibhāga* (pp. 59-60, verses 96 and 97) with only slight variation. The nine metaphors are:

1) the Tathāgata within the calix of a lotus
2) the pure honey within wild mountain trees
3) the purest rice within the coarse husk
4) gold within dirty regions
5) jewel storehouses in the earth

6) great trees which grow from the seed of the mango, within the pit
7) a golden statue which is hidden in the ground by robbers but remains pure
8) an outcaste woman who becomes impregnated by a king, giving birth to a future king but unaware of the caste of her son
9) a golden statue created by an artisan, buried deep within the ground

These metaphors not only explicate the theme of intrinsic purity covered by extrinsic defilement, but also illustrate the permanence and immutability of the Tathāgatagarbha, especially metaphors 4, 5, 6, 7, and 9 which, with the exception of 6, are all geophysical examples, not only exemplifying the permanence and immutability of the Tathāgatagarbha but also illustrating the erroneous but common philological association between *gotra* and mine[66] maintained in a number of Tathāgatagarbha treatises.

Explicating the Tathāgatagarbha in only the most general and simple terms, the *Tathāgatagarbha sūtra* does not discuss in what manner all living beings have the Tathāgatagárbha. From the perspective of exegetical tradition, the level of spiritual attainment represented by the assembly (which consists of Bodhisattvas among whom are Avalokitesvara, Vajraprajñā, Dhāraṇī, Maitreya, and Mañjuśrī, hosts of divinities and 100,000 monks) perhaps indicates that this sermon is only intended for the superior student. However, from the perspective of doctrinal analysis, the *Tathāgatagarbha sūtra* must be considered prior to all other Tathāgatagarbha literature now extant since there is no attempt to analyze the critical relationship between living beings and Buddha-nature. All subsequent literature begins to confront this problem, epitomized in the *Śrīmālādevī-siṁhanāda sūtra* and the *Ratnagotravibhāga*.

Certain characteristics in format which do appear in this sūtra set the precedent for subsequent Tathāgatagarbha literature, which expands on this format:

1) Because of the Bodhisattva's capability to understand the profound teaching of Tathāgatagarbha, a close

association is drawn between Bodhisattvas and the teaching of Tathāgatagarbha.

2) The association of Tathāgatagarbha with meditation, illustrated in the opening of the sūtra. In the first scene of the *Tathāgatagarbha sūtra* the Buddha is seated in meditation (*samādhi*).

3) The description of the radiation of light prior to the explanation of the Dharma. (In addition, ten of the forty-nine Bodhisattvas enumerated have names pertaining to light.) The sūtra also closes with a description of light as the awakening. In the allegory concerning the Buddha Ch'ang-fang-kuang-ming ("Eternal Rays of Light"), his birth is described by the emission of magnificent rays of light from his mother's womb.

4) References to Buddha nature (仏性) (457c) (three occurrences) are interchanged in similar passages with "Essence" or "Container" of the Buddha (仏藏) (three occurrences), nature of the Tathāgata (如来藏) (four occurrences), Tathāgata's dharma-essence (如来法性 (one occurrence), Tathāgata's jewel-treasury 如来宝藏) (two occurrences), Tathāgata's mysteries (如来妙藏) (如来微妙藏) (two occurrences), jewel-treasury of the Great Dharma (大法宝藏 (one occurrence), and the jewel-treasury (宝藏) (two occurrences). However, Tathāgatagarbha is used in the majority of cases. Note the jewel metaphor which will be characteristic of the majority of Tathāgatagarbha literature.

5) Three references to the unlimited elocution of the Buddha to teach the Dharma, two referring to the present Buddha, one to the past Buddha, Ch'ang-fang-kuang-ming.

This sūtra has only some of the doctrinal characteristics of the Tathāgatagarbha theory represented in its complete development in the *Śrīmālādevī-siṁhanāda sūtra* and in the *Ratnagotravibhāga*. The most important of the tenets which are adopted by other texts in the evolution of this thought are delineated below:

a) *Characteristics related to living beings:*

1) All living beings have the Tathāgatagarbha within their defiled selves but are ignorant of this fact.
2) Because of the Tathāgatagarbha, living beings are not different from the Buddha.

b) *Characteristics of the Tathāgatagarbha itself:*
1) The Tathāgatagarbha embodies the nature and wisdom of the Buddha.
2) It is eternal, immutable and inherently pure.
3) It is the basis for all living beings and for the true thoughts of the Bodhisattvas.
4) The Tathāgatagarbha is replete with the virtues of the Buddha.

Deficiencies in doctrine which do not appear in the *Tathāgatagarbha sūtra* but in subsequent Tathāgatagarbha literature:

1) No explicit reference to the Dharma-Body (法身) but many references to the presence of the Tathagatagarbha within the Buddha's Body, suggestive of his Form-Body (*rūpa-kāya*). For example, it is said that the Tathāgata has the jewel treasury of the Great Dharma (大法宝藏) within his body. But because living beings in the five sensory levels of existence do not hear or know (the Tathāgatagarbha), the Buddha appears on behalf of the world to reveal the Tathāgata's dharma-essence (如来法藏) within his body.[67]
2) There are no Pratyeka Buddhas mentioned in the text. The audience is all male although the phrase "good sons and daughters" appears in prescribing the acts of reading, writing, and memorization of the *Tathāgatagarbha sūtra* which are immeasurably meritorious.
3) Only three references to ignorance (*avidyā*) (無明) appear in this sutra, two substituting for defilement (*kleśa*) which covers the Buddhagarbha (458c and 459a), the other referring to the shell of ignorance (無明殼) in which the Tathāgata's jewel-treasury (如来宝藏) resides. In later treatises, Tathāgatagarbha's relation to ignorance is to assume supreme

importance in explaining the realization of the Tathāgata's nature.

4) There is no occurrence of Dharma-nature or Dharma-realm (*Dharmatā* or *Dharma-dhātu*) nor any occurrence of the basis for all phenomena, both conditioned and unconditioned (*sarvadharmāśraya*), but only reference to the basis for living beings (*sattvāśraya*).
5) There is no discussion of the inherently pure mind of living beings. The Tathāgata's inherently pure nature is discussed, but no explication of pure mind (*prabhāsvaracitta*) nor of the living beings' mind (*sattvacitta*) is explicitly developed. It is suggested that living beings are ignorant of the fact that they have the Tathāgatagarbha. Consequently, the Buddha and Bodhisattvas must teach them to become aware of their true nature in the Tathāgatagarbha.
6) There is no mention of Emptiness nor of the One Vehicle (*Ekayāna*).

In summary, the *Tathāgatagarbha sūtra* contributed several vital elements to the Tathāgatagarbha transmission which developed from the concepts of intrinsically pure mind and Buddha nature or lineage (*gotra*) discussed above. To the concept of intrinsically pure mind the *Tathāgatagarbha sūtra* devotes little attention to living beings' minds but rather to the pure nature of the Tathāgata with whom all beings are identical in nature. By implication then, living beings also must share in the nature of the Tathāgata's wisdom which is intrisically pure. However, no explicit discussion of such a claim occurs in this text. The emphasis remains on the defiled nature of living beings whose true nature is the Tathāgata's, but which is beyond their comprehension.

Because the main theme is the Tathāgata nature participated in by all living beings, the *Tathāgatagarbha sūtra* may be considered primarily an innovative text with regard to the concept of *gotra* as seed or essence, for the "pure within the impure" metaphors all demonstrate the pure "essence" or "nature" which is only extraneously covered by defiled elements. Although this universally pure nature is attributed to all living beings, the One Vehicle of universal salvation remains only an implicit tenet. Moreover, the Tathāgatagarbha which remains within the Buddha's body does not clarify the meaning of *garbha* in its common sense of "embryo" or "womb" but instead, appears to be a gloss for *kośa* or *ākara*, i.e. "storehouse" or "container" for the Dharma, exemplified by the Buddha who is the Dharma-Body or Aggregate for the Dharmas. This notion of "storehouse," "treasure," or "container" and *gotra* or "mine" merge in this sūtra, i.e. *garbha* (*kośa, ākara*)→ *gotra* ("storehouse" or "container" → "mine") through the geophysical model. In subsequent literature, the two terms will merge through a physiological model as well, as the identification of garbha ("embryo" or "womb") with *gotra* ("lineage," "inheritance"). With the introduction of *dhātu* as an alternative for both *gotra* and *garbha*, retaining both models, physiologically as "ssed" or "cause" and geophysically as "realm," "world," "sphere," the identity of all three terms will be reinforced.

2. *Pu tseng pu chien ching* (不增不減經) (*Anunatvapurantva-nirdeśa sūtra*) (T. v. 16, no. 668, p. 466)

The *Pu tseng pu chien ching*, quoted in the *Ratnagotravibhāga*, is now extant only in Chinese. Bodhiruci (6th C.) of North India, went to Pei-liang in 508 and translated this text in 525 A.D. Not to be confused with Bodhiruci of T'ang, the translator of the *Ratnakūṭa* anthology, Bodhiruci of N. Wei, the Pure Land patriarch, also translated the *Sukhāvatīvyūha*, *Vajracchedika Prajñāpāramitā*, *Laṅkāvatāra*, *Daśabhūmika-vyakhyāna*. He is also believed to have translated the *Ratnagotravibhāga*, now lost, contemporaneous with Saramati's recension.

The *Pu tseng pu chien ching*, like the *Tathāgatagarbha sūtra*, is very brief in length but is more informative with regard to Tathāgatagarbha thought. After the translation of the *Tathāgatagarbha sūtra* by Fa-chü and Fa-li, more than two hundred years elapsed before the translation of the *Pu tseng pu chien*. Consequently, the evolution of Tathāgatagarbha thought represented by the *Pu tseng pu chien* may have been developing for over two centuries. According to Takasaki Jikido,[68] there are only two Tathāgatagarbha texts prior to the *Śrīmālādevī sūtra* now extant. However, certain other texts, e.g. *Mahāparinirvāṇa sūtra*, also were influenced by the

Tathāgatagarbha doctrine though not considered basically Tathāgatagarbha in intent. These are not within the scope of this study.

The *Pu tseng pu chien ching* opens with Śāriputra asking the Buddha if living beings who transmigrate in the six levels of existence increase or decrease in number. The Buddha then delivers the following exegesis, summarized below:

1) The average deluded person does not know the One World of the Dharma (*ekadharmadhātu*). Therefore, he thinks the world of living beings (*sattvadhātu*) increases or decreases.
2) Five hundred years after the Buddha's parinirvāṇa, there are self-proclaimed monks who really are not the Buddha's disciples.
3) Because living beings understand only the incomplete meaning of the sūtras, they do not comprehend the true meaning of Emptiness.
4) Because living beings do not know the first moment of the awakening of mind (*bodhicitta*) when the Buddha reveals himself, they do not truly understand how to cultivate innumerable merits, nor do they understand the Tathāgata's unlimited qualities, powers. His world (*dhāta*), His sphere (*gocara*), His Dharma mastery (*dharmaiśvarya*),[69] His skillful means, and His differentiated (phenomenal?) world. They cannot participate in the Tathāgata's compassion.
5) They cannot truly know the Tathāgata's Nirvāṇa. When they hear of His Nirvāṇa, they engage in thoughts of nihilism and think the world of living beings decreases. When they see how living beings suffer and forsake all good actions, they believe the world of living beings increases.
6) Living beings have various erroneous ideas concerning Nirvāṇa.
7) The One World of the Dharma is the Tathāgata's mind (*Tathāgatacitta*).
8) Because only the Tathāgatas can understand and have insight into the One World (of the Dharma), the Śrāvakas and Pratyekas cannot know nor meditate upon this world

but can only believe in it. The Oneorld of the Dharma is the supreme truth and is the realm of living beings (*sattvadhātu*), the Tathāgatagarbha, the Dharma-Body.

9) The Dharma-Body means the Tathāgata's merits and inconceivable Buddha-dharmas, which are not different, not severed, not separate [70] (from the one world of the Dharma?), and more numerous than the sands of the Ganges, just as colors and forms are not separate from the jewel itself.

10) The Dharma-Body is neither produced nor destroyed. It has neither a past nor a future but transcends both limits, i.e. there is no time for either its production or its destruction.

11) The Dharma-Body is permanent because it is not different from the Dharma.

12) The Dharma-Body is eternal because it is the perceptual refuge and is equal to the future limit.

13) The Dharma-Body is pure because there is no dualism nor differentiation.

14) The Dharma-Body is immutable because there is neither production nor extinction of the Dharma.

15) The Dharma-Body is covered with unlimited defilements since beginningless time.

16) The Dharma-Body is separate from the life-death cycle (*saṁsāra*). By practicing the ten pāramitās, accepting the 84,000 teachings and cultivating the Bodhisattva practice one becomes a Bodhisattva.

17) The Dharma-Body is separate from defilement and yet is covered by unlimited suffering. Moreover, it is separate from all defilement and is pure.

18) The Dharma-Body is not separate from the world of living beings. The world of living beings are the Dharma-Body. These are only different in name.

19) Based upon the intrinsically pure world of the Dharma, i.e. Suchness, the Buddha teaches the inconceivable, intrinsically pure mind, for the benefit of living beings.

20) Within the world of living beings there are three dimensions to the Tathāgatagarbha:
    a) Its original essence interacts with the pure dharmas.
    b) Its original essence does not interact with impurity but is covered with impurity. Only the Tathāgata's enlightened wisdom can eliminate this impurity.
    c) The Tathāgatagarbha is equal to the future limit, i.e. is eternal and embodies the Dharma, being the foundation of all things. Endowed with all things, the Tathāgatagarbha is not separate nor free from the truth of all things.
21) Living beings are another name for the pure world of the Dharma which is inconceivable, unproduced, permanent, eternal, pure and an immutable refuge.

The major tenets summarized above demonstrate the fact that the *Pu tseng pu chien ching* is a more developed exposition on the Tathāgatagarbha than its predecessor, the *Tathāgatagarbha sūtra*. Certain characteristics in format are shared by both the *Tathāgatagarbha sūtra* and the *Pu tseng pu chien ching*, viz. the jewel metaphor and the absence of the "good sons and daughters." Characteristics or deficiencies in doctrine found in both the *Tathāgatagarbha sūtra* and the *Pu tseng pu chien ching* are:

1) The common man is not aware of the Tathāgatagarbha.
2) The association of Bodhisattva practice with the teaching of the Tathāgatagarbha.
3) The association of Tathāgatagarbha with living beings.
4) Tathāgatagarbha embodies the nature and wisdom of the Buddha.
5) Only one reference to ignorance (*avidyā*).
6) No mention of Dharma-Nature (*dharmadhātu*) per se.
7) No discussion of the One vehicle (*Ekayāna*).

Characteristics found in the *Tathāgatagarbha sūtra* and other Tathāgatagarbha literature but not in the *Pu tseng pu chien ching*:

1) Equation of Buddha-nature with Tathāgatagarbha.
2) The Tathāgatagarbha is the basis for the true thoughts of the Bodhisattvas.

3) The description of the illumination of the Buddha's rays at the time of his teaching.
4) The listing of specific Bodhisattva names.
5) The outline of the nine metaphros.

Most important innovations in the *Pu tseng pu chien ching*:

a) Characteristics related to living beings:
   1) Explicit reference to the Dharma-Body and also to its relationship with the Tathāgatagarbha and with living beings. (#8 through 18, 20)
   2) Discussion of defilement with relation to the Tathāgatagarbha/Dharma-Body. (#15, 17, 20) and the introduction of the beginningless nature of these defilements.
   3) Interrelationship between Dharma-world, world of living beings, and Tathāgatagarbha/Dharma-Body. (#1, 4, 8, 19, 20, 21)
   4) Criticism of self-proclaimed monks who do not understand Emptiness. (#2, 3)
   5) Introduction of *bodhicitta* to understanding the Tathāgata's world. (#4)
   6) Introduction of the inconceivable, intrinsically pure mind. (#19)
   7) Introduction of the theme of erroneous views with regard to Nirvāṇa. (#5, 6)
   8) Śrāvakas and Pratyekas can only believe but not comprehend the Tathāgatagarbha. (#8)
b) Characteristics of the Tathāgatagarbha itself:
   1) The meaning of the Tathāgatagarbha/Dharma-Body is the merits and qualities of the Tathāgata which are not different from, severed from, nor separate from (the world or nature of the Dharma). (#8)
   2) The Tathāgatagarbha/Dharma-Body is neither produced nor destroyed. (#10)
   3) The four qualities (*guṇa*) of the *Tathāgatagarbha/* Dharma-Body are: permanence, eternity, purity, and immutability.[72] (#11-14, 20a)

4) The Tathāgatagarbha is the foundation of all things.[73] (20c)

5) The Tathāgatagarbha/One World of the Dharma is the Tathāgata's mind. Thus, only the Tathāgata can comprehend the Tathāgatagarbha. (#7, 8)[74]

The idea that living beings neither increase nor decrease in number, the theme which gives its name to the *Pu tseng pu chien*, is a singularly peculiar characteristic of this sūtra. Except for this peculiarity, the *Pu tseng pu chien* became a model for all systematized Tathāgatagarbha literature, in particular the *Śrīmālādevī-siṁhanāda sūtra* and the *Ratnagotravibhāga-mahāyānottaratantra śāstra*, the major commentary of this tradition which was greatly influenced by the *Śrīmālādevī sūtra*. The most important contribution made by the *Pu tseng pu chien ching* is the association between the World of the Dharma and the World of living beings, worlds no longer considered distinct because of the Tathāgatagarbha. The problems which arise from the association between the phenomenal world of living beings and the supremely true world of the Dharma become increasingly critical in understanding the Tathāgatagarbhan paradox. The adherents necessarily had to face these problems and attempt to answer them within the Buddhist exegetical tradition, and in particular, to confront the position of the Abhidharmists and the splinter sects. In the *Śrīmālādevī-siṁhanāda sūtra* we see the first text which aims to probe into the nature of the phenomenal world linked to the world of the Dharma by its very nature as Tathāgatagarbha.

CHAPTER II

NOTES

[1]Monier-Williams, Sir Monier. *A Sanskrit-English Dictionary* (Oxford: Clarendon Press, 1970), p. 349b-c.

[2]Cited by Franklin Edgerton, *Buddhist Hybrid Sanskrit Grammar and Dictionary*, vol. II, p. 248.

[3]Richard H. Robinson, *The Buddhist Religion: A Historical Introduction* (Belmont, Calif: Dickenson Publishing Company, Inc., 1970), p. 71.

[4]Robinson, *Ibid.*, p. 71.

[5]Nakamura Hajime, *Shinbutten bukkyō jiten* (*op. cit.*), p. 413.

[6]Ui Hakuju, *Bukkyō jiten* (*op. cit.*), p. 840.

[7]Takasaki Jikidō, "Nyoraizō shisō ni okeru *shōmangyō* no chii" in *Shōmangyō gisho ronshu, Nihom bukkyō genryū kenkyū kiyō*, No. 2, 1965, p. 184.

[8]Ruegg, *La Théorie du Tathāgatagarbha et du Gotra* (*op. cit.*) p. 51.

[9]Ruegg, *Ibid.*, pp. 501-502.

[10]Adapted from Ruegg's annotation of the different translations for *garbha* in *Tathāgatagarbha*, pp. 502-504.

[11]Ruegg, *La Théorie du Tathāgatagarbha et du Gotra* (*op. cit.*), p. 5, p. 50.

[12]See above, p. 9.

[13]Ruegg, *Ibid.*, p. 73.

[14]*Ibid.*, pp. 74-75.

[15]*Ibid.*, p. 109.

[16]*Ibid.*, p. 111.

[17]*Ibid.*, pp. 112-113.

[18]*Ibid.*, p. 125.

[19]Takasaki Jikidō, "Nyoraizō shisō ni okeru *Shōmangyō* no chii" in *Shōmangyō gisho ronshu*, *op. cit.*, p. 174.

[20]Takasaki, *A Study on the Ratnagotravibhāga*, *op. cit.*, p. 32.

[21]Takasaki, *Ibid.*, p. 34

[22]*Ibid.*, p. 57

[23]Takasaki, "Nyoraizō shisō ni okeru *Shōmangyō* no chii" in *Shōmangyō gisho ronshu, op. cit.*, p. 192.

[24]*Ibid.*, p. 192. The *Pu tseng pu chien ching* is no longer extant in Sanskrit but is quoted in the *Ratnagotravibhāga*. Its contribution to the Tathāgatagarbha systemization will be discussed below.

[25]The following is a brief outline of Katsumata's third chapter: "The Development of the Tathāgatagarbha theory" (Nyoraizō shisō no hattatsu) in *Bukkyō ni okeru shinshikisetsu no kenkyū, op. cit.*, pp. 593-635.

[26]*Daśabhūmikasūtra et Bodhisattvabhūmi*, ed. by J. Rahder, (Paris: Paul Guethner, 1926), p. 88.

[27]Katsumata, *Bukkyō ni okeru shinshikisetsu no kenkyū, op. cit.*,p. 602.

[28]Ui Hakuju, *Bukkyō kyōtenshi* (Tokyo: Tōsei shuppansha, 1957), p. 137.

[29]Ui, *Ibid.*, p. 138.

[30]Ui, *Ibid.*, p. 139.

[31]Chinese recension already noted above on page 46. The Chinese recension of the *Ekottarikāgama* may belong to a Mahāsaṅghikan Canon, see above, p. 9.

[32]Akanuma Chizen, *The Comparative Catalogue of Chinese Āgamas and Pāli Nikāyas* (Nagoya: Hajinkaku shobō, 1929), p. 120.

[33]*Bussho kaisetsu daijiten, op. cit.*, v. VII, p. 59.

[34]Akanuma Chizen, *Bukkyō kyōten shiron* (Nagoya: Hajinkaku shobō, 1939), p. 22.

[35]Akanuma, *Bukkyō kyōten, Ibid.*, pp. 27-28.

[36]Akanuma, *Ibid.*, pp. 38-39.

[37]Translation of this passage is from Ruegg's *La Théorie du Tathāgatagarbha et du Gotra*, p. 411.

[38]Ruegg cites R. Sarathchandra, *Buddhist Psychology of Perception* (Colombo, 1958), on the parallelism between *pabhassaramcittam* and *ālaya-vijñāna*. Cf. *La Théorie du Tathāgatagarbha*, p. 411.

[39]For other citations in the Pāli Canon and paracanonical literature concerning the luminous mind, see Ruegg, *Ibid.*,

footnoted pp. 411-412, and Etienne Lamotte, *L'Enseignement de Vimalakīrti* (Louvain: Institut Orientaliste, 1962) in the section discussing the Theravādin luminous mind, p. 56ff, which cites, among others, the *Suttanipāta* (v. III, p. 15), and *Milindapanhā* (IV, 7-2).

40 問何故作此論(阿毘達磨大毘婆沙論)。答為欲分別契經義故說心解脫貪瞋癡。契經雖作是說而不廣分別。何等心解脫為有貪瞋癡心解脫為離貪瞋癡心解脫。契經是此論根本。彼所不分別者今應說之。

...如分別論者彼說心本性清淨客塵煩惱所染污故相不清淨。為止彼執顯示心性非本清淨客塵煩惱所染污故相不清淨。若心本性清淨客塵煩惱所染污故相不清淨者何不客塵煩惱本性染污與本性清淨心相應故其相清淨。若客塵煩惱本性染污雖與本性清淨心相應而相不清淨。亦應心本性清淨不由客塵煩惱相不清淨義相似故。

又此本性淨心為在客塵煩惱先生為俱時生若在先生。應心生已住待煩惱。若爾應經二剎那住有違宗失。若俱時生云何可說心性本淨。汝宗不說有未來心可言本淨。為止如是他宗異執.及顯自宗無顛倒理故作斯論....謂若身中煩惱未斷心未行世不在相續。以心不能自在行世在相續故不名解脫. 若自身中諸煩惱斷爾時此心自在行世相續故名得解脫。

...分別論者彼說染污心其體無異。謂若相應煩惱未斷名染污心。若時相應煩惱已斷名不染污心如銅器等.未除垢時名有垢器等.若除垢已名無垢器等、心亦如是。

[41]Kagawa Takao, "*Shōmangyō* ni okeru bonnōsetsu no seiritsu" in Professor Etani's commemorative volume, *Jōdokyō no shisō to bunka* (Kyoto: Bukkyo University, 1973), p. 1049.

[42]Kagawa, "*Shōmangyō* ni okeru bonnōsetsu," *op. cit.*, p. 1063.

[43]*Ibid.*, p. 1054.

[44]分別論者又說隨眠是纏種子。隨眠自性心不相應。諸纏自性與心相應。纏從隨眠生。纏現前故諸阿羅漢已斷隨眠纏既不生。
(T. v. 27, no. 1545, p. 313a). Cited in Kagawa, *Ibid.*, p. 1059.

[45]Kagawa, *Ibid.*, p. 1059.

[46]Lamotte, *L'Enseignement de Vimalakīrti, op. cit.*, p. 54.

[47]For further discussion, the reader is referred to Ruegg's *La Théorie du Tathāgatagarbha, op. cit.*, and *Takasaki's A Study on the Ratnogotravibhāga*, and Ui Hakuju's *Hōshoron kenkyū* (Tokyo: Iwanami shoten, 1959), pp. 354-429.

[48]Lamotte, *L'Enseignement de Vimalakīrti, op. cit.*, pp. 56, 60.

[49]Takasaki Jikidō, "Kegon kyōgaku to Nyoraizō shisō" in *Kegon shisō* ed. by Nakamura Hajime and Kawada Kumatarō (Tokyo: Hōzōkan, 1960), p. 304.

[50]Ruegg, *La Théorie du Tathāgatagarbha, op. cit.*, p. 110.

[51]*The Kāśyapaprivarta: A Mahāyāna sūtra of the Ratnakūṭa Class*, ed. by Baron A. von Staël-Holstein (Shanghai, 1926), section 103.

[52]For further discussion see Ruegg, *La Théorie du Tathāgatagarbha, op. cit.*, p. 110 ff. in which Lamotte's translation of *Vimalakīrtinirdeśa* appears as reference.

[53]Takasaki, "Kegon Kyōgaku," in *Kegon shisō, op. cit.*, p. 329.

[54]Ruegg, *La Théorie du Tathāgatagarbha, op. cit.*, p. 287ff.

[55]Candrakirti, in the *Madhyamakāvatāra* (1. 5-8) also discusses the Tathāgatagotra in relation to the awakening to the thought of enlightenment (*bodhicittotpada*). In the first Bodhisattva stage, the *bhūmi* in which one has extricated himself from the level of either the common man or the Śrāvakas and Pratyeka-Buddhas, he is born in the path to the Buddha-stages (*Tathāgatabhūmi*) which is called *Samantaprobhā*. See Reugg, *La Théorie du Taṭhagatagarbha*, p. 114. It is interesting to note that Queen Śrīmālā receives the prediction that she will become the Buddha P'u-kuang ("Universal Light"), most likely a translation of Samantaprabhā.

56 Nagao Gadjin, "On the Theory of Buddha-Body (*Buddha-kāya*(" in the *Eastern Buddhist* (Kyoto: Otani University), v. VI, no. 1, May 1973, pp. 29-30.

57 Nagao, "On the Theory of Buddha-Body," *Ibid.*, p. 32.

58 *Ibid.*, p. 31. Professor Nagao bases this interpretation on the *Ch'eng wei shih lun* (成唯識論) (the *Vijñaptimātratā-siddhi*).

59 Ruegg, *La Théorie du Tathagatagarbha, op. cit.*, p. 514.

60 See Takasaki Jikido, "Nyoraizō shisō ni okeru Shōmangyō no chii," p. 187 in *Shōmangyō gisho ronshu, op. cit.*

61 Ruegg, *op. cit.*, p. 4.

62 Tokiwa Daijō, *Gokan yori Sō Sei ni itaru yakkyō sōroku* (Tokyo: Tōhō bunka gakuin tōkyō kenkyūsho, 1938), p. 683, 768-769.

63 The *Tathagatagarbha sutra* appears to be similar to the *Ju-lai hsing-hsien ching* (如来興顯経) (T. v. 10, no. 291, p. 592), translated by Dharmaraksa (Fa-hu) (法護) (266-308) of Western Tsin and incorporated in the *Avataṁsaka sūtra*, the latter being translated in part by Buddhabhadra. The *Ju-lai hsing-hsien ching* was also translated by Śikṣananda of T'ang (T. v. 10, no. 279, p. 1) as a separate sūtra. See Takasaki, "Nyoraizō shisō ni okeru Shōmangyō no chii" in *Shōmangyō gisho ronshu, op. cit.*,p. 187.

64 Not to be confused with Hui-yüan of Sui who composed the *Sheng-man ching i-chi*, a commentary on the *Śrīmālādevī sūtra*.

65 Amogha's translation differs in using both the phrase "good sons and daughters" and in including the lotus metaphor in this passage. See T. v. 16, no. 667, p. 461c.

66 Cf. Franklin Edgerton, *Buddhist Hybrid Sanskrit Grammar and Dictionary* (Delhi: Motilal Banarsidass, 1970), p. 216 in which the allusion to both gold and mine occur in the *Laṅkāvatāra* and the *Mahāyānasutrālaṅkāra*.

67 大法宝蔵在其身内不聞不知耽惑五欲。輪轉生死受苦無量是故諸仏出興于世為開身内如来法蔵。(458b)

68 Takasaki, "Nyoraizō shisō ni okeru Shōmangyō no chii," in *Shōmangyō gisho ronshu, op. cit.*

69 Sanskrit equivalents given here are based upon "Fuzō fugengyō no Nyoraizōsetsu" by Jikidō Takasaki in *Komazawa daigaku bukkyō gakubu kenkyū kiyō*, v. 23, March 1965, p. 89.

70 The importance of the terms *avinirbhāga, avinirmukta* and *sambaddha* will be discussed below in relation to their application in the *Śrīmālādevī sūtra*.

[71]Numbers in parentheses refer to the summary of tenets in the *Pu tseng pu chien ching*, listed above.

[72]Cf. The three qualities of permanence, immutatility, and purity in the *Tathāgatagarbha sūtra*, omitting eternity.

[73]Cf. The Tathāgatagarbha is the basis for all living beings and for the true thoughts of the Buddha in the *Tathāgatagarbha sūtra*.

[74]Cf. The Tathāgatagarbha is the wisdom of the Buddha in the *Tathāgatagarbha sūtra*.

CHAPTER III

TATHĀGATAGARBHA THOUGHT IN THE ŚRĪMĀLĀDEVĪ-SIṀHANĀDA SŪTRA: PART I

The major sūtra of Tathāgatagarbha literature may be considered the *Śrīmālādevī sūtra* for it is in htis text that we see the majority of basic tenets developed in considerable detail. The principal characteristics in format which are transmitted from prior literature are:

1) The meditational opening of the sūtra (TGS).[1]
2) The radiation of light from the Buddha at the beginning of the sūtra (TGS).
3) The two models, geophysical and physiological, for the Tathāgatagarbha (TGS, PTPCC).
4) The "good sons and daughters" of the assembly (TGS).

The major tenets in doctrine which are transmitted from prior literature are:

Relating to living beings:

1) All living beings have the Tathāgatagarbha within their defiled selves but are ignorant of this because of erroneous views (TGS, PTPCC).
2) Because of the Tathāgatagarbha, living beings are not different from the Buddha (TGS, PTPCC).
3) Monks do not truly understand the nature of Emptiness nor of Nirvāṇa (PTPCC).
4) The close association between Bodhisattvas and the teaching of the Tathāgatagarbha (TGS, PTPCC).

Relating to the Tathāgatagarbha itself:

1) The Tathāgatagarbha embodies the nature and wisdom of the Tathāgata (TGS, PTPCC).
2) The Tathāgatagarbha is encowed with the merits and qualities of the Tathāgata and is not different from, severed from, nor separate from (the world of nature of the Dharma) (PTPCC).
3) The Tathāgatagarbha is equal to the Dharma-Body covered with defilement (PTPCC).

4) The Tathāgatagarbha is neither produced nor destroyed (PTPCC).
5) The Tathāgatagarbha is permanent, eternal, pure, and immutable (PTPCC).

The major doctrinal issues which are adumbrated in the *Śrīmālādevī sūtra* will be the subject of the next chapter. The focus of the present chapter will be the format and style of the *Śrīmālādevī sūtra* and in what manner they depict the essence of the Tathāgatagarbha.

1) *The meditational opening of the sūtra:*

In both the *Tathāgatagarbha sūtra* and the *Śrīmālādevī-siṁhanāda sūtra*, the role of meditation is dominant in the opening of the text. In the *Tathāgatagarbha sūtra*, the story opens with the Buddha sitting perfectly in the lotus position, in *samādhi*, with innumerable lotuses falling at his feet. Using the lotuses as a metaphor, the Buddha initiates his discourse on Tathāgatagarbha. In the *Pu tseng pu chien ching* there is no mention of meditation but there is the association of the true view of Emptiness with the awakening to the thought of enlightenment,[2] usually the outcome of meditation.

In the *Śrīmālādevī sūtra* there is a combination of both the act of meditation and the subsequent awakening of the mind to the thought of enlightenment. Queen Śrīmālā, after having received a letter from her parents requesting her to study Buddhist scripture, commences to learn these texts and visualizes the Buddha in meditation. Due to her meditating, she produces the thought of enlightenment and enters the first Bodhisattva stage, professing the ten Bodhisattva vows, and fervently committing herself to the Bodhisattva practice.

The relationship between the awakening of the mind to the thought of enlightenment (*bodhicitta*) and the intrinsically pure mind equated with Tathāgatagarbha is the most important relationship, from the soteriological dimension, in Tathāgatagarbha literature. Due to the intrinsically pure nature of mind, viz. Tathāgatagarbha, the mind conditions itself in awakening to this fact phenomenally, upon meditation on the Dharma. Paradoxically, the Tathāgatagarbha is both cause and effect, stimulating the mind to become aware of its true nature which has been existent from the beginning. Consequently, meditation as the phenomenal activity of Tathāgatagarbha serves the function of introspection upon the mind itself in its true, intrinsically pure nature. Having meditated upon itself, the mind then awakens to the thought of enlightenment, transforming the ordinary mind (*sattvacitta*) which is extrinsically defiled into the commitment to rediscover the ture, luminous mind (*prabhāsvara-citta*), vowing to eliminate all defilements from oneself and from all other living beings.

Therefore, the implication is that meditation initiates the entire process of rediscovering one's own true nature as identical with the Tathāgata through the intrinsically pure mind, viz. the Tathāgatagarbha, the object of meditation. Serving as the initial link between the phenomenal and supreme levels of truth, meditation manifests the nature of the mind on the supreme level, but functions within the phenomenal level.

The role which meditation plays in the context of Tathāgatagarbha after the initial awakening to the thought of enlightenment remains unclear. The translators as well as the commentators of the *Tathāgatagarbha sūtra, Pu tseng pu chien* and *Śrīmālādevī sūtra* without exception, are associated with either devotional (Pure Land) or tantric texts. The translators of the two recensions of the *Tathāgatagarbha sūtra* now extant in Chinese, Buddhabhadra and Amogha (vajra), are associated with devotionalism and tantricism respecitvely, having translated texts accepted by these trends in Buddhism. Bodhiruci of N. Wei, translator of the *Pu tseng pu chien ching*, is both a Pure Land patriarch and translator of the *Vajracchedika Prajñāpāramitā*, a text which emphasizes meditation. The translators of the *Śrīmālādevī-sūtra*, Guṇabhadra and Bodhiruci of T'ang, have both translated the *Sukhāvatīvyūha*. Chi-tsang, the Mādhyamikan master, author of *Sheng-man pao-k'u*, also composed a commentary on the *Sukhāvatīvyūha*, and Hui-yüan, author of *Sheng-man i-chi*, and extremely knowledgeable in various Buddhist trends of thought, also composed a commentary on the *Sukhāvatīvyūha*. The relationship between the development of devotionalism and its potential influence on Tathāgatagarbha, which is not within the scope of this study, would be an investigation proving most valuable to the field of Buddhology.

2) *The radiation of light from the Buddha and other allusions to light:*

Within the context of Tathāgatagarbha literature there are numerous allusions to light filtering from the Buddha's body as well as to names of Bodhisattvas and future Buddhas who are characterized by light. The importance of the symbolism of light with reference to the Buddhas and Bodhisattvas may be paralleled with the luminous quality of the intrinsically pure mind, exemplified most clearly in the Buddhas and Bodhisattvas who have realized or are realizing this nature of mind.

In the *Tathāgatagarbha sutra*, ten of the forty-nine Bodhisattvas have names pertaining to light:

1) Yüeh-kuang (月光) (Candraprabhā?) - "Moonlight"
2) Pao-yüeh (宝月) (Ratnacandra?) - "Jewel-moon"
3) Man-yüeh (滿月) - "Full moon"
4) Erh-tsang (日藏) (Adityagarbha?) - "Sun-storehouse"
5) Wu-pien kuang (無邊光) (Anantaprabhā?) - "Infinite Light"
6) Fang-kuang (放光) - "Light Rays"
7) Nan-kou kuang (離垢光) (Nirmalaprabhā?) - "Immaculate Light"
8) Kuang-te wang (光德王) (Prabhāguṇarāja) - "The King having Brilliant Virtue"
9) P'u-chao (普照) (Samantaprabhā?) - "Universal Light"
10) Yüeh-ming (月明) (Candraprabhā) - "Moonlight"

There is also a Buddha named Ch'ang-fang-kuang-ming (常放光明) ("Eternal Radiance of Light") whose birth is narrated with descriptions of light emanating from his mother's womb.

The illusion to light in the verses describes the transformation of the lotuses into seats for one hundred billion Buddhas seated in *samādhi*, emitting unlimited rays of light in all directions. In addition several Bodhisattvas have names pertaining to meditation, e.g. Dhāranī Bodhisattva (總持菩薩) and Dhāraṇī Iśvararāja Bodhisattva (總持自在王菩薩).

In contrast to the *Tathāgatagarbha sūtra*, the *Pu tseng pu chien* has few allusions to either light or meditation. The only reference to meditation is with reference to the Śrāvakas and Pratyeka Buddhas who are unable to meditate upon nor comprehend the One World of the Dharma. There is no allusion to light but there is the first example given within early Tathāgatagarbha literature of the intrinsically pure mind which is luminously pure, identical with the Buddha's luminously pure nature.

In the *Śrīmālādevī-siṁhanāda sūtra* we see all three constituents--light, meditation, and luminous nature of mind--combined and interrelated. First, Queen Śrīmālā's meditation upon Buddhist scripture awakens her mind to the thought of enlightenment, accompanied by a description in verse of the Buddha's infinite rays of light emanating from his incomparable body. After visualizing the Buddha and producing this first moment of the thought of enlightenment, Queen Śrīmālā receives the prediction of her future Buddhahood in which she will become P'u-kuang, the Buddha "Infinite Light" (Samantaprabhā). According to Hui-yüan,[3] the Buddha Samantaprabhā has everlasting light radiating from her (?) body because the Buddha visualized before her in the first moment of awakening had shed his infinite light upon her.

The correlation between the first awakening to the thought of enlightenment and the inherently pure, luminous nature of mind (*prabhāsvara-citta*) is symbolically represented as the emission of rays of light from the Buddha who teaches the novice Bodhisattva. Therefore, it may be postulated that the symbolism of light, used generally for wisdom, more specifically is employed as a depiction of the luminously pure quality of mind, first realized by living beings at the awakening of the mind to this thought, immediately prior to the Bodhisattva stages.

3) *The two models, geophysical and physiological, for the Tathāgatagarbha:*

As mentioned previously,[4] the compound *Tathāgata-garbha* may be construed as either the "Embryo of the Tathāgata" or the "Womb of the Tathāgata." Both meanings appear in the *Tathāgatagarbha sūtra*, for in the eighth metaphor of this sūtra, in which the outcaste woman gives birth to a prince fathered by a king, the essentially pure nature of the Tathāgatagarbha is represented by the embryo concomitant with the extraneously defiled nature of the mother's womb. Thus, the

Tathāgatagarbha as essentially pure, luminous mind, is metaphorically represented by the embryo of the prince whereas the impure, defiled extrinsic quality of a living being's mind is represented by the outcaste mother's womb. When one refers to the Tathāgatagarbha in a living being's mind, the Tathāgatagarbha may best be construed as the "Womb of the Tathāgata" in that the defiled elements of the living being's mind have extrinsically obfuscated the nature of the Tathāgata. When the living being's mind has awakened to the nature of enlightenment, beginning to progress along the Bodhisattva path whereby he gradually extirpates defilements, the Tathāgatagarbha is construed as the "Embryo of the Tathāgata," gradually attaining his spiritual growth and identification with the Dharma-Body.

In the *Pu tseng pu chien ching* the identity of the world (or nature) of living beings with the world (or nature) of the Dharma is emphasized. The pure nature of both worlds is the focus of attention, thus emphasizing the "nature" (*dhātu*) or "seed" (*hetu*) of the Tathāgata in the living being's mind. The pure nature of the Dharma and of mind is then best construed as "Embryo" or "Essence" of the Tathāgata, as the purity represented by the eighth metaphor of the *Tathāgatagarbha sūtra* which indicates such an interpretation. While the defilement of the living being's mind is hindering the awakening of the mind and preventing the knowledge of the intrinsically pure mind from occurring, the physiological nature of the womb as a container, a passive receptacle, perhaps is suggested, whereas when t-e living being's mind awakens to the luminous nature of mind, the "embryo" as the potentiality for becoming a Tathāgata, begins to grow. The problem concerning the relationship of the container or "womb" as preserving the Tathāgata and the "embryo" as the eventual spiritual growth from a seed to a mature spiritual being, i.e. a Tathāgata, who is the Dharma-Body, will become the central issue in the *Śrīmālādevīsiṁhanāda sūtra*, describing Tathāgatagarbha as not separate from defilements (as Womb) simultaneously with separation from these defilements (as Embryo).

The idea of Buddha-nature (*Buddha-gotra*) used alternatively for Tathāgatagarbha in the *Tathāgatagarbha sūtra*, also indicates the preference for the interpretation of *garbha* as "member," "seed," "lineage," referring to the true sons of the Buddha. The concept of *Buddha-gotra* again, like the concept of the "Embryo of the Tathāgata," focused on the nature or essence of the Tathāgata, reflected in the intrinsically pure nature of mind, and not on the defiled extrinsic nature of the living being's mind. The *Pu tseng pu chien ching* similarly emphasizes the nature of the Tathāgata, de-emphasizing the nature of defilement characteristic of the ordinary man's mind.

In the *Śrīmālādevī-siṁhanāda sūtra* we see the first attempt at a definitive exposition concerning the defiled nature of mind versus the intrinsically pure nature of mind. Consequently, the Tathāgatagarbha, as depicted in this sūtra, assumes both the meaning of "Womb of the Tathāgata" as not separate from defilements and "Embryo of the Tathāgata" as the intrinsically pure nature of mind which is separate from defilements. In both meanings, we are to see the development of a schema for beginningless defilement in parallel with the beginningless nature of the Tathāgata, but concomitantly, without any interaction between the two whatsoever. Because of their concomitant co-existence with the absence of interaction, perhaps the metaphor of womb and embryo represents their mutual co-existing yet difference in nature, being mother and offspring with distinct characteristics yet co-existing in a cause-effect relationship, the womb (or living being's mind) functioning as the means for producing the "embryo" (the pure mind).

However, this may be an extreme interpretation of the physiological metaphor and one which breaks down since the offspring is dependent upon the womb whereas the nature of the Tathāgata is not dependent upon defilement, a conclusion however, which is sometimes paradoxically implied in the *Śrīmālādevī-sūtra's* exposition on beginningless ignorance, to be discussed in the next chapter.

The geophysical metaphor employed for the Tathāgatagarbha serves a function similar to that of the physiological metaphor. For example, in the *Tathāgatagarbha sūtra*, metaphors #4, 5, 7 and 9 are all geophysical examples[5] for the Tathāgatagarbha within defilement. However, in these metaphors *garbha* functions as the earth or dirt from which the pure gold or jewels emerge untainted. Thus *garbha* is construed as a container or storehouse in which the pure nature of the Tathāgata remains enclosed. In the Chinese translation of *tathāgatagarbha* (*ju-lai-tsang*) (如來藏), mentioned above, *tsang*, used as a translation for both *garbha* and *kośa*, clearly illustrates the "container" connotation of *garbha*. In addition, *gotra* later assumes the meaning of "mine,"[6] again functioning as a container in which there are precious jewels or gold enclosed. All of these examples emphasize the co-existence yet non-interaction between the two elements of purity and defilement more clearly than in the physiological metaphor. The element of immutability is superimposed upon the metaphor of gold, thus contributing another attribute to the Tathāgatagarbha.

When *dharma-dhātu* is included within the list of meanings for the Tathāgatagarbha, the metaphors become more complex. In the physiological metaphor, *dharma-dhātu* is construed as the "seed," "cause," or "element" of the Tathāgata. Thus, the Tathāgatagarbha is the "Embryo of the Tathāgata"; viewed in terms of the Dharma, it is the "seed" of the Dharma, the incipience of the development into the spiritual attainment of the Tathāgata at the Dharma-Body. Because the "Embryo of the Tathāgata" is the pure essence within a living being's mind (the container or "Womb of the Tathāgata" covered by defilements), the eventual maturation of this Dharma-Body from the "Embryo" is immanent. The Tathāgatagarbha becomes the cause or seed for manifesting *bodhicitta* and the Dharma-Body within the phenomenal level of existence through meditation.

Because of the Tathāgatagarbha, a pecular development within the *kāya* theory of the Buddha seems to have emerged at this time, resulting in the notion of *prakṛtisthagotra* in the *Ratnagotravighāga*, alluded to above. The Tathāgatagarbha, when identified with the *prakṛtisthagotra*, becomes the cause or seed for the Dharma-kāya itself from which emanates the Rūpa-kāya and Sambhoga-kāya. Becoming a basis, thinly disguised, for the *tri-kāya* itself, the Tathāgatagarbha is the foundation from which the *bodhicitta* is manifested, prior to the Dharma-kāya as the cause for its realization, and identical with the Dharmakāya not only as its result but by its very nature. Thus, the Tathāgatagarbha paradoxically, as the nature of the Buddha

(*Buddhagotra*) (*Buddhadhātu*), is the cause or seed of itself. Stated otherwise, the Tathāgatagarbha is identical with the Dharma-Body in nature but on the phenomenal level, the former, covered by defilement, causes its own evolution towards the Dharma-Body with the cessation of defilements.

The *dharma-dhātu* as the seed or cause (*hetu*) for the Dharma reinforces this notion of Tathāgatagarbha, "Embryo of the Tathāgata" contained within the world of living beings (*sattvadhātu*), since the "seed of the Dharma" is identical with the "Embryo of the Dharma-Body" in the mind of living beings. Dharma-dhātu and Tathāgatagarbha then are identical with the world of living beings who contain this seed.

When the notion of the identification of Tathāgatagarbha and Dharma-Body is explained by a geophysical model, the *dharma-dhātu* becomes the world of realm of the Dharma, containing all the qualities of the Dharma. In the geophysical model, the *garbha* or *gotra* represents the earth as a mine or container holding the pure and precious gold or gem within it. The notion of Tathāgatagarbha as "storehouse" or "container" of the Tathāgata then illustrates the pure and precious qualities of the Tathāgata who is the World or Sphere of the Dharma.

The notion of Tathāgatagarbha appears as a microcosm for the Dharma-Body (Dharma-kāya) in both the physiological and geophysical models. The Tathāgatagarbha is the "Embryo" or "Essence" of the Tathāgata in every living being, identical with the intrinsically pure mind. This intrinsically pure mind apprehends the World of the Dharma. When existing within defilement, the Tathāgata nature, being identical with the Dharma-nature, signifies the identity between Dharma-dhātu and Dharma-kāya, or the embodiment of Dharma nature, i.e. each individual living being who possesses the Tathāgata-nature, represents the embodiment of the Dharma (Dharma-kāya), of the entire realm of the Dharma (Dharma-dhātu).

Geophysically, the Tathāgatagarbha as "container" or "storehouse" of the Tathāgata also illustrates that the nature of the Tathāgata is stored within the living being's mind, intrinsically pure in nautre, but obscured by "dust" (*kleśa*) as if buried within the earth. The Tathāgata as the Dharma-kāya or aggregate of dharmas, of Dharma-nature, is the container for all these Dharma-qualities. Thus, Tathāgatagarbha (= storehouse of the Tathāgata) is equal to the Dharma-kaya (= aggregate of the Dharma itself) when defilements are removed. Because the Tathāgata embodies the aggregate of the Dharma, the Tathāgatagarbha becomes "a storehouse of the aggregate of the Dharma," i.e. living beings contain the embodiment of the Dharma-World due to their intrinsically pure nature of mind.

Therefore, it appears that the physiological and geophysical models for the Tathāgatagarbha are basically functioning in an identical manner. The physiological model demonstrates more concretely than the geophysical model, the manner in which the living being's mind and the Tathāgata's mind are identical, the living being containing the essence or pure nature of the Tathāgata in embryo. The Tathāgata as a personification of the Dharma, as the Dharma-kāya, is more easily illustrated by the employment of this physiological model; however, the Tathāgatagarbha as "storehouse" or "container" also serves the function of illustrating the fact that the Tathāgata is the "container of the Dharma."

The distinction between "container" and the "essence or contained itself" collapses not only because of the nature of the terms *garbha*, *gotra*, and *dhātu* themselves, but also because the distinction between subject and object no longer is feasible within the schema of Emptiness, perhaps suggesting the deliberate choice of words connoting both meanings. Thus *garbha* signifies both the "essence" or "contained," viz. the embryo and the "container" or "storehouse," viz. the womb. Likewise, *gotra* is the heritage or direct descent in a particular clan as well as the members of the clan collectively. Further expanded etymologically in Buddhist literature, *gotra* then assumes the meaning of mine or container for the jewels or gold hidden within, as well as for the jewels or gold themselves.

4) *The "good sons and daughters"*

The term *kuladuhitṛ*, "good daughter" and *kulaputra*, "good son," both appear in the *Aṣṭasāhasrikā-prajñāparamitā sūtra*. Only *kulaputra* appears in the *Vimalakīrtinirdeśa sūtra*. In the *Tathāgatagarbha sūtra*, *Pu tseng pu chien ching* *Śrīmālādevī-siṁhanāda sūtra*, we find the texts at variance in the manner in which they use these two compounds.

In the *Tathāgatagarbha sūtra*, the assembly consists of 100,000 monks, Bodhisattvas numbering sixty times the sands of the Ganges, and one hundred billion Buddhas who are all gathered on Mt. Gṛdhakūṭa. No women apparently are included in the assembly although one Bodhisattva is named the "Bodhisattva who transforms into a woman" (Chuan nü shen p'u-sa) (轉女身菩薩) (t. v. 16, no. 666, p. 457a). The only metaphor which refers to a woman is that of the womb of an outcaste woman symbolizing the impure element, representing defilement, in contrast to the male embryo destined to be a king, which represents the pure "Embryo of the Tathāgata."

The entire discourse on the nine metaphors is addressed to the "good sons" only. After the discourse has ended, the Buddha promulgates the benefits for all good sons and daughters who read, transcribe, and honor the *Tathāgatagarbha sūtra* (T. v. 16, no. 666, p. 459b). The reading of this sūtra and its subsequent merits are then open to all followers of the Dharma of both sexes.[7]

The only ot-er imagery involving a woman occurs in the description of the birth of Bodhisattva Ch'ang-fang-kuang-ming who emerges from his mother's womb, emitting rays of light in all directions.

In the *Pu tseng pu chien ching* the assembly consists of 1250 monks and innumerable Bodhisattvas gathered on Mt. Gṛdhrakūṭa with Śāriputra leading the inquiry into the nature of the world of living beings. No women are in the assembly which is addressed as "true disciples of the Buddha") (*chen fo ti tzu*) (眞仏弟子), more literally rendered "true sons of the Buddha" (*bhagavataḥ putrā aurasā*). No reference to "good daughter" occurs nor are there any allusions to women throughout the discourse.

In the *Śrīmālādevī-siṁhanāda sūtra* the assembly consists entirely of laymen and laywomen who are the attendants in Queen Śrīmālā's court. Queen Śrīmālā, developing spiritually from the first stage of awakening to the thought of enlightenment to a fullfledged Bodhisattva having professed the ten major vows, is the central figure in the sūtra, expounding on the Tathāgatagarbha, the true Dharma, in the presence of the Buddha. The entire exposition is addressed to both the good sons and daughters who love and accept the true Dharma, teaching all other living beings to do likewise. The emphasis in the first half of the text is upon total commitment to the propagation of the Dharma through relentless compassion and skillful means on behalf of all beings. These good sons and daughters are compared to a great rain cloud pouring forth innumerable benefits and rewards, reminiscent of the parable in the *Saddharma-puṇḍarīka*. They are also compared to the great earth which carries the weight of the sea, mountains, vegetation, and sentient life, bestowing compassion like the great Dharma-mother of the world.

In the second half of the text which is comprised of an analysis of the mind in error and its subsequent realization of its true, intrinsically pure nature, the "true sons of the Buddha" are mentioned in reference to correctly comprehending the Dharma-Body. Neither "good sons" nor "good daughters" are mentioned. After the description of the three kinds of "true sons of the Buddha" delineated by the Buddha to Queen Śrīmālā, the latter refers to these as "those three kinds of good sons and daughters" (T. v. 12, no. 353, p. 222c) and the reference to "good sons" and "good daughters" continues throughout the remainder of the text.

After the discourse, the order of the conversion of the citizens of Ayodhya to Mahāyāna is extraordinary. First, the women of the city seven years of age and older are converted; *then*, Queen Śrīmālā's husband, King Mitrayaśas; and then the men of the city who were seven years of age and older. Finally, the citizens of the entire kingdom are converted. The preeminence of women over men in the order of conversion may either suggest a concession for the sake of the narration since Queen Śrīmālā, being a woman, is the central figure, or it may suggest a preeminence of women in the society in which this text was composed.

In addition, to explicate the doctrine of Tathāgatagarbha, a physiological metaphor in which the woman's womb is a major symbol is employed. Perhaps, the delegation of a woman to further reinforce the female symbolism was intentional. The author may have wanted to acknowledge the social position of women in the place of his residence as well. Given a setting in which women were devout and fervent Buddhist patronesses, a natural product of this patronage would be a text as testimony to the epitome of the Buddhist woman and her role in teaching the Dharma. Moreover, the entire tone of supporter, acceptor, and compassionate Dharma-Mother is strongly reinforced throughout the text in proclaiming "the Acceptance of the true Dharma." Because of the physiological metaphor of *garbha* which borrows the concept of receptacle from the imagery of the womb and the embryo, the female symbolism personified as a woman who teaches this doctrine is a natural outcome. The later implications of Tathāgatagarbha and the expansion of its female symbolism in tantric texts would be a valuable future study for the field of Buddhist studies in general.

CHAPTER III

NOTES

[1] The initials TGS and PTPCC in parentheses are abbreviations for the *Tathāgatagarbha sūtra* and *Pu tseng pu chien ching* respectively.

[2] 遠離如實空見故不如實知如來所證初發心故 (T. no. 668, v. 16, p. 466b).

[3] *Sheng-man i-chi* in *Dainihon zokuzōkyō*, p. 284a.

[4] See Chapter II.

[5] These metaphors are listed on pp. 67-68 above.

[6] See Chapter II, footnote 66.

[7] In Amogha's recension of the *Tathāgatagarbha-sūtra*, both the good sons and daughters will become Buddhas (464b).

CHAPTER IV

TATHĀGATAGARBHA THOUGHT IN THE ŚRĪMĀLĀDEVĪ-SIṀHANĀDA SŪTRA: PART II

In Chapter III the major doctrinal tenets transmitted from prior literature and retained in the Śrīmālādevī-siṁhanāda sūtra were outlined, divided into 1) the relationship between living beings and the Tathāgatagarbha and 2) the concept of Tathāgatagarbha itself. Four factors were developed in the *Tathāgatagarbha sūtra* and the *Pu tseng pu chien ching* related to living beings and the Tathāgatagarbha:

1) The ignorance of living beings obfuscates the knowledge of Tathāgatagarbha.
2) The nature of living beings is identical to that of the Buddha.
3) The ordinary monk also cannot understand the Tathāgatagarbha because he misinterprets both the nature of Emptiness and of Nirvāṇa.
4) The Bodhisattva is the essential means by which living beings are instructed in the profound teaching of the Tathāgatagarbha.

These four factors approximate the first half of the text of the Śrīmālādevī sūtra in which the Bodhisattva, in his relationship with the true Dharma, is able to assist and convert all suffering and ignorant beings. The Bodhisattva and his relationship to living beings will be discussed below in the sections "Acceptance of the true Dharma" and "The One Vehicle."

The five factors which are an analysis of the Tathāgatagarbha per se, developed in the *Tathāgatagarbha sūtra* and *Pu tseng pu chien ching* and expanded in the *Śrīmālādevī sūtra* are the following:

1) The nature and wisdom of the Tathāgata are the Tathāgatagarbha.
2) The Dharma-Body extrinsically covered by defilement is the Tathāgatagarbha.

3) The merits and qualities of the Buddha which are complete in the Tathāgatagarbha are not different from, severed from, nor separate from the nature of the Dharma.
4) The Tathāgatagarbha is neither produced nor destroyed.
5) The Tathāgatagarbha is permanent, eternal, pure, and immutable.

These five factors approximate the last half of the text in which the Tathāgatagarbha is described both from the dimension of the supreme and absolute knowledge of the Buddha and from the phenomenal and conventional level of living beings who must be guided by the Godhisattva. The two dimensions of Tathāgatagarbha will be discussed below under the headings "'The One Noble Truth' and 'The One Basis'" and "The meaning of Emptiness."

A. *The Acceptance of the True Dharma*

1) *The Bodhisattva Stages*

The essential agent through whom living beings are instructed in the profound teaching of the Tathāgatagarbha is the Bodhisattva. Described in both the *Tathāgatagarbha sūtra* and the *Pu tseng pu chien ching* to be developed extensively in the *Śrīmālādevī sūtra*, the Bodhisattva path is the path to realize the meaning of Tathāgatagarbha.

Queen Śrīmālā becomes a Bodhisattva who explains Tathāgatagarbha in the presence of the Buddha, due to her parents sending a letter requesting her to study the Dharma. Awakening to the thought of enlightenment,[1] meditating upon the Buddha, she visualizes him and expresses the wish to follow the Bodhisattva path. Receiving the prediction of her future Buddhahood from the Buddha, she enters the path of the true Dharma, the incipience of Bodhisattva practice. (T. v. 12, no. 353, p. 217b).

According to the *Bodhisattva bhūmi*, the first stage Bodhisattva declares the ten aspirations and then declares many others from these. In the seventh stage, the Bodhisattva is said to have perfected the ten pāramitā,[2] whereas in the *Śrīmālādevī sūtra* only six are outlined. If the original number of *bhūmi* were seven,[3] the first six corresponding to the six pāramitā, the seventh stage then becomes the apex of Bodhisattvahood, and closely proximates Buddhahood. The

Daśabhūmika, in contrast to the *Bodhisattva-bhūmi*, still reflects this original schema because the seventh stage is considered the perfection of all ten pāramitā although three stages and three pāramitā remain unrealized. The four additional pāramitā to the original six are superfluous since the seventh through tenth stages are very near to perfection.

The difficulty in differentiating between the higher stages of the Bodhisattva path is well-illustrated in the commentaries on the *Śrīmālādevī sūtra*. According to the *Sheng-man i-su ben-i* (勝鬘義疏本義) and the *Sheng-man pao-k'u* Queen Śrīmālā is an eighth stage Bodhisattva. The *Sheng-man pao-k'u*, based upon the *Mahāprajñāpāramitā śāstra* (*Ta-chih tu-lun*) (大智度論), refers to the eighth *bhūmi* as that of the Dharma-Body Bodhisattiva. Chi-tsang also cites another commentator who interprets Queen Śrīmālā's level of attainment as at the eighth stage, based upon the *Daśabhūmika*.[5] In contrast with the *Sheng-man i-su ben-i* and the *Pao-k'u* the *Shōmangyō gisho* considers Queen Śrīmālā a seventh stage Bodhisattva about to enter the eighth *bhūmi*.[6]

According to the *Sheng-man-ching i-chi*[7] the opening verses of the *Śrīmālādevī-siṁhanāda sūtra* depict the awakening to the thought of enlightenment, prior to the first *Bodhisattva-bhūmi*. Because no other mention of the *bhūmi* occurs, Queen Śrīmālā must be considered a first stage Bodhisattva according to this commentary.

The controversy which arose concerning Queen Śrīmālā's level of attainment reflects the original schema of seven Bodhisattva bhūmi, instead of ten, in the following manner:

1) At the seventh stage, the Bodhisattva is considered to have perfected all the pāramitās. The *Śrīmālādevī sūtra* does not explicitly stage whether Queen Śrīmālā is vowing to perfect the practice of the pāramitās or has actually begun achieving such perfection. Consequently, certain commentators interpreted the state of Queen Śrīmālā's spiritual attainment as the perfection of the six pāramitā, i.e. the seventh *bhūmi*.

2) At the seventh stage a Bodhisattva still retains a material body. Depending upon whether or not the commentator acknowledged Śrīmālā as a woman or a male Bodhisattva would determine the stage of attainment. If Śrīmālā were a male

Bodhisattva transformed into the likeness of a woman, then the Bodhisattva would necessarily be of the eighth stage or above in order to accomplish such a transformation.

3) At the eighth stage, the Bodhisattva may be considered a Buddha because he has attained the stage of perfection, no longer capable of regressing from the path to Buddhahood. He is considered a Dharma-Body Bodhisattva since his knowledge of the Dharma-Body is perfected and his body is no longer material in form. Because certain commentators considered Śrīmālā a male Bodhisattva in a woman's form, Queen Śrīmālā would then be an eighth stage Bodhisattva.

4) The twelfth bhūmi, one of the two Buddha stages, is sometimes called Samantaprabhā, the name given to Queen Śrīmālā at the time she receives the prediction of her future Buddhahood. If the seventh and eighth *bhūmi*, as construed in the original model of seven *bhūmi*, are considered the highest level of Bodhisattvahood and Buddhahood respectively, the seventh and eighth *bhūmi* are very close in nature, the eighth being originally the Buddha-stage Samantaprabhā and the seventh only infinitesimally different from this Buddha stage. Thus, the controversy which developed in the commentaries centered on the seventh and eighth stages is due to the differentiation between the last step of Bodhisattvahood, represented by Queen Śrīmālā as a living being, and the assured-of-Buddhahood stage, the non-retrogressive eighth stage in which Samantaprabhā, the future Buddha, is immanent.

In the text the Śrāvakas and PratyekaBuddhas cannot comprehend the mysteries of the Tathāgatagarbha but can only have faith in them (p. 222a). Bodhisattvas who have recently entered the path also cannot comprehend this most profound teaching (p. 219a). The implication is that Queen Śrīmālā must be a Bodhisattva at a higher level of spiritual attainment, e.g. the seventh or eighth *bhūmi* instead of the first, since she is capable of understanding the teaching of the Tathāgatagarbha. Because of the interrelationship between Tathāgatagarbha and the Dharma-Body, the main theme of this text, it is reasonable to postulate that Queen Śrīmālā is either at the eighth stage, the Dharma-Body Bodhisattva stage, or quickly approaching that stage from the seventh.

2) *Bodhisattva Practice*

Queen Śrīmālā's first major discourse on the Dharma after professing her Bodhisattva vows is the "Acceptance of the true Dharma" (*saddharmaparigraha*), the definition given to Bodhisattva practice in this sūtra. The head-noun *parigraha* signifies "laying hold on all sides, surrounding, enclosing... comprehending...totality, accepting, acquisition...property... root, origin, foundation."[8] In Buddhist Sanskrit, *parigraha* refers to "property,"..."acquisition" and *parigrahaka* refers to "completely grasping, comprehending" when used with Mahāyāna or *saddharma*.[9] *Parigraha* is sometimes glossed as *anuparigraha* which signifies "embracing (in one whole), uniting"..."tending, cultivating, favoring" the *saddharma*, while *anuparigrahaka* means "helping," sometimes glossed as *para* + *anugrahah*, "favor, kindness...conferring benefits...assistance" for others.[11] The Chinese translation of *parigraha*, *she-shou* (攝受), illustrates both the meanings of *parigraha* and its gloss, *anuparigraha*. *She* signifies "uniting in one person, to assist," to "take or hold up." *Shou* signifies "to receive," "to accept."[12]

The compound *saddharma-parigraha* then connotes the total acceptance of and commitment to the true Dharma, as one's origin and foundation. In comprehending this true Dharma, one will cultivate and nurture it by helping and receiving all beings. The total devotion to and embracing of the true Dharma will then be exemplified in the Bodhisattva, synonymous with the Bodhisattva practice, and exemplified perfectly in the Buddha who has totally accepted and embraced the true Dharma.

In the *Aṣṭasāhasrikā* several passages (x224; ix 251) refer to *buddhaparigraha*, the "assistance of the Buddha" in teaching the Bodhisattvas about wisdom (*prajñā*). *Saddharma-parigraha* also occurs, particularly with reference to the eighth grade Bohisattva who cannot regress in spiritual practice:

punar aparaṁ subhūte avinivartanīyo bodhisattvo mahāsattvaḥ, saddharmaparigrahasya kṛtaśa ātmaparityāgam api karoti, jīvitaparityāgam api karoti/ tasmād bodhisattvo mahāsattvo 'vinivartanīyah saddharmaparigrahāya param udyogam āpadyate atītānāgatapratyutpannānāṁ buddhānāṁ bhagavatāṁ premnā ca gauraveṇa ca/ dharmakāyā buddhā bhagavanta iti dharma prema ca gauravaṁ copādayā saddharmaparigrahaṁ karoti/ nāyaṁ kevalam atītānām eva buddhānāṁ bhagavatāṁ saddharmaparigrahaḥ pratyutpannānām api buddhānāṁ bhagavatām eṣa eva saddharmaparigrahaḥ, anāgatānām api buddhānāṁ bhagavatām eṣa eva saddharmaparigrahaḥ --aham api tatra teṣām anāgatānāṁ buddhānāṁ bhagavatāṁ saṁkhyāṁ guṇanāṁ praviṣṭa iti, aham api tatra vyākṛto 'nuttarāyāṁ samyaksaṁbodhau, mamāpy eṣa eva saddharmaparigraha iti/ sa imam apy arthavaśaṁ saṁparśyan saddharmaparigrahasya kṛtaśa ātmaparityāgam api karoti jīvitaparityāgam api karoti/ xvii, pp. 338-339.

"Moreover, Subhūti, the Bodhisattva-Mahāsattva who is incapable of regressing (from the path) abandons his body and life for the sake of the Acceptance of the true Dharma. Therefore, the Bodhisattva-Mahāsattva who is incapable of regressing exerts himself still furt-er for the Acceptance of the true Dharma with love and respect for the past, present, and future Buddhas who are lords, viz. the Buddha-Lords who are the Dharma-Body. Based upon the love and respect for the Dharma, he accepts the true Dharma. The Acceptance of the true Dharma belongs not only to the past Buddha-Lords but also to the present Buddha-Lords and the future ones. Only this is the Acceptance of the true Dharma. I, who have entered (the Complete and Supreme Enlightenment), predict the Supreme Complete Enlightenment for all the future Buddhas who have innumerable qualities. Only this is the Acceptance of the true Dharma. Seeing this goal of the Supreme, Complete Enlightenment, one abandons his body and life for the sake of the Acceptance of the true Dharma."

The above statement is echoed in the *Śrīmālādevī sūtra*:

"In accepting the true Dharma, may I abandon body, life, and property, and uphold the true Dharma" (T. v. 12, no. 353, p. 218a).

"...The Buddha praised Śrīmālā:... 'Your explanation of the Acceptance of the true Dharma is that which the Buddhas of the past, present, and future have explained, now explain, and will explain. Having realized the Supreme, Complete Enlightenment, I also speak of this Acceptance of the true Dharma." (p. 218a)

Because the Bodhisattva understands that the Acceptance of the true Dharma is Supreme, Complete Enlightenment he is able to totally devote himself to save all other beings through the pāramitās, expressed in the three actions of abandoning body, life, and property, mentioned in both the *Aṣṭasāhasrikā prajñāpāramitā* and the *Śrīmālādevī sūtra*.

The Acceptance of the true Dharma involves total and complete commitment to the Dharma, even to the abandonment of body, life, and property, in order to accept and embrace all living beings. Because of this total commitment, the Bodhisattva is no longer separate from the true Dharma itself because he has vowed always to uphold and to follow the path of the Dharma. Therefore, the Dharma as all the merits of the Buddhas and Bodhisattvas is identical with the total commitment and all-encompassing devotion to the Dharma. This is the Acceptance of the true Dharma.

The totality of the merits of the Buddhas and Bodhisattvas then, is the Acceptance of the true Dharma and for that reason, no merits are produced outside the Acceptance of the true Dharma for it is the container as well as the source of all merits and virtue. Being the totality of all that is good, the Buddhas and Bodhisattvas are identical to the Acceptance of the true Dharma.

The virtuous acts of the Buddhas and Bodhisattvas of past, present, and future, represented by the abandonment of body, life, and property and by the pāramitās, also are identical with the Acceptance of the true Dharma. The one who practices the path represented by the pāramitās and the three abandonments is identical with the true Dharma itself for the true Dharma is the totality of all that is good in living beings. Thus, the Acceptance of the true Dharma is the practicing of the true Dharma, that is, the one who totally embraces all living beings, teaching them to love the Dharma. The personification of this totality of good actions then, is the Buddha or his true disciple the Bodhisattva, and the culmination of his vows is the Acceptance of the true Dharma:

yāny apīmāni bhagavan gaṅgānadīvālikāsamāni bodhisattva-praṇidhānāni tāni ekasmin mahāpraṇidhāne upanikṣiptāny antargatāni anupratiṣṭhāni yad uta saddharmaparigraha/ evam mahāviṣayo bhagavan saddharmaparigraha iti. (*Sikshasamuccaya*, p. 42, ll. 12-14; citation from ŚDS.)

"Ō Lord, these Bodhisattva vows, which are as numerous as the sands of the Ganges, are all contained and incorporated in the one great vow called the 'Acceptance of the true Dharma'. The Acceptance of the true Dharma truly has a great sphere."[13]

The *Daśabhūmika sūtra* also discusses the act of acceptance in Bodhisattva practice which entails the complete understanding of the Dharma and mastery of the Buddha powers:

1) Mahākaruṇāpūrvaṁgamaṁ prajñājñānādhipateyam upāyakauśalya-parigṛhītam āśayādhyāśayopastabdhaṁ tathāgatabalāprameyaṁ satvabalabuddhibalasuvicitavicayam asambhinnajñānābhimukhaṁ svayambhūjñānānukūlaṁ sarvabuddhadharmaprajñājñānāvavādasamprat-yeṣakaṁ dharmadhātuparamam ākāśadhātusthitakam aparāntakoṭin-iṣṭham. (p. 11, T.)

"Preceded by great compassion (the Bodhisattva's mind) has controlled wisdom and knowledge, having been assisted by skill-ful means, based upon his resolution and intention, as well as (accomplishing) the infinite number of the Tathāgata's powers, thorough investigation into the powers of enlightenment and powers for living beings (*satva*), turned towards pure knowledge, inclined towards independent knowledge, having the reception of instruction in wisdom and knowledge of all Buddha dharmas, and being the ground of the utmost limit, the one who abides in space, the excellence of the Dharma-realm."

2) Yad uta sarvatathāgatabhāṣitadharmanetrīsamdhāranāya sarvabuddhabodhisatvasuparigrahāya sarvasamyaksambuddha-śāsanaparirakṣanāya buddhotpāda saddharmaparigrahāya[14] dvitiyam. (p. 14, EE)

This is the second of the ten Bodhisattva ordinational vows (*mahāpraṇidhānāni*). "Namely, (one professes) the second (vow) by the Acceptance of the true Dharma (which causes) the awakening to (the thought of) enlightenment by the preservation of the teaching of all the completely Enlightened Ones, by total support to all the Buddhas and Bodhisattvas, and by upholding the way of the Dharma which was explained by all the Tathāgatas."

Both citations from the *Daśabhūmika* refer to the total comprehension of the Dharma which the Buddha has taught and the preservation of His discipline. Queen Śrīmālā's profession of the ten vows also are a commitment to practice both for her own sake and for others. (T. v. 12, no. 353, p. 217c)

The implication of the Acceptance of the true Dharma for Bodhisattva practice is also found in the *Bodhisattvabhūmi*:

1) punaḥ parigrahaśīlena bodhisattvaḥ sattvāṇāṁ gaṇaparikarṣaṇayogena parigrahaṁ kurvaṁ pūrvaṁ tāvat niśrayaṁ dadāti nirāmiṣeṇa cittenānukampācittam eva saṁpuraskṛtya. (p. 147)

"Moreover, the Bodhisattva, through the discipline of acceptance, gives support to living beings, having formerly actualized his acceptance through the practice of caring (*parikarṣaṇa*) for the multitude, manifesting a compassionate heart without a profane attitude (*nirāmiṣeṇa cittena*).

2) kathaṁ ca bodhisattvaḥ apakāriṣu sattveṣu parigrahasaṁjñāṁ bhāvayati./ iha bodhisattva idaṁ pratisaṁśikṣate/ mayā khalu sarvasattvā bodhāya cittam utpādayatā kaḍatrabhāvena parigṛhītāḥ/ sarvasattvānāṁ mayārthaḥ karaṇīya iti. (p. 191)

"How does the Bodhisattva manifest the idea of acceptance among ignorant living beings? In such a case the Bodhisattva realizes perfectly well that: 'I, having awakened to the thought of enlightenment, have accepted all living beings as my family. I will act for the benefit of all beings.'"

One of the metaphors mentioned in the *Śrīmālādevī sūtra* compares the Bodhisattva who accepts the true Dharma with the great earth which supports four weights, perhaps based upon the second citation from the *Bodhisattvabhūmi* quoted above in which the Bodhisattva, through the acceptance of the Dharma, cares[15] for the multitude of living beings with great compassion. The *Śrīmālādevī sūtra* describes the Acceptance of the true Dharma as the basis and support for all living beings in the following passage:

"Thus, Bhagavan, good sons and daughters who accept the true Dharma, build the great earth, and carry the four responsibilities, become friends without being asked, for the sake of all living beings. In their great compassion they comfort and sympathize with living beings, becoming the Dharma-mother of the world." (T. v. 12, no. 353, p. 218b).

3) saptavidho dharmaparigrahaḥ/ ratnatrayapūjopasthānaṁ gurupūjopasthānaṁ dharmāṇāṁ udgrahaṇam udgṛhītāṇāṁ pareṣāṁ vistareṇa deśanā vistareṇa svareṇa svādhyāyakriyā ekākino rahogatasya samyakcintanā tulanaupaparikṣaṇā yogamanasikāra-samgṛhītā śamathavipaśyanā bhāvanā ca/ asmiṁ saptākāre dharma-parigrahe bodhisattvasya vyāyacchamānasya yad duḥkham utpadyate/ tad apy adhivāsayati/ na can tan nidānaṁ vīryaṁ sraṁsayati. (pp. 193-194)

"There are seven kinds of Acceptance of the Dharma: 1) service and reverence to the three jewels, 2) service and reverence to one's teacher, 3) comprehension of the phenomena, 4) instruction in other things which have been comprehended in detail, 5) the performance of other studies in detail, 6) the investigation, consideration, correct thinking done privately, and 7) the accomplished states which are insight and tranquillity controlled by mental comprehension and practice. In these seven forms of the Acceptance of the true Dharma which belong to the Bodhisattva who has exerted himself (*vyāyacchamānasya*), suffering which occurs will be endured. For that reason he will not fail in perseverance."

4) tatra katamo bodhisattvasya parānugrahaḥ/ iha bodhisattvaḥ catvāri saṁgrahavastūni niśritya dānaṁ priyavā-ditām arthacaryāṁ samānārthatāṁ ca tad ekatyānāṁ sattvānāṁ hitam apy upasamharati/ hitasukham apy upasamharati/ ayam bodhisattvānāṁ parānugrahasya samāsanirdesaḥ/ vistaranirdeśaḥ punaḥ pūrvavad veditavyaḥ/ tad yathā svaparārthapaṭale. (p. 309).

"Then, what is the acceptance of others by a Bodhisattva? The Bodhisattva, based upon the four all-embracing acts of giving, kind words, conduct for the benefit of others, and the same objective (for both oneself and others), brings well-being to certain living beings. He also brings happiness. He brings both happiness and well-being. This is the instruction in equality (*samāsa*) of the acceptance of others by the Bodhisattvas. The extensive teaching (*vistaranirdeśaḥ*) again is to be known as mentioned previously in the section on (practice for) oneself and others."

In the above citations from the *Bodhisattvabhūmi*, the Bodhisattva is described as accepting all ignorant beings, forgiving their ignorant ways with understanding and patience, and enduring all suffering for their behalf. Queen Śrīmālā expresses her earnest wish to accept and assist all living beings first through the profession of the ten ordinational vows, in which she expresses her sympathy towards the suffering condition of others, and then through the commitment to practice the six pāramitās, describing more exactly the acceptance of all beings regardless of their faults, encouraging others to follow the Dharma according to individual disposition. The fourth citation mentioned above is reiterated in the seventh and eighth ordinational vows professed by Queen Śrīmālā:

Seventh vow: "I will practice the four all-embracing acts for all living beings, and not for myself. I accept all living beings without lust, without satisfaction, and without prejudice."

Eighth vow: "When I see living beings who are lonely, imprisoned, sick, and afflicted by various misfortunes and hardships, I will never forsake them, even for a moment, for I must bring them peace. Through my good deeds I will bring them benefits and liberate them from their pain. Only then will I leave them." (p. 217a)

In the *Śrīmālādevī-siṁhanāda sūtra* the Acceptance of the true Dharma is also defined in terms of one's personal understanding of the Buddha's teaching and perfection of his discipline on the one hand, with the concomitant commitment to accept and assist all other living beings in order to enable them to accept the true Dharma as well. The dual function of the Acceptance of the true Dharma is to attain one's own spiritual realization and to teach others to attain spiritual enlightenment.

The Acceptance of the true Dharma, then, is the total commitment to assuring all other beings' enlightenment as well as one's own. These two dimensions of the Acceptance of the true Dharma are first illustrated in Queen Śrīmālā's ten ordinational vows which are different from the Bodhisattva vows in the *Daśabhūmika*. The first five vows refer to Queen Śrīmālā's observance of moral precepts for her own spiritual perfection, the next four vows refer to her assisting and teaching others, and the last vow is the perfect vow, viz. the Acceptance of the true Dharma, because it is the integration of both perfection of self and perfection of others.

The three vows Queen Śrīmālā professes after her ordinational vows, refer only to the perfection of others, having perfected herself in virtuous deeds. The culmination of a Bodhisattva's total commitment to the Dharma, however, is expressed in the act of the Acceptance of the true Dharma which encompasses all other Bodhisattva vows.

The unlimited extension and infinity of merits which constitute the Acceptance of the true Dharma are alluded to in both the *Bodhisattvabhūmi* and *Daśabhūmika*. In the *Bodhisattvabhūmi* the Acceptance of the good was equated with all the virtues and merits of the Bodhisattvas, Śrāvakas, Pratyeka-buddhas, and living beings. The acceptance of all others is considered the "extensive teaching" (*vistaranirdeśaḥ*), parallel with the "extensive exposition" (*mahāvaipulya sūtra*), which Śrīmālā delivers on the Acceptance of the true Dharma. Queen Śrīmālā explains: "...the innumerable worlds of Mahāyāna, the superpowers of all the Bodhisattvas, the peace and happiness of all worlds, the magical omnipotence of all the worlds, and the peace of the transcendental worlds which has not been experienced by gods and men from the time of creation--all these emerge from the Acceptance of the true Dharma." (218b)

Queen Śrīmālā describes this great extension or sphere of the Acceptance of the true Dharma in four metaphors: 1) the great cloud, 2) the great waters, 3) the great earth which carries four weights, and 4) the great earth which contains four jewel storehouses. The great cloud symbolizes the source for all good merits of the Dharma pouring forth on all beings, reminiscent of the parable in the *Saddharma-puṇḍarīka*. The great waters are the source of creation for all the merits of Mahāyāna, the transcendental, and mundane worlds. The great earth carries all things just as the true Dharma carries all beings. The great earth also contains all treasures just as the true Dharma includes all beings who are its jewels.

In all four of these metaphors, the Acceptance of the true Dharma functions as the receptacle or container of all merits in the same manner in which the Tathāgatagarbha will be described later. The Acceptance of the true Dharma is also the source of all merit just as the Tathāgatagarbha is the source of the Bodhisattva practice.

The Acceptance of the true Dharma as the cause for enlightenment is interpreted in the *Śrīmālādevī-siṁhanāda sūtra* as the Tathāgatagarbha itself. This association between *saddharma-parigraha* and Tathāgatagarbha appears for the first time in this text. The terms *saddharma-parigraha* and *Tathāgata-garbha* are identical in meaning in the *Śrīmālādevī sūtra*. *Saddharma* is the "good" or "holy" or "true" law which the Tathāgata taught while *parigraha* was defined above as the total enclosure or embracing of the Dharma, manifested in total commitment to all living beings by assisting them and accepting them through the Bodhisattva practice.

Garbha, also a derivative from *grah*, refers both to the enclosure or container which preserves (or "holds on to") the nature of the Tathāgata, as well as to the contained or "embryo" which will mature and become aware of its own true nature. The first moment of this awareness, in which one accepts the true Dharma and realizes one contains the Buddha's nature, is the moment of awakening to the thought of enlightenment, the initial step in entering the Bodhisattva path. The cause of this moment of enlightenment is alternatively called the "Acceptance of the Dharma" or the "Tathāgatagarbha" in the *Śrīmālādevī sūtra*, in a re-interpretation of *saddharma-parigraha*. Since the Acceptance of the true Dharma includes all good actions and is the cause for the awakening to the thought of enlightenment, it is considered the source or reservoir of all merit. In cultivating merit, one is accepting the true Dharma either directly as a Bodhisattva or indirectly, unaware that his good act is due to the Acceptance of the true Dharma. Consequently, the Acceptance of the true Dharma, the totality of good actions, implies the universal Buddha vehicle which belongs to all who perform good acts.

B. "The One Vehicle"

In Chapter 5, "Ekayāna," Queen Śrīmālā equates the Acceptance of the true Dharma with the Acceptance of Mahāyāna, thus claiming that all good acts which are included in the Acceptance of the true Dharma are included in the Acceptance of Mahāyāna, through identity of the true Dharma with Mahāyāna. The subsequent discourse explains the relationship between the Arhat's path and Mahāyāna, the former being a step towards

Mahāyāna because the Arhat seeks refuge in the Tathāgata. However, the Arhat has not perfected all the merits which only a Tathāgata can perfect. Therefore, he only attains a partial Nirvāṇa. The two vehicles of the Arhat and Pratyeka-buddha then, are the skillful means of the Buddha to encourage them to enter the path of the true Dharma, namely the path of Mahāyāna.

The Arhats, Pratyeka-buddhas, and also the Bodhisattvas cannot entirely know suffering (defilement), eliminate the source of suffering, entirely extinguish suffering, nor practice the entire path because of the impediment that is the stage of beginningless ignorance. The Arhats and Pratyeka-buddhas are turned towards enlightenment and will attain the Supreme, Complete Enlightenment because they enter Mahāyāna which is the true Dharma, the Buddha's vehicle, the One Vehicle. In seeking refuge in the Dharma, Saṅgha, and Buddha, they ultimately are seeking refuge in the Buddha who signifies both the Dharma and Saṅgha. The Bodhisattvas, having already entered Mahāyāna, will also attain the Supreme, Complete Enlightenment because they have entered the Buddha's vehicle.

The author of the *Śrīmālādevī-siṁhanāda sūtra* is sometimes ambivalent in attitude towards the Bodhisattva in comparison with the Arhats and Pratyeka-buddhas. In the first four chapters of the text, the focus is on the Bodhisattva who totally commits himself to the Acceptance of the true Dharma. Although all living beings who practice virtuous actions are subsumed under the Acceptance of the true Dharma, it is the Bodhisattva who is the hero, abandoning his body, life and property out of compassion for suffering beings. The focus dramatically shifts in Chapter 5, however, in which the exposition on the One Vehicle is contrasted with the three vehicles of the Arhat, Pratyeka-buddha, and Bodhisattva, emphasizing the Buddha's Supreme, Complete Enlightenment in contrast with the partial enlightenment of the three vehicles.

Mahāyāna is identified with the true Dharma, accepted totally by the Bodhisattva. The Arhats and Pratyeka-buddhas endeavor to realize the fruits of enlightenment, purifying themselves in accordance with the true Dharma. Their Nirvāṇa however is partial in contrast with the ultimate Nirvāṇa of the Buddha. Yet, when the spiritual powers of the Arhats and

Pratyeka-buddhas are described they are identical with the Bodhisattvas. All three vehicles have the powers of the inconceivable death of transformation and mind-produced bodies, powers usually attributed to Bodhisattvas alone who assume these bodies for the purpose of saving living beings. However, in the teaching of the One Vehicle, the Arhats and Pratyeka-buddhas enter Mahāyāna, implying their Bodhisattvahood, which is a possible reason for attributing a Bodhisattva's powers to them.

The ordinary death of mortals is contrasted to the transformational death (for a purpose) which is a power belonging to the Arhats, Pratyeka-buddhas, and Bodhisattvas (T. v. 12, no. 353, p. 219c). In the course of their ordinary existence within the triple world, the Arhats and Pratyeka-buddhas who have eliminated defilements due to the psycho-physical forces (*skandhas*) will no longer be reborn. Although they are capable of transformational death due to their mind-produced bodies, the Arhats and Pratyeka-buddhas, as well as the Bodhisattvas, are incapable of eliminating beginningless ignorance. Consequently, they do not attain the Supreme, Complete Enlightenment of the Tathāgata, but only a partial enlightenment due to remaining defilements. Because the Buddha's wisdom and His Vehicle, viz. the One Vehicle, are being contrasted to the three vehicles, the higher level of spiritual attainment which the Bodhisattva exemplifies in comparison with the two vehicles, is not the central issue.

For the first time in Tathāgatagarbhan literature, the identity of the Buddha's nature with the One Vehicle appears. A natural culmination of a doctrine in which all living beings possess the Buddha-nature is the teaching of universal salvation, the One Vehicle. While the first Ekayānist sūtra, the *Saddharma-puṇḍarīka sūtra*, proclaimed universal salvation (*Ekayāna*) and the *Tathāgatagarbha sūtra* and *Pu tseng pu chien ching* proclaimed universal Buddha-nature, the *Śrīmālādevī sūtra* is the first text in which the integration of universal salvation (*Ekayāna*) with universal Buddha-nature (Tathāgatagarbha) demonstrates that no one can lost the Buddha-nature once he is born for his enlightenment is immanent.

Because of this identity of the One Vehicle with Tathāgatagarbha, Mahāyāna no longer is a distinct path placed over and above the Arhats and Pratyeka-buddhas. Instead, Mahāyāna as the Acceptance of the true Dharma, is identical with the One Vehicle because of this total inclusion of all living beings without distinction of path. Ultimately there is only one path towards the Supreme, Complete Enlightenment.

SANGHA:

Arhats	Mahāyāna
Pratyeka-buddhas	One Vehicle
	Buddha's Vehicle (Tathāgatagarbha)

DHARMA:

One Vehicle = Tathāgatagarbha

BUDDHA = Dharma-Body = Tathāgatagarbha

Figure 3. The Three Jewels in the ŚDS

C. "The One NOble Truth" and "The One Refuge"

The distinction is made between the Buddha who has achieved the Supreme, Complete Enlightenment and those who are still struggling along the path, based upon an analysis of defilement. The Buddha alone can eliminate the most subtle and fundamental defilement, beginningless ignorance, which is the most fundamental characteristic of the sentient consciousness. In a parallel analysis to the One Vehicle, the One Noble Truth and the One Refuge designate the Buddha who includes all living beings under his guidance. The pre-eminence of the Buddha over the other two refuges, as the embodiment of the Dharma, the Dharma-Body, is explained in terms of the absolute truth in comparison with the incomplete or limited truth.

The absolute truth refers to the purity of the Buddha's nature, i.e. the purity of His enlightened wisdom which is identified with the extinction of the most subtle defilement, viz. beginningless ignorance. In contrast, the limited truth is the purity of the three vehicles who have eliminated all defilements except beginningless ignorance. In order to understand the most profound teaching, the Tathāgatagarbha, one must understand the nature of defilement which obscures the intrinsically pure nature of mind equated with the Tathāgata's wisdom.

The various kinds of defilement are divided into two major classes:

"There are two kinds of defilements. What are the two? They are latent defilement and active defilement. There are four kinds of latent defilements. They are:

1) the stage of all (false) views of monism
2) the stage of desiring sensuous pleasures
3) the stage of desiring forms
4) the stage of desiring existence.

From these four kinds of (defilement) stages, there are all the active defilements. 'What is active' is momentary and associated with the momentariness of mind. O Lord, the mind does not associate with the stage of beginningless ignorance (in the same manner)." (T. v. 12, no. 353, p. 222a)

The interaction between the intrinsically pure mind and defilements is vehemently denied.

"This Tathāgatagarbha, which is inherently pure, is the inconceivable realm of the Tathāgata which has been contaminated by alien defilements (*āgantu kleśa*) and other virulent defilements. Why? The good mind is momentary and not contaminated by defilements. The evil mind is also momentary but is not contaminated by defilements either. Defilements do not affect ('touch') the mind. Then, how does the mind, which is unaffected by nature, become defiled? O Lord, there are defilements and there are defiled minds. The fact that there is defilement in a mind which is inherently pure is difficult to comprehend." (p. 222b)

Because active defilement is momentary and the active consciousness is momentary they interact with each other. Since beginningless ignorance is not momentary, but is the basis (*anuśaya-kleśa*) for all momentary, active defilement (*paryavasthāna-kleśa*) it is not associated with the active, momentary mind. Only the Buddha who complete comprehends Tathāgatagarbha is able to extirpate beginningless ignorance, the very last attachment or propensity which obscures knowledge of the intrinsically pure mind. The nature of beginningless ignorance however, is ignored. It is the basis for all defilement and conditions the active defilements which in turn interact with the momentary consciousness. Yet, the character of beginningless ignorance itself is not momentary and does not interact with the mind in either its active, defiled state or its quiescent, intrinsically pure state. Moreover, beginningless ignorance, being the basis for all defilements is not discussed in relation to the Tathāgatagarbha which is the basis for all conditioned and unconditioned phenomena. If, as stated, beginningless ignorance is a conditioned phenomena, one is forced to conclude that Tathāgatagarbha is also the basis for beginningless ignorance, or beginningless ignorance is of a separate nature from intrinsically pure mind, perpetuating itself in parallel with the mind's activity but never affecting the mind's nature.

If the mind is intrinsically pure, as maintained in the *Śrīmālādevī sūtra*, the problem of defilement is a crucial one. To assert the purity of the mind yet also the impurity of the non-liberated state of mind, one must explain why the intrinsically pure nature of mind has been temporarily impeded by ignorance. The *Śrīmālādevī sūtra* admits that the unaffected nature of mind which co-exists with defilement is difficult to comprehend. Momentariness is associated with activity, viz. a defiled or ignorant state, and disassociated from the quiescent state of the intrinsically pure mind. The last impediment which stirs the mind from its original purity is referred to as the propensity of beginningless ignorance, which being non-momentary, is not active yet conditioned.

The dominant tendency presented in the *Śrīmālādevī sūtra* is to consider defilement as unreal or extraneous since there is only one mind, intrinsically pure in nature, but manifested in an active and momentary manner. The defiled nature of mind which interacts with the active moments of consciousness is essentially unreal, since all phenomena are identical in quality (to the intrinsically pure mind).

"O Lord, there is no attainment of Nirvāṇa because of (the differentiation between) inferior and superior phenomena. O Lord, there is the attainment of Nirvāṇa because of the equality of all phenomena. Because of the equality of knowledge, one attains Nirvāṇa. Because of the equality of liberation, one attains Nirvāṇa. Because of the equality of purity, one attains Nirvāṇa. Therefore, Nirvāṇa has one and the same quality which is that of liberation.

O Lord, if the stage of ignorance is not ultimately eliminated, then one does not attain the one and the same quality of knowledge (*vidyā*) and liberation." (T. v. 12, no. 353, p. 220b)

Based upon beginningless ignorance, the most formidable obstacle to attaining liberation, the momentary mind differentiates phenomena as inferior and superior, thus impeding the realization of the wisdom of the intrinsically pure mind. Consequently, the oneness of all phenomena is identical with the intrinsically pure, luminous mind which, in the *Aṣṭasāhasrikā prajñāpāramitā* was referred to as no-mindedness (*acittatā*).

The author of the *Śrīmālādevī sūtra* emphasizes the oneness of phenomena as the ultimate wisdom of the Tathāgata, reinforcing the unity of all phenomena by the themes of One Vehicle, One Noble Truth, and One Refuge. As mentioned above, there is only One Vehicle, the Buddha's Vehicle, because there is no differentiation of paths for all good acts and merits are included in the Acceptance of the true Dharma.

The introduction of two kinds of noble truths indicates that the elimination of defilement by the three vehicles is only partial. Consequently, their spiritual realization is only Nirvāṇa with remainder. Their understanding of the noble truths is only conditioned, and not the ultimate wisdom of the unconditioned, which belongs only to the Buddha.

Among the conditioned and unconditioned noble truths, only one truth is the supreme truth, viz. the one unconditioned noble truth of the extinction of suffering, all other truths being implied and serving as means to comprehending the unconditioned. The extinction of suffering is identical with the elimination of beginningless ignorance, the last distinct characteristic which differentiates the mind of the Buddha from that of living beings.

The differentiation between the intrinsically pure mind of living beings and that of the Buddha occurs only on the conditioned level of existence. The three vehicles, being within the life-death cycle, must contend with the defilements of such an existence. From the unconditioned level of existence, in which the Buddha's ultimate and absolute wisdom is manifested, the intrinsically pure mind of living beings is identical with His nature. Consequently, the wisdom of the Tathāgatagarbha is the wisdom of both the conditioned and unconditioned levels of existence because the Tathāgatagarbha as covered by defilement is conditioned and as the nature of the Buddha is unconditioned. The true Dharma which is the Tathāgatagarbha is manifested both in the conditioned and unconditioned, in much the same way as Emptiness is manifested both in *saṁsāra* and *Nirvāṇa*.

> Le même *tathāgatagarbha*--ou le *dhatū*--est la Base des deux séries de *dharma*, qui correspondent aux deux plans du *nirvāṇa* et du *saṁsāra*, en vertu de la connexion impensable (et en quelque sorte "irrationnelle") entre le *saṁkleśa* et le *vyavadāna*.[16]

The *Śrīmālādevī sūtra* explains the Tathāgatagarbha, as the identity of both the conditioned and unconditioned, in the following manner:

"In explaining the Tathāgatagarbha, one explains the Dharma-Body of the Tathāgata, the inconceivable Buddha-realms, and skillful means. The mind which attains this determination, then believes and understands the twofold noble truths...they are referred to as the 'conditioned' noble truths and the 'unconditioned' noble truths.

....O Lord, the life-death cycle (*saṁsāra*) is both conditioned and unconditioned; Nirvāṇa likewise is (conditioned and unconditioned), being (Nirvāṇa) with remainder (i.e. conditioned) and (Nirvāṇa) without remainder (i.e. unconditioned)." (p. 221b)

Because the one noble truth of the extinction of all suffering is accomplished by the Tathāgata alone, the one noble truth is identified with the Buddha, who also is the one refuge. Among the twofold noble truths only this one unconditioned noble truth is a refuge because it is permanent and is the supreme truth.

"The one noble truth, viz. the extinction of suffering, is separate from the conditioned. What is 'separate from the conditioned' is permanent. What is 'permanent' is not false and deceptive in nature. What is 'not false and deceptive in nature' is true, permanent, and a refuge. Therefore, the noble truth of the extinction (of suffering) is the supreme truth." (p. 222a)

The last fetter which binds living beings to *saṁsāra* is beginningless ignorance. When this ignorance is eliminated one no longer is bound to *saṁsāra* but can freely live in *saṁsāra* as identical with Nirvāṇa. In the *Śrīmālādevī sūtra* only the Buddha has such spiritual freedom for He realizes that the Tathāgatagarbha is identical with the Dharma-Body in nature, due to His elimination of beginningless ignorance. Consequently, the impediment of beginningless ignorance, regardless of its subtlety, binds even the high level Bodhisattva, preventing him from realizing complete freedom. The Bodhisattva is the intermediary agent who illustrates that he still has attained only partial enlightenment in contrast with the Buddha and functions as the model for living beings to follow.

Although the Bodhisattva has not realized the one noble truth, he is the link between the conditioned and unconditioned. The Bodhisattva, who has not yet realized the unconditioned, is no longer attached to the conditioned in the same manner as other living beings. Because he is only a short distance from the Supreme, Complete Enlightenment, he is a model to living beings that enlightenment is possible, encouraging them to follow the way of the Dharma, the path of the One Vehicle.

In Tathāgatagarbha literature, with the exception of the *Ratnagotravibhāga*, no *trikāya* theory occurs. However, three constituents of the Buddha's body are developed as another interpretation of the personification of the Dharma. The Tathāgatagarbha, as the seed or cause for awakening to the thought of enlightenment, will eventually culminate in the realization of the Dharma-Body. Therefore, the Tathāgatagarbha is the cause for the Dharma-Body and its emanation, the Form-Body. The Bodhisattva, in bridging the gap between the conditioned and unconditioned, is a mirror-image of the Tathāgatagarbha in its conditioned manifestation, revealing

the intrinsically pure state of mind still subtly defiled.

Stated otherwise, the Dharma-Body as the embodiment of the true Dharma itself, is abstract, unconditioned, and absolute. In contrast to the Buddha who has attained the Dharma-Body, the Bodhisattva, in his peregrination within *saṁsāra* still struggles for immeasurable periods of time out of compassion for living beings concomitant with the difficult path he has vowed to undertake for his own purification. As he removes the subtler forms of the conditioned, defiled mind, the Bodhisattva begins to close the gap between the conditioned and unconditioned. Consequently, he has not completely understood Tathāgatagarbha but he has partially understood its nature.

The interpretation of the various stages of defiled mind in the *Śrīmālādevī sūtra* represents a sophisticated analysis over that of its two predecessors, the *Tathāgatagarbha sūtra* and the *Pu tseng pu chien ching*. The emphasis on gross defilements, illustrated by the nine metaphors in the *Tathāgatagarbha sūtra*, are absent from Queen Śrīmālā's exposition, demonstrating the fact that the intention of the *Śrīmālādevī sūtra* is to explicate the nature of the Buddha's absolute purity as contrasted even to the subtlest impurity of the Bodhisattva, without emphasizing the coarseness and ignorance of living beings.

In the *Pu tseng pu chien ching* self-proclaimed monks were not really the Buddha's disciples, because they did not truly understand the meaning of the sutras. In the *Śrīmālādevī sūtra* Queen Śrīmālā has a more compassionate view towards the Arhats who have endeavored to follow the Buddha's teaching, gradually approaching Mahāyāna which has been reinterpreted as Ekayāna. In the *Pu tseng pu chien* the ignorance of living beings towards the Buddha's nature is due to their not having experienced the first moment of the awakening of mind to the thought of enlightenment. In the *Śrīmālādevī sūtra*, due to its interpretation of Tathāgatagarbha in the context of Ekayāna, living beings will experience the first moment of awakening, resulting in their gradual understanding of the Buddha's nature and the subsequent attainment of the Supreme, Complete Enlightenment, having sought refuge in the ultimate refuge, the Buddha.

D. *The Meaning of Emptiness*

Tathāgatagarbha is equated with Emptiness for the first time in the *Śrīmālādevī sūtra*, analyzed in two dimensions, the phenomenal and the absolute, corresponding to the conditioned (*saṁsāra*) and the unconditioned (*nirvāṇa*), which are ultimately identical in nature, all phenomena being of one and the same essence which is Emptiness.

In Vijñānavāda Emptiness is interpreted in terms of three levels of being (*trisvabhāva*) in which the second level of being, conditioned existence (*paratantra-svabhāva*) is Emptiness in its phenomenal manifestation.[17] In the *Śrīmālādevī sūtra* there are only two dimensions of being, the Empty and the Non-Empty ascribed to the non-real and the real respectively, collapsing the second and third levels (*paratantra-svabhāva* and *pariniṣpannasvabhāva*) in the Vijñānavāda schema into one. What is Empty is what is devoid of reality, viz. the defilements obscuring the real. What is Non-Empty are the pure Buddha-dharmas, the truly existent, the unconditioned reality.

Because of false and antithetical views (*viparyāsa*) concerning Emptiness, the wisdom of the Tathāgatagarbha is impeded. These false views which are impediments to the knowledge of Emptiness are due to beginningless ignorance, which tenaciously adheres to the two extreme views of nihilism and eternalism with regard to Emptiness. The extinction of such views is the extinction of suffering, i.e. the extinction of beginningless ignorance, and the complete apprehension of Emptiness--the One Noble Truth realized only by the Buddha. The forerunner for this equation of the One Noble Truth with Emptiness is found in the *Mūlamadhyamaka-kārika* of Nāgārjuna:[18]

> eva (mukte) mañjuśrīḥ kumārabhūto bhagavantam etad avocat/ deśayatu bhagavān kasyo 'palambhataḥ sattvāḥ saṁsāraṁ nātikrāmanti// bhagavān āha/ ātmātmīyopalambhato (mañjuśrīḥ) sattvāḥ saṁsāram nātikrāmanti/ tat kasya hetoḥ/
>
> yo hi mañjuśrīr ātmānaṁ paraṁ ca samanupaśyati tasya karmābhisaṁskārā bhavanti/ bālo mañjuśrīr aśrutvān pṛthagjano 'tyantaparinirvṛtān sarvadharmān aprajñānāna ātmānaṁ paraṁ copalabhate, upalabhy-(ā)-bhinivaśate, abhiniviṣṭaḥ san rajyate iṣyate muhyate/ sa rakto iṣṭo mūḍhaḥ san trividhaṁ karmābhisaṁskaroti kāyena vācā manasā/ so 'satsamāropeṇa vikalpayati/ ahaṁ rakto 'haṁ iṣṭo 'haṁ muḍha iti/ tasya tathāgataśāsane pravrajitasyaivaṁ bhavati, ahaṁ śīlavān aham brahmacārī, ahaṁ saṁsāraṁ samatikramiṣyāmi, ahaṁ nirvāṇam anuprāpsyāmi, ahaṁ

duḥkhebhyo mokṣyāmi/ sa kalpayatīme dharmāḥ kuśalā ime dharmā akuśalā iti, ime dharmāḥ prahātavyā ime dharmāḥ sākṣātkartavyāḥ duḥkhaṁ parijñātavyam samudayaḥ prahatavyo nirodhaḥ sākṣātkartavyo mārgo bhāvayitavyaḥ/ sa kalpayati, anityāḥ sarvasaṁskārā ādīptāḥ sarvasaṁskārāḥ yannvahaṁ sarvasaṁskārebhyaḥ palāyeyaṁ/ tasyaivam avekṣamānasyo 'tpadyate nirvitsahagato manasikāraḥ animittapurogataḥ.

"When that was spoken, Mañjuśrī, the eternal youth, spoke to the Lord: 'Indicate, Lord, what living beings who do not transcend existence apprehend?' The Lord spoke: 'Apprehending I and Mine, Mañjuśri, living beings do not transcend existence. Why? He who perceives himself and others, Mañjuśri, becomes engaged in action. Without understanding that all phenomena are entirely extinguished, the common person, being ignorant and foolish, apprehends himself and others, becoming involved in these apprehensions. Having become involved, he is impassioned, desirous and deluded. Having become impassioned, desirous and deluded, he engages in the three kinds of actions f body, speech, and mind. He discriminates by imputation on what is non-existent. 'I am impassioned.' 'I am desirous.' 'I am deluded.' Having renounced his home he is engaged in the rules of the Tathāgata: 'I am a practitioner of morality.' 'I am a practitioner of holiness.' 'I will transcend existence.' 'I will obtain Nirvāṇa.' 'I will be liberated from suffering.' He discriminates: 'These things are good.' 'These things are bad.' 'These things must be abandoned.' 'These things must be realized.' 'Suffering must be thoroughly learned.' 'The source (of suffering) must be eliminated.' 'The extinction (of suffering) must be realized.' 'The path must be practiced.' He discriminates: 'All conditioned states are impermanent.' 'All conditioned states are ablaze. I will flee from all those conditioned states.' Observing (conditioned states) in such a manner, he has a mental attitude preceded by that of signlessness, together with aversion (for conditioned states).'"

Similarly, in the *Śrīmālādevī sūtra* erroneous views regarding Emptiness prevent the wisdom of the Tathāgata:

agocaro 'yam bhagavaṁs tathāgatagarbhaḥ satkāyadṛṣṭipatitānāṁ viparyāsābhiratānāṁ śūnyatāvikṣiptacittānāṁ iti (Cited in RGV, p. 74, ll. 5-6)

"O Lord, the Tathāgatagarbha is not a realm for those who have fallen into the view of a substantial body, are contented with contrary views, or have minds which are bewildered by Emptiness."

In the analysis of Emptiness as the Tathāgatagarbha presented in the *Śrīmālādevī sūtra* both negative and positive qualities are presented, re-interpreting Emptiness in order to avoid the accusation of either the extreme view of nihilism or eternalism.

1) Emptiness: Negation of Defilement

"O Lord, the Tathāgatagarbha which is Empty is separate from, free from, and different from the stores of all defilements." (Guṇabhadra) (T. v. 12, no. 353, p. 221a)

"The Tathāgatagarbha which is Empty is separate from knowledge which is not of liberation and from the stores of all defilement." (Bodhiruci) (T. v. 11, no. 310, p. 677a)

The Tathāgatagarbha which is Empty describes the essence of the Buddha-nature through the negation of defilement. "Empty" is interpreted as the "absence of," and conversely, "Non-Empty" is the "complete presence of." The absence of defilement is identical to the One Noble Truth, "the extinction of suffering."

"Defilement" or "suffering" refers to even the most subtle impediments to the wisdom of Emptiness, when the three vehicles discriminate phenomena as inferior or superior, "I" and "mine," "existent" and "non-existent." From the level of sentient consciousness in which the three vehicles are struggling, the Emptiness of the Tathāgatagarbha is not yet known due to the tenacity of beginningless ignorance.

"O Lord, the wisdom of Tathāgatagarbha is the Tathāgata's wisdom of Emptiness. O Lord, the Tathāgatagarbha has not been seen nor attained originally by all the Arhats, Pratyeka-buddhas, and powerful Bodhisattvas.

...O Lord, the various great Śrāvakas can believe in the Tathāgata with reference to the two wisdoms of Emptiness. All the Arhats and Pratyekabuddhas revolve in the realm of the four contrary views because of their knowledge of Emptiness. Thus, the Arhats and Pratyeka-buddhas do not originally see nor attain (the wisdom of the Tathāgatagarbha)." (T. v. 12, no. 353, p. 221c)

The emphasis is on the intrinsically pure mind which never interacts with adventitious defilements. The idea of complete severance and total disassociation from defilements, the dominant feature of Tathāgatagarbha literature, is expressed as being "Empty" of defilement, i.e. Empty of beginningless ignorance. In the *Pao-k'u* Chi-tsang cites a commentator who explains that the defiled mind which contains the Tathāgatagarbha is "Empty" because it lacks real existence, being adventitious.[19] Consequently, the defiled, conditioned mind is really non-existent while the Tathāgatagarbha as the unconditioned, intrinsically pure mind is truly existent, i.e. "Not Empty."

Nevertheless, the defiled, conditioned mind of living beings co-exists with the Tathāgatagarbha on the phenomenal level although absolutely non-existent from the absolute level of truth:

> ayam eva ca bhagavaṁs tathāgatadharmakāyo 'vinirmuktakleśakośas tathāgatagarbhaḥ sūcyate. (RGV, p. 12, l. 14; citation from ŚDS)

"This Dharma-Body of the Tathāgata, O Lord, is called the Tathāgatagarbha when it has the stores of defilement which have not yet been separated (from it)."

Consequently, the Tathāgatagarbha specifically refers to phenomenal, conditioned aspect of mind, viz. the sentient, discriminating consciousness when it is being contrasted with the Dharma-Body, though in essence, the mind is only one, the intrinsically pure mind identical with that of the Tathāgata.

In a paradoxical manner, the basis for all phenomena, conditioned and unconditioned, is the Tathāgatagarbha, which is the wisdom of the Tathāgata. When one understands the Tathāgatagarbha, one realizes that the defiled nature of mind has always been adventitious and unreal, i.e. "Empty," and that all phenomena viewed by the Buddha are comprehended as equal in nature and as truly existent, i.e. "Not Empty."

> asaṁbaddhānām api bhagavan vinirbhāgadharmānāṁ muktajñānāṁ saṁskṛtānāṁ dharmānāṁ niśraya ādhāraḥ pratiṣṭhā tathāgatagarbha iti. (RGV, p. 73, ll. 3-5; citation from ŚDS).

"The Tathāgatagarbha is also the basis, support, and foundation for all conditioned phenomena which are the knowledge separated from, divided from, and not connected with (the Tathāgatagarbha)."

The above citation from the *Śrīmālādevī sūtra* is used to explain the passage from the *Mahāyanābhidarma sūtra* mentioned above, viz. "The causal element which continues from beginningless time is the basis for all phenomena. Because of its existence, there are all levels of existence as well as the attainment of Nirvana." In the *Ratnagotravibhāga* the *Śrīmālādevī sūtra* is the authority cited for equating the "causal element which continues from beginningless time" with the Tathāgatagarbha. While the Vijñānavādins were to identify the causal element with the *Ālaya-vijñāna* necessitating its revolution in order to realize Nirvāṇa, the Tathāgatagarbha exponents believed defilement was fictive from beginningless time, requiring only a different orientation towards phenomena which is intrinsic to the mind and yet accomplished only by the Buddhas. Consequently, while the Tathāgatagarbha is never associated with the defiled mind, the fictive mind is imagined until the Buddha's nature is realized, vis-à-vis the awareness of the originally pure mind. If the original nature of mind is identified with the Buddha's, the superimposition of a beginningless propensity for creating a fictive mind attáched to conditioned existence remains unexplained in Tathāgatagarbhan texts.

2) "Not Empty": Affirmation of the Buddhadharmas

The Tathāgatagarbha which is not empty is equivalent to the unconditioned, viz. all the Buddha-dharmas which comprise the Buddha's wisdom:

> Aśūnyo gaṅgānadīvālikāvyativṛttair avinirbhāgair amuktajñair acintyair buddhadharmair iti. (RGV, p. 76, ll. 9-10, citation from ŚDS).

"(The Tathāgatagarbha which is) Not Empty is due to its identity with ('nondistinction from') the inconceivable Buddhadharmas which are the knowledge not separated (from the Tathāgatagarbha), being more numerous than the sands of the Ganges."

The affirmation of the Tathāgatagarbha is described in Chapter 12 of *ŚDS* in terms of the four highest qualities (*guṇapāramitā*), a re-interpretation of the four contrary views (*viparyāsa*) which Arhats and Pratyeka-buddhas strive to eliminate.

> viparyastā bhagavan sattvā upātteṣu pancasutpādānaskandheṣu/ te bhavanty anitye nityasaṁjñinaḥ/ duḥkhe sukhasaṁjñinaḥ/ anātmany ātmasaṁjñinah/ aśubhe śubhasamjñinaḥ/ sarvaśrāvakapratyeka-buddhā api bhagavan śūnyatājñānenādṛṣṭapūrve sarvajñajñānaviṣaye tathāgatadharmakāye viparyastāḥ/ ye bhagavan sattvāḥ syur bhagavataḥ putrā aurasā nityasamjñina ātmasamjñinaḥ sukhasamjñinaḥ śubhasamjñinas te bhagavan sattvāḥ syur aviparyastāḥ/ syus te bhagavan samyagdṛśinaḥ/ tat kasmād hetoḥ/ tathāgatadharmakāya eva bhagavan nityapāramitā sukhapāramitā ātmapāramitā śubhapāramitā/ ye bhagavan sattvās tathāgatadharmakāyam evaṁ paśyanti te samyak paśyanti/ (RGV, pp. 30-31, ll. 19-21, ll. 1-5; citation from ŚDS).

"O Lord, living beings are confused (by contrary views) when they have acquired the five constituents of an individual (form, feeling, name, conditioned states, and consciousness).[20] The transitory is known as eternal. Suffering is known as happiness. Non-self is known as a substantial self. The impure is known as pure. Even all the Śrāvakas and Pratyekabuddhas are confused by their knowledge of Emptiness with reference to the Dharma-Body of the Tathāgata, the realm of the knowledge of all knowledges which has not been previously seen. O Lord, those living beings who are the legitimate sons of the Bhagavat know the permanent, self, happiness, and the pure and are living beings who are not confused (by contrary views). They have the correct view, O Lord. Why? Because only the Dharma-Body of the Tathāgata is the pāramitā of permanence, the pāramitā of bliss, the pāramitā of a substantial self, the pāramitā of the pure. O Lord, those living beings who see the Dharma-Body of the Tathāgata in this way, correctly see."

Since the time of early Buddhism, the four contrary views had been an impediment to Arhatship. In the *Śrīmālādevī sūtra* the early view is retained with regard to conditioned existence but re-interpreted in terms of the Absolute. The two vehicles have the four contrary views when they attempt to understand the affirmation of the Tathāgatagarbha as not Empty.[21] Because the two vehicles have endeavored to eliminate the four contrary views, they cannot understand the affirmation of the truly existent Tathāgatagarbha, but consider it Empty, viz. impermanent, suffering, non-self, and impure. They see Emptiness where there is non-Emptiness and consequently become attached to the former.

The Tathāgatagarbha is not described in terms of the contrary views applied to conditioned existence. Paradoxically, the *Śrīmālādevī sūtra* employs attributes regarded as erroneous views for conditioned existence to the Absolute reality of the Tathāgatagarbha as the unconditioned to demonstrate that the conditioned does not interact with the unconditioned. The path of the two vehicles is partial because it is conditioned. The noble truths studied by the two vehicles are limited because they are conditioned. The consciousness of all living beings is defiled because it is conditioned. In contrast, the One Vehicle is complete and perfect because it is unconditioned. The One Noble Truth of Extinction is unlimited because it is unconditioned. The intrinsic nature of mind is pure because it is unconditioned.

Consequently, one cannot apply positive attributes from the conditioned, phenomenal level of knowledge to the unconditioned, absolute level of the Buddha's knowledge in the same manner:

"O Lord, the Tathāgatagarbha is not a substantial self nor a living being, nor 'fate' nor a person. The Tathāgatagarbha is not a realm for living beings who have degenerated into the belief of a substantially-existent body or for whose who have contrary views, or have minds bewildered by Emptiness." (T.v. 12, no. 353, p.222b)

The Tathāgatagarbha as the nature of the Buddha who has attained Supreme, Complete Enlightenment, is unconditioned and is the basis for all of his good qualities. Therefore, it is not the realm of living beings nor do the categories "eternity," "happiness," "substantial self," and "purity" as understood by living beings apply.

The absolute truth of the one world of the Dharma viewed by the Buddha is eternally true, and therefore is the perfection of permanence for the truth is immutable. The mind which has grasped this truth has viewed the world in radically different categories from those applied to the phenomenal world conditioned by defilement. The eternal in the conditioned defiled world is a contrary view but the eternal in the world as unconditioned is the perfect view of the Buddha. The pure cannot be found in a conditioned defiled world but in the world of the Tathāgata. The substantial ego as a permanent, immutable essence, similar to the eternity of the world as unconditioned, is the perfect view which the Buddha possesses, having realized the permanent and eternal truths of the Dharma. Happiness is not attained within the three vehicles which are attached to existence but in the unattached, unconditioned supreme and complete enlightenment.

The One Noble Truth or One Refuge which is the unconditioned truth of the Tathagatagarbha is attained by the intrinsically pure mind which is itself the Tathāgatagarbha. The defiled mind which is tied to tbe phenomenal is unable to bridge the gap between the absolute and the phenomenal whereas the Tathāgatagarbha as the absolute, intrinsically pure mind is paradoxically able to co-exist in the phenomenal world remaining uncontaminated by it because the mind no longer discriminates between inferior and superior, conditioned and unconditioned.

CHAPTER IV

NOTES

[1]See Har Dayal, *The Bodhisattva Doctrine, op. cit.*, pp. 58-64 for a description of *Bodhicittotpāda*.

[2]Har Dayal, *Ibid.*, p. 281.

[3]*Ibid.*, p. 271. According to Har Dayal, ten *bhūmi* and ten *pāramitā* were probably substitutes for the original seven and six respectively sometime after the invention of the decimal system in the third of fourth century A.D. (p. 167).

[4]Koizumi Enjun, "*Shōmangyō gisho hongi*" in *Shōtoku taishi kenkyū*, v.V, *op. cit.*, p. 15.

[5]T.v. 37, no. 1744, p. 3a.

[6]*Shōmangyō gisho*, Hōryūji blockprint, p. 5a.

[7]*Dainihon zokuzokyo*, p. 283.

[8]Sir Monier Monier-Williams, *A Sanskrit-English Dictionary, op. cit.*, p. 593a.

[9]Franklin Edgerton, *Buddhist Hybrid Sanskrit Grammar and Dictionary*, v. II, *op. cit.*, p. 312b.

[10]Edgerton, *Ibid.*, p. 29a.

[11]Monier-Williams, *A Sanskrit-English dictionary, op. cit.*, p. 32a. In the *Bodhisattvabhūmi*, ed. by Unrai Wogihara (Tokyo: Sankibō Buddhist Bookstore, 1971), p. 307, *kauśalaparigraha* is glossed as *kauśalaṁ parānugrahaḥ*.

[12]R. H. Mathews, *Mathews' Chinese-English Dictionary* (Cambridge: Harvard University Press, 1969), p. 788c and p. 824b-c.

[13]Both Chinese recensions give *i ta-yüan* (一大願), "the one great vow" or *ekamahāpranidhāna* instead of *mahāviṣaya*.

[14]Although Rahder has edited the passage as two separate compounds, I have construed these two phrases as one compound, i.e. *buddhotpādasaddharmaparigrahāya*.

[15]The Sanskrit *parikarṣana*, translated as "care," refers originally to a mother's caring for and nursing of her child. Cf. Edgerton, *Buddhist Hybrid Sanskrit Dictionary, op. cit.*, p. 320b.

[16]Ruegg, *La Théorie du Tathāgatagarbha, op. cit.*, p. 359.

[17]See "'What Remains' in Śūnyatā: A Yogācārin Interpretation of Emptiness" by Gadjin M. Nagao (soon to be published in Richard Robinson's commemorative volume), for an analysis of

the positive meaning of Emptiness in the Yogācārin treatises, which is not discussed in the present study.

[18] *Mūlamadhyamakakarikā*, ed. by Louis de la Vallée Poussin (St. Petersburg, 1903), p. 516.

[19] 空知者能照之智離相。故名空智。...又空如來藏即是明如來藏是中道義。空藏明煩惱畢竟空。(p. 73b)

[20] The five Sanskrit equivalents are *rūpa*, *vedanā*, *samjñā*, *saṁskāra*, and *vijñāna*.

[21] *Pao-k'u*: ...於不空如來藏起四倒也。不空藏具常樂我淨四德而彼謂苦無常空無我也。...又於不空藏而見空故是轉倒。(p. 74c)

CONCLUDING REMARKS

The *Śrīmālādevī-siṁhanāda sūtra* reinterpreted the meaning of Emptiness presented in the *Prajñāparamitā* in terms of Tathāgatagarbha, focusing on the relationship between the intrinsically pure mind and the extraneous defilements which impede the awareness of this true nature of mind. In the *Aṣṭasāhasrikā* and the *Vimalakīrtinirdeśa* pure mind was equated with Emptiness, denying any ground to the phenomenal world. In Tathāgatagarbha literature the equation of intrinsically pure mind with Emptiness was retained but this mind became the ground for all phenomena, both conditioned and unconditioned, interpreting Emptiness as a positive and affirmative apprehension of the Dharma-nature, represented in the intrinsically pure minds of all living beings. Dharma-nature itself was equated with Tathāgatagarbha and Ekayāna.

Prior to the *Śrīmālādevī* Tathāgatagarbha literature was shown to have emphasized Buddha nature, the intrinsically pure nature of mind, without discussing the erroneous or confused sentient consciousness. The author of the *Śrīmālādevī sūtra* within the context of Tathāgatagarbha thought, attempts for the first time to analyze the nature of defilement and its relationship with the intrinsically pure mind. Although the defiled mind was claimed to be adventitious and unreal ("empty"), the sentient consciousness in its everyday activity tenaciously adhered to this defiled state (beginningless ignorance), discriminating and losing sight of the Dharma-nature. The evolution of the notion of Tathagatagarbha in the *ŚDS* culminated in the merging of luminous, intrinsically pure mind as the basis of the phenomenal (linking this mind with the world of living beings) with the world of the Tathāgata, the world of the Dharma itself, being the basis for the unconditioned.

The *Śrīmālādevī sūtra* confronts the problem of ignorance or discriminative thinking as fictive in nature, imagined by the deluded mind. However, the struggle which the sentient consciousness continually undertakes in order to overcome ignorance, precludes the acceptance of ignorance as merely "adventitious." The author of the text was aware of this dilemma and encouraged living beings, through the merits of the Acceptance of the true Dharma, to persevere in their efforts to understand the Tathāgatagarbha. In the final analysis, however, the nature of all phenomena, being identical in nature with the Dharma, rendered the defiled mind non-existent and imagined.

The intrinsically pure mind and the theory of extraneous defilements outlined in Tathāgatagarbha literature were traced to the Mahāsaṅghikan sects in south India, centered in Āndhra. The female symbolism peculiar to the concept of Tathāgatagarbha concomitant with the selection of a woman as the main character in this text indicated that matriarchal societies such as those found in Āndhra would be receptive to this teaching. In addition, the first known occurrance of the term "Tathāgatagarbha" appears in the introduction to the *Ekottarikāgama*, most probably a composition of a Mahāsaṅghika. Moreover, according to Paramartha, the *Śrīmālādevī sūtra* was known and accepted by certain Mahāsaṅghika.

The Central Asian countries which devoutly patronized Buddhist studies undoubtedly initiated the full-scale translation of Tatbagatagarbha texts such as the *Śrīmālādevī* and introduced them to North China whose hegemony at that time belonged to non-Chinese clans. Their influence on Tathāgatagarbha literature and its subsequent development and dissemination is of vital importance in understanding the evolution of Tathāgatagarbha thought, a study which would encounter complex problems due to the lacunae in information concerning the exportation of texts from India to all parts of central and east Asia.

Although many gaps still persist with relation to the evolution of Tathāgatagarbha thought, an analysis of its initial form has been attempted by analyzing key passages of other Buddhist literature having an affinity of ideas with Tathāgatagarbha. The culmination of Tathāgatagarbha thought, evidenced in the *Śrīmālādevī sūtra*, is later assimilated with Vijñānavāda in the *Ratnagotravibhāga*, retaining the *Śrīmālādevī sūtra* as its primary textual authority but amending that sūtra's tenets in accordance with both Mādhyamika and Vijñānavāda ideas thus terminating the independent innovative re-interpretation of Emptiness by a southern school of Mahāyāna.

Outside influences on Tathāgatagarbha literature such as the impending Brahmanic renaissance of the Guptan Age and the Dravidian folk religions of the southern regions are a subject for future research would would prove most valuable for scholars not only in Tathāgatagarbha literature but also for those studying Tantric texts, some of which incorporated Tathāgatagarbha ideas. The role of devotionalism and the importance of this role for those who believed in the universality of the Buddha-nature is also a critical issue, especially since the chief translators of Tathāgatagarbha literature were interested in both devotional and meditational texts. In addition, the *Śrīmālādevī sūtra* advocates fervent faith if one cannot comprehend the mysteries of the Tathāgatagarbha.

Investigating the intermediary development of Buddhism between its two greatest schools Mādhyamika and Vijñānavāda not only provides a better understanding of the misconceptions and dilemmas which certain Buddhists experienced after the development of the concept of Emptiness in the *Prajñāpāramitā* period but also furnishes an outline of the subsequent development of Vijñānavāda from certain Tathāgatagarbha tenets which were not satisfactorily explained. Tathāgatagarbha thought thus performed a role as an alternative world view to that of the Mādhyamika, affirming the nature of mind more positively and, from its perspective, more comprehensibly, for the Buddhist audience.

For today's student of world religions the view provided by Tathāgatagarbha literature in general is a unique example of the physiological and geophysical metaphors for the sentient consciousness in its struggle to understand its conditioned existence and its identity with the truly existent. In its universal acceptance of humanity as equal in nature, the *Śrīmālādevī sūtra* is extremely valuable as an altruistic and compassionate depiction of living beings in their daily struggle for survival and their yearning for freedom from existence-in-bondage.

CHAPTER V

THE TEACHING OF QUEEN ŚRĪMĀLĀ WHO HAD THE LION'S ROAR:

A comprehensive text that teaches the skillful means of the One Vehicle

Translated by the Central Indian Tripiṭaka master Guṇabhadra (c. 394-468)

[Chapter 1 - "The merits of the Tathagata's true doctrine"][1]

Thus have I heard: One time the Buddha was residing in the Jeta garden in the city of Śrāvasti[2] in the kingdom Kośala. At that time King Prasenajit and Queen Mallikā, who had only recently attained the faith in the Dharma, said these words together: "Śrīmālā, our daughter, is astute and extremely intelligent. If she has the opportunity to see the Buddha she will certainly understand the Dharma without doubting (its truth). Sometime we should send a message to her to awaken her religious state of mind."

His queen spoke: "Now is the right time." The king and queen then wrote a letter to Śrīmālā praising the Tathāgata's immeasurable merits, dispatching a messenger named Candirā[3] to deliver the letter to the kingdom of Ayodhyā (where Śrīmālā was queen). Entering the palace, the messenger respectfully conferred the letter to Śrīmālā who rejoined upon receiving it, raising the letter to her head (as a sign of reverence). She read and understood it, arousing a religious mind of rare quality. Then she spoke to Candirā in verses:

"I hear the name 'Buddha,'
The One who is rarely in the world.
If my words are true (that the Buddha is now in the world)
Then I will honor Him.

Since I humbly submit that the Buddha-Bhagavan
Came for the sake of the world,
He should be compassionate with me
Allowing me to see Him."[4]

At that very moment of reflection,
The Buddha appeared in heaven,
Radiating pure light in all directions,
And revealing His incomparable body.

Śrīmālā and her attendants
Prostrated themselves reverently at His feet;
And with pure minds,
They praised the true merits of the Buddha:

"The body of the Tathāgata, excellent in form,
Is unequalled in the world,
Being incomparable and inconceivable.
Therefore, we now honor You.

The Tathāgata's form is inexhaustible[5]
And likewise His wisdom.
All things eternally abide (in Him).
Therefore, we take refuge in You.

Having already exorcised the mind's defilements[6]
And the four kinds (of faults) in body (and speech)[7]
You have already arrived at the undaunted stage.[8]
Therefore, we worship you, the Dharma-King.

By knowing all objects to be known,
And by the self-mastery of Your Body of wisdom,
You encompass all things.
Therefore, we now honor You.

We honor You, the One who transcends all measures
(of space and time).
We honor You, the One who is incomparable.
We honor You, the One who has the limitless Dharma.
We honor You, the One beyond conceptualization."

(Śrīmālā:)

"Please be compassionate and protect me,
Causing the seeds of the Dharma to grow (within me).
In this life and in future lives,
Please, Buddha, always accept me."

(The Buddha:)

"I have been with you for a long time,
Guiding you in former lives.

I now again will accept you.
And will do likewise in the future."

(Śrīmālā:)

"I have produced merits
At present and in other lives.
Because of these virtuous deeds[9]
I only wish to be accepted."

Then Śrīmālā and all of her attendants prostrated themselves before the Buddha's feet. The Buddha then made this prediction among them:[10] "You praise the true merits of the Tathāgata, because of your virtuous deeds. After immeasurable periods of time, you will become iśvara-kings among the gods. In all lives you will continually see me and praise me in my presence, in the same manner as you are doing now. You will also make offerings to the immeasurable numbers of Buddhas, for more than 20,000 immeasurable periods of time. Then you (Śrīmālā) will become the Buddha named "Universal Light" (Samanta-prabhā?), the Tathāgata, Arhat, Perfectly-Enlightened One.

Your Buddha-land will have no evil destinies and no suffering due to old age, sickness, deterioration, torments, etc. There will be no evil whatsoever. Those who are in your land will have the five desires (of the senses fulfilled), longevity, physical power, and beauty, and will be happier than even the *paranirmitavaśavartin*[11] gods. They all will be exclusively Mahāyāna, having habitually practiced virtuous deeds, and assemblying in your land."

When Queen Śrīmālā had received this prediction, the innumerable gods, men, and other beings, vowed to be born in her land. The Lord predicted to everyone that they all would be born there.

CHAPTER V

NOTES

[1]The chapter headings given in the *Taishō* have been bracketed since the oldest manuscripts at Tun-huang contained no chapter headings. The commentaries gradually developed chapter headings but they differed greatly. For convenience in locating the text in the *Taishō*, these headings have been retained here. For a discussion concerning the development of chapter headings in the *Śrīmālādevī-sūtra* see Koizumi Enjun, "Shōmangyō gisho hongi," pp. 3-4 and Fujieda Akira, "Hokuchō ni okeru Shōmangyō no denshō," p. 331, both in *Tōhō Gakuhō*, v. XL (Kyoto: Jimbun Kagaku Kenkyūsho, 1972).

[2]Śrāvastī is "a city situated north of the Ganges and founded by King Śrāvastā (it was the ancient capital of Kośala and said to have been the place where the wealthy merchant Anāthapiṇḍika built the Buddha a residence in the Jeta-vana monastery which became his favorite retreat during the rainy seasons)." Monier-Williams, Sir. Monier (*Sanskrit-English Dictionary*, Oxford: Clarendon Press, 1964), p. 1098. It is now located in the present Sahet-Maheth in Oudh.

[3]The Chinese transliterations 旃提羅, Chan-ti-lo, and 眞提羅 Chen-ti-lo (Guṇabhadra and Bodhiruci's translations respectively) may both be translated as Candra, Candrā, Candira, Candirā--all names pertaining to the moon.

[4]Bodhiruci: 令我觀眞相 --"causes me to see the mark of truth." Cf. 必令我得見

[5]The Tathāgata's form is inexhaustible because He appears to all beings who are mindful of Him.

[6]The ten evil actions (十悪, 十不善業):

a. killing (*prāṇātipāta*) 殺生
b. stealing (*adattādana*) 偸盗
c. sexual misconduct (*kāmamithyācāra*) 邪婬
d. false speech (*mṛṣāvāda*) 妄語
e. idle talk (*saṁbhinna-pralāpa*) 綺語
f. harsh speech (*pāruṣya*) 悪口
g. slander (*paiśunya*) 兩舌
h. covetousness (*abhidhyā*) 貪欲
i. evil intent (*vyāpāda*) 瞋恚
j. wrong views (*mithyādṛṣṭi*) 邪見

[7]The commentaries vary. *Gisho*: The four kinds of misleading ways refer to 身三口四 in which the three faults of the body are killing, stealing, and sexual misconduct and the four faults of speech refer to false speech, slander, harsh speech, and idle talk (7b). *Pao k'u*: The four kinds of misleading ways refer to birth, sickness, old age, and death. Professor Tsukinowa claims that *catvara* (四種) is a corruption of *vacana* (口四) which coincides with the *Gisho*. (Tsukinowa Kenryū, *Shōmangyō hōgatsu-dōji-shomongyō*, Kyoto: 1940, p. 2 fn. 1 for p. 9).

[8]The "undaunted stage" is referred to as "the inconceivable stage" (不思議地) in Bodhiruci's translation. The *Gisho* refers to this stage as the Vajra stage (金剛心位), the tenth Bodhisattva stage and at other times as the Buddha stages (7b). The fact remains, in either case, that this stage has conquered the ten evil actions and the four kinds of faults of body and speech.

[9]Bodhiruci:由斯善根力 --"because of tbe power of these virtuous deeds." Cf.女是衆善本 (G̣unabhadraB

[10]Bodhiruci:授勝鬘夫人阿耨多羅三藐三提記。 "he predicted Queen Śrīmālā's Supreme, Perfect Enlightenment." Cf.即為受記 (Guṇabhadra)

[11]The paranirmitavaśavartin heaven is a place where there is "the constantly enjoying [of] pleasures provided by others." Monier-Williams, *A Sanskrit-English Dictionary*, p. 586. According to E. J. Thomas, *The History of Buddhist Thought*, *op. cit.*, p. 111, these gods have "power over the transformation of others."

[Chapter 2 - "The ten ordinational vows"[1]]

At that time Śrīmālā, having received the prediction, respectfully arose to take the ten major ordination vows.[2]

"O Lord, from now until I am enlightened:[3]

1) I will not transgress the discipline (*śila*) which I have received.

2) I will have no disrespect towards the venerable elders.

3) I will not hate living beings.

4) I will not be jealous of others with regard to either their physical appearance or their possessions.[4]

5) I will not be stingy although I have little sustenance.[5]

O Lord, from now until I am enlightened:

6) I will not accumulate property for my own benefit.[6] Whatever I receive will be used to assist living beings who are poor and suffering.

7) I will practice the four all-embracing acts[7] for all living beings, and not for myself. I accept all living beings without lust, without satiation, and without prejudice.

8) When I see living beings who are lonely, imprisoned, sick, and afflicted by various misfortunes and hardships, I will never forsake them, even for a moment, for I must bring them peace. Through my good deeds[9] I will bring them benefits and liberate them from their pain. Only then will I leave them.

9) When I see those who hunt or domesticate animals, slaughter, or commit other such offenses[10] against the precepts, I will never forsake them. When I obtain this power[11] (to teach all beings), I will restrain those who should be restrained and assist those who should be assisted[12] wherever I see such living beings. Why? Because by restraining and assisting them, one causes the eternal continuation of the Dharma.[13] If the Dharma continues eternally, gods and men shall flourish and the evil destinies shall diminish in number. Then the Dharma-Wheel which is turned[14] by the Tathāgata will again be turned. Because I see these benefirs I will save, and never quit (teaching living beings).[15]

O Lord, from now until I am enlightened,

10) I accept the true Dharma, never forgetting it. Why? Because those who forget the Dharma, forget Mahāyāna. Those who forget Mahāyāna, forget the Pāramitās.

> Those who forget the Pāramitās, do not desire Mahāyāna. If the Bodhisattvas are not committed to Mahāyāna, they cannot have the desire to accept the true Dharma. Acting according to their pleasure, they will not be able to transcend the level of the common man.[16]

Because I have seen, in this way, the immeasurably great errors (of man) nad have seen the immeasurable merits of the Bodhisattva-Mahāsattvas[17] who will accept the true Dharma, I accept these great ordination vows.[18]

Bhagavan, the Lord of the Dharma, manifested before me, is my witness. Even though the Buddha-Bhagavan presently witnessed (my testimony), living beings' virtuous deeds are superficial. Some of them are skeptical and extremely difficult to save through these ten ordination vows. They engage in immoral activities[19] for long periods of time and are unhappy. In order to bring peace to them, I now declare, in Your presence, that my vows are sincere.

If I receive these ten major vows and practice them as I have stated them by (the power of) these true words, heavenly flowers will rain down and divine music will ring out upon this assembly."

Just when she proclaimed these words, a shower of heavenly flowers poured from the sky and divine music rang out: "It is so! It is so! What you have said is true, not false." Having seen these wondrous flowers and having heard this music, the entire assembly no longer was skeptical, rejoicing immeasurably and expressing their wish: "We wish to stay with Queen Śrīmālā and together we would like to join in practice with her."

The Buddha predicted to all that their wish (to stay with Queen Śrīmālā) would be fulfilled.

CHAPTER 2

NOTES

[1]十受 refers to 十戒, the Bodhisattva major vows according to the *Gisho* (9b).

[2]Bodhiruci: 十弘誓--"the ten universal vows." Cf. 十大受 (Guṇabhadra).

[3]Items 1 through 5 below refer to the prohibitory rules of the Bodhisattva discipline (*śīla*) according to the *Mahāyāna Brahmajāla sūtra*, among others. Both the *Gisho* and the *Pao-k'u* refer to these five items of ordination as the prohibitory rules. The *Pao-k'u* also makes reference to the *Ying-lo-ching* (瓔珞經) indicating that these ten items of ordination are the Bodhisattva interpretation of the *śīla* (20b). Both of these commentaries further divide the next five items. The *Gisho* refers to items 6-9 as the *śīla* of compassion (11b) and the last item as the perfect *śīla* (12b); the *Pao-k'u* reverses the names of these two subdivisions (21a).

[4]Bodhiruci: 於諸勝己及諸勝事不起妬 "I will not be jealous of either superiors or of the accomplishments (of others)." Cf. 於他身色及外衆具不起疾(嫉)心 (Guṇabhadra)

[5]Guṇabhadra: 於内外法不起慳心 "I will not be attached to inner and outer things." The translator has chosen Bodhiruci's text instead of Guṇabhadra's for the sake of clarity. Both texts refer to non-attachment to material possessions. According to the *Pao-k'u*, "the inner things" refer to one's own possessions, "the outer" to others' possessions. Another interpretation gives one's wife and children's possessions for the latter (22b) (*Gisho*).

[6]Bodhiruci: 不求恩報 --"not seeking reward for (my own) kindness." Cf. 不自為己 (Guṇabhadra)

[7]The "four all-embracing acts" (四攝法) are giving (布施) (*dāna*), kind speech (愛語) (*priyavacana*), benefitting others (利行) (*arthakṛtya*), and cooperation towards leading all beings to virtuous deeds (同事) (*samānārthata*).

[8]The *Gisho* amends 無厭足心 to 無瞋心 "without hate" (12a).

[9]Bodhiruci: 以善 --"through good (deeds)." Cf. 以義 --"by justice" (Guṇabhadra) The translator has chosen Bodhiruci's text here.

[10]Bodhiruci: 毀犯如来清浄禁戒 "and violate the Tathāgata's discipline which prohibits acts against purity." Guṇabhadra omits this sentence.

[11]Bodhiruci omits 我得力時 --"when I attain this power."

[12]"Restraining" (折伏) and "assisting" (攝受) refers to the two methods of overcoming defilement (*kleśa*). According to

the *Gisho*, Śrīmālā receives two kinds of power at this time: the power of strength (勢力) which restrains (折伏) more virulent forms of defilement and the power of the path (道力) which assists (攝受) in overcoming lesser forms of defilement (12b).

[13]Bodhiruci: 則正法久住 --"then there will be the eternal continuation of the true Dharma." Cf. 令法久法 (Guṇabhadra)

[14]The phrase 能於如來 ...has been amended, omitting *neng* (能) in accordance with the Tun-huang manuscript (S. 2526)

[15]Bodhiruci omits 而得隨轉、見是利故、救攝不捨。

[16]Bodhiruci: 便不堪任超凡夫境則為大失。"Unable to transcend the realm of the common man they will be lost." Cf. 欲隨所樂入永不堪任越凡夫地 (Guṇabhadra)

[17]Bodhisattva refers to the nature of being enlightened, whereas Mahāsattva refers to the magnanimous heart of one who saves others. (Cf. *Kokuyaku-issaikyō, hōshaku-bu shichi, op. cit.*, p. 97, fn. 41.

[18]Bodhiruci: 現在未來攝受正法諸菩薩等具足無邊..益 "The present and future Bodhisattvas who accept and will accept the true Dharma are endowed with limitless and vast merits." Cf. 我見如是無量大過又見未來攝受正法菩薩摩訶薩無量福利。(Guṇabhadra)

[19]Bodhiruci: 習不善法 Cf. 非義饒益。"immoral excesses" (Guṇabhadra). The translator has chosen Bodhiruci's text here.

[Chapter 3 - "The three vows"]

At that time Śrīmālā again, in the presence of the Buddha, professed the three great vows.

"By hte power of my earnest desire, may I bring peace to innumerable and unlimited living beings. By my virtuous deeds, throughout all rebirths may I attain the wisdom of the true Dharma." --This is called the first great vow.[1]

"Having attained the wisdom of the true Dharma, for the sake of all living beings, may I explain (the Dharma) without wearying."--This is called the second great vow.[2]

"In accepting the true Dharma, may I abandon body, life, and property, and uphold the true Dharma."--This is called the third great vow.[3]

At that time the Bhagavan prophesied to Śrīmālā: "With reference to the three great vows,--just as all forms are contained in space, so likewise, the Bodhisattva vows, which are as numerous as the sands of the Ganges, are all contained in these three great vows. These three vows are the truth and are extensive."

CHAPTER 3

NOTES

[1]*Gisho*: The first great vow is called "the wisdom of the Dharma" (正法智) *Koku-yaku-issaikyō*, hōshaku-bu, p. 97, ft. 46.

[2]*Ibid*.: The second great vow is called "the wisdom of explaining" (說智) *Ibid*., p. 97, ft. 46.

[3]*Ibid*.: The third great vow is called "the protection of the Dharma" (護法) One then attains the Vajra-kāya. *Ibid*., p. 98, ft. 47.

[Chapter 4 - "The Acceptance"]

At that time Queen Śrīmālā said to the Buddha: "Having received the Buddha's power, I will now explain the great vow which is controlled[1] (by the principle of the true Dharma), being the truth without error."

The Buddha spoke to Śrīmālā: "I permit you to explain as you wish."

Śrīmālā said to the Buddha: "The Bodhisattva vows, which are as numerous as the sands of the Ganges, are all contained in the one great vow which is called 'the Acceptance of the true Dharma. The Acceptance of the true Dharma truly is the great vow."[2]

The Buddha praised Śrīmālā: "Excellent! Excellent! Your wisdom and skillful means are most profound and subtle! You have already, for a long time, increased in virtue. In the future, living beings who develop such virtue will be able to understand you. Your explanation of the Acceptance of the true Dharma is that which the Buddhas of the past, present, and future have explained, now explain, and will explain. Having realized the Supreme, Complete Enlightenment, I also speak of this Acceptance of the true Dharma. I explain that the Acceptance of the true Dharma has merits which cannot be limited. The Tathāgata's wisdom and eloquence also are without limits. Why? Because in this Acceptance of the true Dharma, there are great merits and great benefits."[3]

Queen Śrīmālā spoke to the Buddha: "Again, having received the Buddha's power, I shall further explain the extension of the Acceptance of the true Dharma."

The Buddha spoke: "Then please explain."

(1. Immeasurable)

(a. Like a Great Cloud:)

Śrīmālā said to the Buddha: "The extension of the Acceptance of the true Dharma is immeasurable. It includes all Buddhadharmas, consisting of 84,000 discourses.[4]

Like a great cloud which appeared at the time of creation, showering down a multi-colored rain and many kinds of jewels, the Acceptance of the true Dharma rains forth innumerable rewards and innumerable virtues.[5]

(b. Like the Great Waters:)

Bhagavan, at the time of creation, the three thousand great worlds[6] and the forty million kinds of continents emerged from the great waters. Similarly, the innumerable worlds of Mahāyāna, the super-powers of all the Bodhisattvas, the peace and happiness of all worlds, the magical omnipotence of all worlds, and the peace of the transcendental worlds which has not been experienced by gods and men from the time of creation--all these emerge from the Acceptance of the true Dharma.[7]

(c. Like the Great Earth, the "Supporter":)

Moreover, the Acceptance of the true Dharma is like the Great Earth which supports four weights. What are the four? The great seas, the mountains, vegetation, and living beings.[8] Similarly, like that Great Earth, the good sons and daughters[9] who accept the true Dharma build the great earth and carry four responsibilities.[10] Who are the four?

1) Living beings who have parted from good friends (*kalyana mitra*), have not heard (the Dharma), or are without the Dharma. By advising them to cultivate the good deeds of men and the gods, they (the good sons and daughters) prepare them (for entering the path).[11]

2) To those who seek Śrāvakahood, they present the Śrāvaka vehicle.

3) To those who seek Pratyeka-buddhahood, they present the Pratyeka vehicle.

4) To those who seek Mahāyāna, they present Mahāyāna.

These are the good sons and daughters who accept the true Dharma, build the great earth, and carry the four responsibilities.

Thus, Bhagavan, good sons and daughters who accept the true Dharma, build the great earth, and carry the four responsibilities, become friends without being asked, for the sake of all living beings. In their great compassion, they comfort and sympathize with living beings, becoming the Dharma-mother of the world.

(3. Like the Great Earth which has four storehouses:)

Again, the Acceptance of the true Dharma is like the Great

Earth that has four kinds of jewel-storehouses. What are the four? 1) the priceless, 2) the supremely valuable, 3) the moderately valuable, 4) the slightly valuable[12]--these are the Great Earth's four kinds of jewel-storehouses.

Similarly, the good sons and daughters who accept the true Dharma and build the great earth, obtain the four kinds of most precious jewels, viz. living beings. Who are the four?

1) Those who have not heard (the Dharma) or are without the Dharma to whom the good sons and daughters who have accepted the true Dharma present the (cultivation of) merits and virtuous deeds of men and the gods.

2) Those who seek Śrāvakahood are presented with the Śrāvaka vehicle.

3) Those who seek Pratyeka-buddhahood are presented with the Pratyeka vehicle.

4) Those who seek Mahāyāna are presented with Mahāyāna.

Thus, all the good sons and daughters who obtain the great jewels, viz. living beings, realize extraordinarily rare merits because of the Acceptance of tbe true Dharma. Lord, the great jewel-storehouse is the Acceptance of the true Dharma.[13]

(4. Identical with the true Dharma itself)

Lord, "the Acceptance of the true Dharma"[14] means the tru Dharma (itself) is not different from the Acceptance of the true Dharma. The true Dharma (itself) is identical with the Acceptance of the true Dharma.[15]

(5. Identical with the Pāramitās)

Lord, the Pāramitās are not different from the one who accepts the true Dharma.[16] The one who accepts the true Dha is identical with the Pāramitās. Why?

1) The good sons and daughters who accept the true Dha give even their body and limbs for those who respo giving. By protecting these (living beings) inten tions, they teach them. When they are thus taught caused to abide[17] in the true Dharma, this is cal the Dāna Pāramitā.

2) The good sons and daughters teach the protection six senses, the purification of action, speech, a thought, and the cultivation of the four correct postures (in walking, standing, sitting and recl to those who respond to discipline. By protecti these (living beings) intentions, they teach th

When they are thus taught and caused to abide in the true Dharma, this is called the Śīla Pāramitā.

3) The good sons and daughter teach non-hatred, liberality, supreme patience, and neutrality in facial expression to those who respond to patience. By protecting these (living beings) intentions, they teach them. When they are thus taught and caused to abide in the true Dharma, this is called the Kṣānti Pāramitā.

4) The good sons and daughters do not teach indolence, but the desire (to practice),[18] supreme perseverance, and the cultivation of the four correct postures to those who respond to perseverance. By protecting these (living beings) intentions, they teach them. When they are thus taught and caused to abide in the true Dharma, this is called the Vīrya Pāramitā.

5) The good sons and daughters teach tranquillity, constant mindfulness not conditioned by external objects, and recollection of all actions and speech over long periods of time, to those who respond to meditation. By protecting these (living beings) intentions, they teach them. When they are thus taught and caused to abide in the true Dharma, this is called the Dhyāna Pāramitā.

6) The good sons and daughters, when questioned concerning the meaning of all things, extensively teach all treatises and all arts, without trepidation, causing those who respond to wisdom to reach the ultimate in science and art. By protecting these (living beings) intentions, they teach them. When they are thus taught and caused to abide in the true Dharma, this is called the Prajñā Pāramitā.

Therefore, O Lord, the Pāramitās are not different from the one who accepts the true Dharma. The one who accepts the true Dharma is identical with the Pāramitās.

O Lord, now receiving the Buddha's power, I will further explain the greatness (of the true Dharma)."

The Buddha spoke: "Please do so."

(6. Identical with the One Who Accepts the True Dharma)

Śrīmālā said to the Buddha: "'The Acceptance of the true Dharma' means the Acceptance of the true Dharma is not different from the one who accepts the true Dharma.[19] The good sons and daughters who accept the true Dharma are identical with the Acceptance of the true Dharma. Why? Because the good sons and daughters who accept the true Dharma, abandon three things for the sake of the Acceptance of the true Dharma. What are the three? They are body, life, and property.

When the good sons and daughters abandon the body, they become equal to the last limit of the life-death cycle (*saṁsāra*). Having parted from old age, sickness, and death, they realize the indestructible, eternal, unchanging and inconceivable merits of the Tathāgata's Dharma-Body.

When they abandon life, they become equal to the last limit of the life-death cycle. Ultimately having parted from death, they realize limitless, eternal, and inconceivable merits, penetrating all the profound Buddha-dharmas.

When they abandon property, they become equal to the last limit of the life-death cycle. Having realized the inexhaustible, indestructible, ultimately eternal, inconceivable and complete merits which are not common to all other living beings, they obtain the excellent offerings of all living beings.

Lord, the good sons and daughters who have abandoned these three and have accepted the true Dharma, will always obtain the predictions of all the Buddhas (concerning their Buddhahood), and will be honored by all living beings.

Furthermore, O Lord, the good sons and daughters who accept the true Dharma without distortion and without deception or misrepresentation,[20] will love the true Dharma and accept the true Dharma, entering the Dharma friendship when monks, nuns, laymen, and laywomen are forming rival factions, which cause the destruction and dispersion (of the Sangha). Those who enter the Dharma friendship will certainly receive the prediction (of their future Buddhahood) by all the Buddhas.

O Lord, I see that the Acceptance of the true Dharma has such great powers. Because the Buddha is the eye of truth, the wisdom of truth, the source of the Dharma and penetrates all things,[21] he is the basis for the true Dharma and knows all things."

At that time, the Lord was joyous over Śrīmālā's explanation concerning the great powers of the Acceptance of the true Dharma. (And He spoke:) "Śrīmālā, what you have said is true. The great powers of the Acceptance of the true Dharma are like a very strong man who briefly touches the (vulnerable) part of the body and causes great pain. Similarly, Śrīmālā, barely accepting the true Dharma causes suffering to Māra, the Evil One. I do not see even one remaining good act which can cause suffering to Māra in the manner that barely accepting the true Dharma does.[22]

Moreover, the bull-king has a form without equal, surpassing all other bulls. Similarly, barely accepting the true Dharma in Mahāyāna is superior to all the virtuous deeds of the two vehicles (*dviyāna*) because it is so extensive.

The majestic bearing and uniqueness of great Mt. Sumeru surpasses all other mountains. Similarly, the (merit of) abandonment of body, life, and property in Mahāyāna--accepting the true Dharma with a benevolent heart[23] surpasses (the merit of) those who have just engaged in the virtuous deeds of Mahāyāna but do not abandon body, life, and property. Because of its extensiveness, of course it is superior to the two vehicles.

Thus, Śrīmālā, through the Acceptance of the true Dharma, explain (this teaching) to living beings, teach and convert living beings, and make living beings confirmed (in the Dharma).

Therefore, Śrīmālā, the Acceptance of the true Dharma has these great benefits, these great blessings, and these great fruits. Śrīmālā, even if I explain the merits and benefits of the Acceptance of the true Dharma for innumerable periods of time, I shall not reach the end (of explaining). Therefore, the Acceptance of the true Dharma has immeasurable and unlimited merits."

CHAPTER 4

NOTES

[1]*Gisho*: "Control" (調伏) here refers to constantly following the right principle (viz. the true Dharma). (16b)

[2]Cf. *Śikshasamuccaya: A Compendium of Buddhistic Teaching*, ed. by Cecil Bendall (Hague: Mouton & Co., 1957), p. 42, ll. 12-14:

> *yāny apīmāni bhagavan gaṅgānadīvālikāsamāni bodhisattva-praṇidhānāni tāny ekasmin mahāpraṇidhāne upanikṣiptāny antargatāny anupratiṣṭhāni yaduta saddharmaparigrahe/ evam mahāviṣayo bhagavan saddharmaparigraha iti/*

[3]*Gisho*: Because the Acceptance of the true Dharma produces omniscience on the supreme level and can convert living beings on the common level, its merits and benefits are inexhaustible and cannot be limited. (17b)

[4]Bodhiruci states that there are 80,000 practices (*saṁskāra-skandha*) (行蘊)

[5]Bodhiruci:如是攝受正法善根之雲、能雨無量福報之雨

> "In like manner the cloud of virtuous deeds of the Acceptance of the true Dharma rains forth innumerable rewards." Cf.如是攝受正法雨無量福報及無量善根之雨. (Guṇabhadra)

[6]The binome *chieh-tsang* (界藏) has been amended to *shih-chieh* (世界) in accordance with the *Pao-k'u* (31b).

[7]The metaphor of the great waters simplies that the Acceptance of the true Dharma is the source of all goodness just as water is the source of nature.

[8]*Gisho*: The sea is a metaphor for the Bodhisattvas who receive without end. The mountains are the Pratyeka vehicle who are tall and upright. The vegetation are the Śrāvaka vehicle who are numerous. Living beings are the men and deity vehicle who only reside in *saṁsāra*. (20b)

Pao-k'u: Cites a commentary which reverses the order, i.e. the sea is equivalent to the living beings, etc. However, Chi-tsang disagrees with this interpretation because the metaphor is directly proportionate with the weight of one's virtue, i.e. the heaviest object, the sea, is compared to the "weight" of a Bodhisattva's virtue. (32b)

[9]*Gisho*: The good sons and daughters are the Bodhisattvas of the eighth *bhūmi* and above. (20b)

[10]*Gisho*: The earth carries forms only, not like the Bodhisattvas who carry forms as well as spirit, causing the transformation of evil and the practice of good. (21a)

[11]Cf. *Pao-k'u* (32b).

[12]*Gisho*: The "priceless" is the Bodhisattva vehicle, the "supremely valuable" is the Pratyeka vehicle, the "moderately valuable" is the Śrāvaka vehicle, and the "slightly valuable" is the man and deity vehicle. (22a)

[13]Bodhiruci: 出大宝者名為眞實攝受正法.

> "The source of the great jewels is the truth, the Acceptance of the true Dharma."
> Cf. 大宝藏者即是攝受正法 (Guṇabhadra)

[14]In Guṇabhadra's recension: 攝受正法攝受正法者無異正法 the first phrase is used for emphasis only, and has been omitted here. Cf. Bodhiruci: 言攝受正法者謂無異正法

> "When one speaks of the Acceptance of the true Dharma this is not different from the true Dharma (itself)."

[15]*Gisho*: This sentence is equivalent to "the acceptance of the true Dharma is identical with the acceptor of the true Dharma. (攝受正法攝受正法者→所攝萬行正法 and 能攝之心 respectively) (22b). There is no bifurcation between subject and object, actor and act. For the Bodhisattva of the eighth *bhūmi* and above, such a unity of subject and object is possible because he is the Dharma-Body (24b)

[16]*Pao-k'u*: The principle of the true Dharma (the pāramitās) is identical with the practice of the one who accepts the true Dharma. (33c)

[17]The translator has chosen Bodhiruci's text (安住) instead of Guṇabhadra's (建立).

[18]Cf. *Pao-k'u*, 35b.

[19]Bodhiruci: 攝受正法者無異攝受正法。無異攝受正法者。

> "The acceptance of the true Dharma is not different from the Acceptance of the true Dharma nor different from the one who accepts the true Dharma."
>
> Cf. 攝受正法攝受正法者無異攝受正法.無異攝受正法者
>
> The first phrase is used for emphasis only and has been omitted here. See ft. 14 above.
>
> *Gisho*: This sentence is equivalent to "The Dharma is man." (攝受正法攝受正法者→法 and 人 respectively.) (26a)
>
> *Pao-k'u*: The one who accepts the true Dharma accepts the result which is the Dharma-Body. Therefore, the acceptor and the accepted (Dharma) are identical. (36a)

[20]Both recensions are nearly identical. The subject which "loves and accepts the true Dharma" is not clearly indicated, being either the groups of monks, nuns, etc. or the good sons and daughters. Because the latter receive the

predictions of the Buddhas in the previous paragraph, they have been chosen as the preferred subject based on context.

[21]Bodhiruci: 為引導法為通達法 --"he leads (one) to the Dharma and pervades all things." Cf. 為通達法 (Guṇabhadra)

[22]Cf. *Śikshasamuccaya, op. cit.*, p. 42:

syad yathāpi nāma devi mahābalavato 'pi purusasyālpo 'pi marmaṇi prahāro vedhanīyo bhavati vādhākaraś ca/ evam eva devi mārasya pāpīyasah paritto 'pi saddharmaparigraho vedhanīyo bhavati śokāvahaḥ paridevakaraś ca bhavati/ nāham devi anyam ekam api dharmam kuśalaṁ samanupaśyāmi mārasya pāpīyasa evaṁ vedhanīyaṁ śokāvahaṁ paridevakaraṁ ca yathāyam alpo 'pi sadharmaparigraha iti/

[23]Bodhiruci: 以饒益心 --"with a benevolent heart." Cf. 以攝受心 "with an accepting heart"--Guṇabhadra.

Cf. *Śikshasamuccaya, op. cit.*, p. 43:

syad yathāpi nāma devi sumeruḥ parvatarājaḥ sarvān kula-parvatān abhibhavann abhirocate ca samabhirocate coccatvena vipulatvena ca/ evam eva devi mahāyānikasya kāyajīvita-nirapekṣasya na ca gṛhītacittasya saddharmaparigraho navayānasamprasthitānām api kāyajīvitasāpekṣānām mahāyānikānāṁ sarvān kusalān dharmān abhibhavatīty ādi/

The interpretation of *gṛhītacittasya*--"a mind which has been seized" is problematic. *Gṛhītaka* refers to "one that has been caught or taken." (Edgerton, p. 214) The suffix *-grāha* refers to "belief (in), holding (to)" heretical or false views (Edgerton, p. 219). The most basic meaning of *gṛhīta*, however, is "grasped, taken, seized, caught...received, accepted... received completely into one's mind"; *gṛhītacetas*--"one whose mind or heart is captivated" (Monier-Williams, p. 362c).

In both the editions by Bendall and P. L. Vaidya (*Buddhist Sanskrit Texts* No. 11, Darbhanga: Mithila Institute, 1961), p. 27, ll. 11 (*na cāgṛhīta*) the negative *na* appears negating the present active verb *abhibhavati*. However, from both the two Chinese recensions and the Tibetan (*Bstan-Hgyur*, p. 197, 37a, 3) no negative appears before this verb equivalent to "surpassing" (*abhibhavati*). The main subject of this passage, the Acceptance of t-e true Dharma, by "the mind which has (not) been seized" surpasses those who are novices in Mahāyāna, according to the Chinese and Tibetan. Therefore, the negative *na* which does not appear in these transmissions may be a transcriber's error. Furthermore, both Chinese recensions translate *agṛhītacitta* (*gṛhītacitta*) as positive, lacking a privative, and connoting benevolence or acceptance. Since *gṛhīta* connotes a state often considered undesirable, i.e. a state in which one is seized or captivated by false views, *gṛhītacitta* appears to be concerned with life and body while *agṛhītacitta* is benevolent and kind, no longer "seized" by such concerns. Perhaps the gloss *anugrahacitta* is intended.

Consequently, if *gṛhītacitta* is construed as an undesirable state of mind, the negative *na* must be omitted from Vaidya's edition and Bendall's remains unchanged. The Chinese and

Tibetan editions would be amended with the addition of *na*, rendering the generally positive Chinese equivalents to obscure negative meanings.

However, if *na* is considered a transcriber's error, the suggested reading of the Sanskrit is:

> ...*mahāyānikasya kāyajīvitanirapekṣasya cāgṛhītacittasya saddharmaparigraho...mahāyānikānāṁ sarvān kuśalān dharmān abhibhavatīty ādi.*

Gṛhītacitta would retain a negative connotation.

If *gṛhītacitta* is construed as positive in meaning, the Chinese recensions which do not demonstrate the original nature of the compound as positive or negative, but only as positive in meaning, could be construed as either *gṛhītacitta agṛhītacitta*, retaining the meaning of the passage. However, both Sanskrit recensions would have to be amended as well as the Tibetan. Therefore, the simplest amendation to the text is the one suggested above with Bendall's edition reading *cāgṛhītacittasya*, not *na ca gṛhītacittasya*, and Vaidya's edition also reading *cāgṛhitacittasya*, not *na cāgṛhītacittasya*. The Chinese and Tibetan recensions would remain unchanged.

[Chapter 5 - "Ekayana"]

The Buddha spoke to Queen Śrīmālā: "Now you should further explain the Acceptance of the true Dharma which was taught by all the Buddhas."[1]

Queen Śrīmālā spoke to the Buddha: "Very well, O Lord, I will, upon receiving Your exhortation." Then she said to the Buddha: "O Lord, the Acceptance of the true Dharma is (the Acceptance of) Mahāyāna. Why? Because Mahāyāna brings forth all the good acts of the world and of the transcendental, of the Śrāvakas and of the Pratyeka-buddhas. O Lord, just as the eight[2] great rivers flow from the Anavatapta[3] lake, so likewise all the good acts of the world and of the transcendental, of the Śrāvakas and of the Pratyeka-buddhas, emerge from Mahāyāna.[4]

O Lord, moreover, just as all seeds are able to grow (only) when they depend upon the earth, so likewise all the good acts of the world and of the transcendental, of the Śrāvakas and of the Pratyeka-buddhas, are able to increase (only) when they depend upon Mahāyāna. Therefore, O Lord, abiding in Mahāyāna, one accepts Mahāyāna--this is identical with abiding in the two vehicles and accepting all the good acts of the world, of the transcendental, and of the two vehicles.

What are the six stations which the Lord explains? They are 1) the continuity of the true Dharma, 2) the destruction of the true Dharma, 3) the rules of pratimokṣa, 4) the discipline of the Vinaya, 5) the renunciation of one's home, and 6) the ordination.[5] On behalf of Mahāyāna the Lord preaches these six stations. Why? Because the continuity of the true Dharma is explained for the sake of Mahāyāna. Continuity of Mahāyāna is continuity of the true Dharma. The extinction of Mahāyāna is the extinction of the True Dharma.[7]

The rules of Pratimokṣa and the discipline of the Vinaya have the same meaning even though they are different in name. The discipline of the Vinaya is learned by Mahāyānists. Why? Because one renounces his home and becomes ordained for the sake of the Buddha. Therefore, the conduct of Mahāyāna, which is the śīla, is the Vinaya--the renunciation of home and ordination.[8]

Consequently, in the case of the Arhat, there is no renunciation of home nor ordination (as a separate vehicle from Mahāyāna).[9] Why? Because the Arhat renounces his home and is ordained for the sake of the Tathāgata.[10] The Arhat, seeking refuge in the Buddha, is afraid. Why? Because the Arhat lives in a state of fear towards all conditioning forces,[11] as if a man holding a sword desired to cause him harm. Therefore, the Arhat has no ultimate happiness. Why? O Lord, being a (final) refuge, one does not seek a refuge. Living beings who are without a refuge, having this or that fear, seek a refuge because of these fears. Likewise, the Arhats who have fears seek refuge in the Tathāgata because of these fears.[12]

O Lord, Arhats and Pratyeka-buddhas are afraid. Because these Arhats and Pratyeka-buddhas still have not extinguished their lives, these (psycho-physical forces) continue.[13] They still have not completed the practice of purity, remaining impure. Because their actions are not ultimate, they still have actions to perform. Because they have not reached that (final stage) they still have defilements which should be severed. Because these are not severed, one is far from the realm of Nirvāṇa. Why? Because only the Tathāgata-Arhat-Completely Enlightened One attains final Nirvāṇa (*parinirvāṇa*), being endowed with all merits. The Arhats and Pratyeka-buddhas are not endowed with all merits. When it is said that they attain Nirvāṇa, this is the skillful means of the Buddha.[14]

Because only the Tathāgata attains final Nirvāṇa, being endowed with inconceivable merits, the Arhats and Pratyeka-buddhas are only endowed with conceivable merits. When it is said that they attain Nirvāṇa, this is the skillful means of the Buddha.

Because only the Tathāgata attains final Nirvāṇa, eliminating transgressions which should be eliminated, and endowed with supreme purity, the Arhats and Pratyeka-Buddhas who still have transgressions are not supremely pure. When it is said that they attain Nirvāṇa, this is the skillful means of the Buddha.

Only the Tathāgata attains final Nirvāṇa, is revered by all living beings, and surpasses the Arhat, Pratyeka-buddha and Bodhisattva realms. Therefore, the Arhats and

Pratyeka-buddhas are far from the realm of Nirvāṇa. When it is said that the Arhats and Pratyeka-buddhas meditate on liberation, have the four wisdoms,[14] and have ultimately attained their resting place, this is also the skillful means of the Tathāgata and is taught as the incomplete meaning. Why? There are two kinds of death. What are the two? They are ordinary death and the inconceivable death of transformation (for a purpose).[16] The ordinary death refers to living beings who live in unreality. The inconceivable death of transformation (for a purpose) refers to the mind-made bodies of the Arhats, Pratyeka-buddhas, and greatly powerful Bodhisattvas, until the time of their Supreme, Complete Enlightenment.

Within these two kinds of death, it is the ordinary death through which tbe Arhats and Pratyeka-buddhas have completely attained the knowledge said to have 'extinguished their lives.' Because they attain realization (Nirvāṇa) with remainder, it is said that 'the practice of holiness has been completely upheld.' Because their errors and defilements have been eliminated, it is said that 'their actions have been completed,' actions which the common men, gods, and seven kinds[17] of educated men are incapable of performing. Because the Arhats and Pratyeka-buddhas cannot be reborn since their defilements are eliminated, it is said that 'they are not reborn.' When it is said that 'they are not reborn,' this is not because they have eliminated *all* defilements nor exhausted *all* births.[18] Why? Because there are defilements which cannot be eliminated by the Arhats and Pratyeka-buddhas.

There are two kinds of defilements. What are the two? They are latent defilement and active defilement. There are four kinds of latent defilements. They are:

1) the stage of all (false) views of monism
2) the stage of desiring sensuous pleasures[19]
3) the stage of desiring forms[20]
4) the stage of desiring existence[21]

From these four kinds of (defilement) stages, there are all the active defilements. 'What is active' is momentary and associated with the momentariness of the mind. O Lord, the mind does not associate with the stage of beginningless ignorance (in the same manner).

O Lord, the power of these four latent defilements are a basis for all active[22] defilements but cannot possibly be compared in number, fraction, counting, similarity, nor resemblance to ignorance (in power).[23]

O Lord, such is the power of the stage of ignorance! The power of the stage of ignorance is much greater than the other stages represented by the fourth stage of desire for existence.[24] The power of the stage of ignorance is like that of the wicked Evil One (Māra), whose form, power, longevity, and retainers are both superior to and more powerful than (the gods of) the paranirmitavaśavartin heaven. Its power is far superior to that of the other stages of defilement represented by the fourth stage of desire for existence. This basis for the active defilements, more numerous than the sands of the Ganges, causes the four kinds of defilements to continue for a long time. The Arhats and Pratyeka-buddhas' wisdom cannot eliminate it. Only the Tathāgata's enlightenment-wisdom can eliminate it. Yes, O Lord, the stage of ignorance is extremely powerful!

O Lord, the three states of existence arise, conditioned by clinging to existence and by defiled actions. In like manner, O Lord, the three forms of mind-made bodies of the Arhats, Pratyeka-buddhas, and greatly powerful Bodhisattvas are conditioned by the stage of ignorance and by pure actions. In these three levels (i.e. the Arhat, Pratyeka-buddha, and Bodhisattva stages), the three kinds of mind-made bodies and pure actions are based upon the latent stage of ignorance. Because all things are conditioned and not unconditioned,[25] the three kinds of mind-made bodies and pure actions are conditioned by the stage of ignorance.

O Lord, thus the other stages of defilement, represented by the fourth stage of desiring existence, are not identical with the stage of ignorance with respect to action.[26] The stage of ignorance is different from the four stages and is eliminated by the Buddha stages and by the enlightenment-wisdom of the Buddha. Why? The Arhats and Pratyeka-buddhas eliminate the four kinds of stages but their purity is not completed for they have not attained autonomy nor have they accomplished their realization (of enlightenment).

'Their purity which is not completed' refers to the stage

of ignorance. O Lord, the Arhats, Pratyeka-buddhas, and the Bodhisattvas in their very last body do not know and do not awaken to the various phenomena[27] because of the impediments of the stage of ignorance. Because they are not aware (of these phenomena) they cannot absolutely eliminate what should be eliminated. Because they do not eliminate (all defilements) they are 'liberated with remaining faults,' which is not 'liberation separated from all faults.'[28] They have 'purity with remaining (purification to be done)' which is not purity in its entirety. They 'accomplish merits with remaining (merits to be accomplished)' which is not entirely meritorious. Because they accomplish liberation with remainder, purity with remainder, and merits with remainder, the Arhats, Pratyeka-buddhas, and Bodhisattvas know suffering (*duḥkha*) with remainder, eliminate the source of suffering (*samudaya*) with remainder, attain the extinction (*nirodha*) of suffering with remainder, and practice the path (*mārga*) with remainder. This is 'attaining the partial Nirvāṇa.'

Those who attain the partial Nirvāṇa are 'turned towards the Nirvāṇa realm.' If one knows all suffering, entirely eliminates the source of suffering, attains the complete extinction (of suffering), and practices the entire path, one will attain the permanent Nirvāṇa in a world which is impermanent and decadent, impermanent and distressed. In a world without protection, a world without a refuge, there is a protector and a refuge. Why?[29] O Lord, there is no attainment of Nirvāṇa because of (the differentiation between) inferior and superior phenomena. O Lord, there is the attainment of Nirvāṇa because of the equality of all phenomena. Because of the equality of knowledge, one attains Nirvāṇa. Because of the equality of liberation, one attains Nirvāṇa. Because of the equality of purity, one attains Nirvāṇa. Therefore, Nirvāṇa has one and the same quality which is that of liberation.

O Lord, if the stage of ignorance is not absolutely eliminated, then one does not attain the one and the same quality of knowledge and liberation. Why? If the stage of ignorance is not absolutely eliminated, then the phenomena more numerous than the sands of the Ganges which should be eliminated will not be absolutely eliminated. Because the phenomena more numerous than the sands of the Ganges which should be eliminated are not eliminated, the phenomena more numerous than the sands of the Ganges which should be attained will not be attained and which should be manifested will not be manifested. Therefore, the accumulation (of defilements) in the stage of ignorance produces both the defilements which are severed by the practice of the entire path and the virulent defilement, as well as the virulent defilements of the mind, of meditation, of concentration, of contemplation, of insight, of skillful means, of wisdom, of the results (of the path), of the attainment, of power, and of fearlessness. These are all the active defilements more numerous than the sands of the Ganges which are eliminated by the enlightenment-wisdom of the Tathāgata.

All these defilements are due to the stage of ignorance. All the active defilements which arise are caused by and conditioned by the stage of ignorance. O Lord, among the defilements which arise the mind and its various faculties arise together momentarily. O Lord, the mind does not associate with the stage of beginningless ignorance (in the same manner).

O Lord, all the phenomena more numerous than the sands of the Ganges which should be eliminated by the Tathāgata's enlightenment-wisdom are supported and sustained by the stage of ignorance. For example, all the seeds which depend on the earth for their life, sustenance, and growth would be ruined if the earth were ruined. Similarly, all the phenomena more numerous than the sands of the Ganges which should be eliminated by the Tathāgata's enlightenment-wisdom are based upon the stage of ignorance for their life, sustenance, and growth.

If the stage of ignorance is eliminated, all the phenomena more numerous than the sands of the Ganges which should be eliminated by the Tathāgata's enlightenment-wisdom will be eliminated. If all defilements and virulent defilements are eliminated, all phenomena more numerous than the sands of the Ganges will be attained by the Tathāgatas, who penetrate them without obstruction.[30] Omniscience is separate from all transgressions, attaining all the merits of the Dharma-King, the Dharma-Lord, attaining autonomy and manifesting the stage of autonomy from all phenomena.

O Tathāgata, Arhat, Completely Enlightened One, who has the Lion's Roar, the complete extinction of one's life, 'the complete practice of holiness,' 'the completion of actions,' and the 'non-acceptance of rebirth' have been explained up until now, based upon Your Lion's Roar, for their complete meaning.

O Lord, there are two kinds of knowledge which do not accept rebirth. First there is the knowledge of the Tathāgatas who, by means of their unsurpassed powers, subdue the four Evil Ones,[31] appear in all worlds, and are worshipped by all living beings. They attain the unthinkable[32] Dharma-Body, all spheres of knowledge, and unobstructed autonomy in all things.[33] In this stage there is no action nor attainment which is higher. Having the ten magnificent powers[34] (of knowledge) they ascend to the supreme, unexcelled, fearless stage. With their omniscient, unobstructed knowledge, they understand without relying on another.[35] This wisdom which does not accept rebirth is the Lion's Roar.

O Lord, second, there is the knowledge of the Arhats and Pratyeka-buddhas who cross over the fears of life and death and gradually attain the happiness of liberation with this thought: 'I have parted from the fears of life and death, and no longer experience the suffering of life and death.' Lord, when the Arhats and Pratyeka-buddhas meditate, they do not accept rebirth and have insight into the supremely restful stage of Nirvāṇa.

O Lord, those who first attained that stage (of Nirvāṇa) were not ignorant of the Dharma[36] and were not dependent upon others.[37] They also knew they had attained the stages with remainder through their own efforts,[38] and would inevitably attain the Supreme, Complete Enlightenment. Why? Because the Śrāvaka and Pratyeka-buddha vehicles are included in Mahāyāna. Mahāyāna is the Buddha's vehicle. Therefore, the three vehicles are the One Vehicle (*ekayāna*).

Those who attain the One Vehicle attain the Supreme, Complete Enlightenment. The Supreme, Complete Enlightenment is the realm of Nirvāṇa. The realm of Nirvāṇa is the

Dharma-Body of the Tathāgata.[39] Attaining the absolute Dharma-Body is (attaining) the absolute One Vehicle. The Tathāgata is not different from the Dharma-Body. The Tathāgata is identical with the Dharma-Body.[40] If one attains the absolute Dharma-Body then one attains the absolute One Vehicle. The absolute (One Vehicle) is unlimited and unceasing.[41]

O Lord, the Tathāgata, who is not limited by time, is the Tathāgata, Arhat, Completely Enlightened One, equal to the utmost limit (of the life-death cycle). The Tathāgata is without limitation. His great compassion also is unlimited,[42] bringing peace and comfort to the world. His unlimited great compassion brings unlimited peace and comfort to the world.[43] This explanation is a good explanation concerning the Tathāgata.[44] If one again speaks of the inexhaustible Dharma, the eternally abiding Dharma which is the refuge of all worlds--this is also a good explanation concerning the Tathāgata.[45] Therefore, in a world that has not been saved,[46] a world without a refuge, there is an inexhaustible, eternally abiding refuge equal to the utmost limit (of the life-death cycle), viz. the Tathāgata, Arhat, Completely Enlightened One.

The Dharma is the path of the One Vehicle. The Saṅgha is the assembly of the three vehicles. These two refuges (i.e. the Dharma and the Saṅgha) are not the ultimate refuge. They are called 'the partial refuge.' Why? The Dharma[47] of the path of the One Vehicle attains the absolute Dharma-Body. Furthermore, there can be no Dharma-Body[48] other than that of the One Vehicle.

The assembly of the three vehicles (viz. the Saṅgha), being afraid, seeks refuge in the Tathāgata. These students who go out to practice[49] turn towards the Supreme, Complete Enlightenment. Therefore, these two refuges are not the ultimate refuge but are limited refuges.

If there are living beings who are subdued by the Tathāgata, they will seek refuge in the Tathāgata, attain the permeation of the Dharma, and will have faith and happiness, seeking refuge in the Dharma and the Saṅgha. These two refuges (however) are not two refuges[50] for they seek refuge in the Tathāgata. Seeking refuge in the supreme truth is seeking refuge in the Tathāgata.

The supreme truth of these two refuges is the ultimate refuge, the Tathāgata. Why? Because the Tathāgata is not different from the two refuges. The Tathāgata is identical with the three refuges. Why? Because of the path of the One Vehicle. The Tathāgata, who has perfected the four states of fearlessness,[51] is the one who teaches with the Lion's Roar. The Tathāgata, according to individual dispositions, teaches through skillful means. This is Mahāyāna and not the three vehicles. The three vehicles enter the One Vehicle. The One Vehicle is the supreme vehicle."

CHAPTER 5

NOTES

[1]Bodhiruci: 汝今復応演我所説摂受正法一切諸仏.... "Now again extensively explain the Acceptance of the true Dharma which was taught by me and which is loved by all the Buddhas together."

Cf. 汝今更説一切諸仏所説摂受正法 (Guṇabhadra)

[2]All Chinese recensions and commentaries have "eight rivers" (八河) but this is an error. It should read "four rivers" (四河). See the following footnote.

[3]The Anavatapta lake is north of the Himālayan mountains, between the Himālayas and Mt. Gandha-mādana, where the Nāga king Anavatapta lived. In Indian myths this lake, described as having banks decorated with gold, silver, lapis lazuli, and crystal, is considered the source of the Ganges river on the east, the Sindhu (Indus) river on the south, the Vakṣa river on the west, and the Sītā river on the north. (Cf. Nakamura, Hajime. *Shinbukkyō jiten, op. cit.*, p. 10).

Some scholars now consider a lake located at the foot of Mt. Gangdisishan (the legendary Mt. Kailāśa), named Lake Manasaluowochi, identical to the mythical Lake Anavatapta. (*Bukkyō daijiten*, v.II, p. 46b-c).

[4]*Gisho*: Just as the water of the eight rivers (which flow from the Anavatapta lake) are that lake's water...the four vehicles are Mahāyāna and not different vehicles. (31b)

The *Gisho* and *Pao-k'u* illustrate the fact that the metaphor originally involved the number four but due to their faulty understanding of the mythical Lake Anavatapta, the commentators believed eight rivers, and not four, flowed from that lake.

[5]The paths of the two vehicles are not separate from Mahāyāna but are an unrefined form of Mahāyāna. (*Kokuyaku-issaikyō, op. cit.*, p. 103, ft. 81).

Cf. *Gisho*: Just as seeds depend on the earth, the four vehicles depend on Mahāyāna. Because the seeds depend on the earth they are not separate from the earth. Because the five vehicles (the three Buddhist vehicles, the gods, and man) depend on Mahāyāna, they are not separate from Mahayana. (31b)

[6]"Ordination" (具足) (*upasampadā* or *upasampādana*) refers to both the monk's discipline (of 250 items) and the nun's discipline (of 348 items).

[7]If Hīnayāna is nothing other than Mahāyāna, the implication is that the flourishings of the Dharma in the 500-year period after the Buddha's parinirvāṇa is the flourishing of Mahāyāna and likewise, the decline of the Dharma after this

period is the decline of Mahāyāna. (*Kokuyaku-issaikyō*, *op. cit.*, p. 103, ft. 82).

[8]Bodhiruci:是故大乘戒蘊是毘奈耶。是正出家是受具足。
"Therefore, the actions of Mahāyāna which are the śīla are the Vinaya--the true renunciation of home and ordination." Cf.是故說大乘威儀戒是比尼是出家是具足。(Guṇabhadra)

[9]*Pao-k'u*:小乘人無別出家受具足依大乘仏出家受具足戒。
"The Hīnayānist does not have a separate renunciation of home nor a separate ordination because he renounces his home and becomes ordained for the sake of the Buddha who teaches Mahāyāna."
是故毘尼出家受具足郎以大乘也。
"Therefore, the Vinaya, renunciation of home, and ordination are identical to that of Mahāyāna."
離大乘之法無別小乘法、示離大乘菩薩無別小乘羅漢。
"There is no Hīnayāna Dharma which is separate from that of Mahāyāna nor is there any Hīnayānist Arhat who is distinct from the Mahāyānist Bodhisattva for the teaching of the Hīnayānist is included in the Mahāyānist teaching which is identical with the One Teaching."

[10]Bodhiruci:不為如來出家受具足故。
"Because the Arhst renounces his home and becomes ordained not (solely) for the sake of the Tathāgata (but from fear)." Cf.阿羅漢依如來出家受具足故。
Guṇabhadra states the dependence of the Arhat upon the Tathāgata in a positive manner here. In the following sentence of the text, both recensions discuss the negative aspects of the Arhat's dependence.

[11]Bodhiruci:阿羅漢於一切行住怖畏想。
Guṇabhadra inserts the negative *wu* (無) between *chieh* (切) and *hsing* (行) which is an error. See the following footnote.

[12]Cf. *Ratnagotravighaga*, p. 19, ll. 8-13:
Yasmād arhantām api kṣīṇapunarbhavānām aprahīṇatvād vāsanāyāḥ satatasamitaṁ sarvasaṁskāreṣu tīvrā bhayasamjñā pratyupasthitā bhavati syād yathāpi namo 'tksiptāsike vadhakapuruse tasmāt te 'pi nātyantasukhaṇiḥsaraṇam adhigatāḥ/ na hi śaraṇaṁ śaraṇaṁ paryeṣate/ yathaivā śaraṇāḥ sattvā yena tena bhayena bhītās tatas tato niḥsaraṇaṁ paryeṣante tadvad arhatām apy asti tadbhayaṁ yatas te bhayād bhītās tathāgatam eva śaraṇam upagacchanti/ yaś caivaṁ sabhayatvāc charaṇam upaggacchaty avaśyaṁ bhayān niḥsaraṇaṁ sa paryeṣate/

"Because even the Arhats who have severed transmigration have an extreme awareness of fear which exists perpetually and constantly in all their actions because they have not eliminated the subconscious influences (*vāsanāyāḥ*) (of the defiled mind) just as when a hunter is waving a sword (over him). Thus, this is not the attainment of the ultimate blissful salvation. A refuge does not seek a refuge. As living beings are without a refuge, being frightened by this or that fear, and seek salvation, so likewise the Arhats are frightened, having this or that fear. Because of their fear, they seek refuge in the Tathāgata./ Therefore, one who seeks refuge because of his fear, will necessarily seek salvation from fear."

[13]These four accomplishments of the Buddha which are the aspiration of the Arhat are found in the *Mahānidāna sutta, Digha Nikāya*, xv, no. 32 (Pāli Text Society): *khīnā jāti, vusitam brahmacariyaṁ, kataṁ karaṇīyam, nāparam itthattāyāti.*

[14]The following section of the text in which the Tathāgata's Parinirvāṇa is contrasted with the partial Nirvāṇa of the two vehicles is only briefly mentioned by Bodhiruci. The skillful means of the Buddha is considerably more emphasized in Guṇabhadra's translation.

[15]Although the four wisdoms are not delineated in the text, they may refer to the four wisdoms of the Buddha: *ādarśajñāna*, "wisdom of all the dharmas"; *samatā-jñāna*, "compassion for all living beings"; *pratyaveksanā-jñāna*, "insight into all dharmas," and *kṛtyānuṣṭhāna-jñāna*, "knowledge which converts the two vehicles."

[16]Ordinary death belongs to the triple world of tramsmigration. The inconceivable death of transformation may be conceived as the Bodhisattva's transference of merit for the purpose of saving all living beings, even giving away his life, body, and property for the benefit of others. (*Kokuyaku-issaikyō, op. cit.*, pp. 105-106, ft. 102-103). In the case of the Arhats and Pratyeka Buddhas, they gain such powers only after they have entered Mahāyāna. (*Pao-k'u*, p. 49a).

[17]The "seven kinds of educated men" refer to the four stages of the Theravādin path with each entrance and result, excluding the result of the Arhat, resulting in seven kinds of men educated in that path with the last stage not yet realized.

[18]Bodhiruci: 世尊說生不受後有智者謂阿羅漢及辟支仏。不能斷於一切煩惱不了一切受生之智。何以故。是阿羅漢及辟支仏有餘煩惱不斷盡故不能了知一切受生。

> "O Lord, those who have knowledge by which one is not reborn refer to the Arhats and Pratyeka-buddhas. They cannot sever all defilements nor complete knowledge of all births. Why? These Arhats and Pratyeka-buddhas cannot completely understand all their births because they have not entirely eliminated all their remaining defilements."

Cf. 阿羅漢辟支仏所斷煩惱更不能受後有故說不受後有。非盡一切煩惱亦非盡一切受生故說不受後有。

[19]The stage of all false views is eliminated before the stage of desire. Both stages belong to the world of desire in the triple world. (Cf. *Kokuyaku-issaikyō, op. cit.*, p. 106, ft. 106).

[20] The stage of desiring forms belongs to the world of form in the triple world. (Cf. *Kokuyaku-issaikyō, op. cit.*, p. 106, ft. 106).

[21] The stage of desiring existence belongs to the world of formlessness in the triple world. (Cf. *Kokuyaku-issaikyō, op. cit.*, p. 106, ft. 106).

[22] Bodhiruci's translation has been chosen because it is consistent with the classification of defilements listed above.

四住地力能遍起煩惱所依。

Guṇabhadra's translation replaces "active" defilements with "virulent" defilements (*shang*) (上):

此四住地力一切上煩惱依種。

Pao-k'u: 四住所起煩惱麁强名上。

"The defilements which arise from the four latent stages are called *shang* because they are virulent." (p. 52b)

[23] The entire series, common in many Buddhist texts, may be found in the *Vajracchedikā Prajñapāramitā*, ed. by Edward Conze (Roma: Serie Orientale Roma, 1957), v. XIII, p. 81.

[24] The following classification of defilements is not Abhidharmist, as delineated in the *Abhidharmakośa*. The stage of ignorance (*avidyā-vāsabhūmi*) is not the same concept of ignorance which is described in the *Abhidharma-kośa* as mind-associated (*citta-samprayukta-dharma*). The stage of ignorance in the ŚDS is the basis for all defilements, the most powerful to eliminate, and the very last impediment to Buddhahood. Moreover, it is mind-disassociated because it is prior to consciousness, i.e. prior to the momentary cognition of the "active" mind. Prior to the active mind, there are five subconscious or latent stages of mind which are mind-disassociated: 1) the stage of all (false) views of monism, 2) the stage of desiring sensuous pleasures, 3) the stage of desiring forms, and 4) the stage of desiring existence which are based upon 5) the stage of ignorance. The first four, listed in increasing order of strength, characterize all subconscious qualities of the sentient mind. The fifth stage, ignorance, is the final stage, the most fundamental stage, which characterizes the subconscious mind.

According to the *Hsieh-chu sheng-man-ching*, the oldest extant commentary on the *Śrīmālādevi sūtra* (T.v. 85, no. 2763, p. 279b), the stage of ignorance and the four latent stages of defilement are considered "mind-disassociated" because they are not active. However, when they become activated, they are "mind-associated" with the Āryan mind of the three vehicles and not with the ordinary sentient mind. Consequently, the four latent stages of defilement and the stage of ignorance are the subtle propensities which still must be eliminated by the three vehicles, being associated with their highly spiritual mind and not with the mind of the ordinary being.

The fourth and fifth latent stages of the subconscious mind were known to Nāgārjuna (See Tsukinowa, *Shōmangyō hōgatsu dōji shomongyō, op. cit.*, p. 10) but the other three latent stages were not. Moreover, the *Ratnagotravibhāga* and *Laṅkāvatāra* refer only to *avidyā-vāsabhūmi* and not to the other four *vāsabhūmi*.

[25]Bodhiruci: 彼雖有緣亦能為緣。

"Although they (the three kinds of mind-made bodies and pure actions) are conditioned they also can become the conditioner."

Cf. 有緣非無緣 (Guṇabhadra)

[26]*Pao-k'u*: 四住之業唯作分段，無明之業能作變易。故曰不同也

"The action of the four latent stages produces only the ordinary (death). The action of ignorance produces the transformational (death). Therefore they are not the same." (p. 54b)

The ordinary death belongs to the triple-world and is the three vehicles' means for eliminating the four latent stages of defilement. The very last stage of conditioned existence, belonging to the sentient mind, is the stage of ignorance through which the three vehicles (epitomized in the eighth stage Bodhisattva and above) produce their mind-made bodies, capable of transformational death.

[27]*Pao-k'u*: 於彼彼法不知不覺是無治也。如來藏中恒沙仏法是彼彼法。是無明覆故，不知不覺。

"...'(they) do not know, and do not awaken to the various phenomena' refers to what they have not controlled. The Buddha dharmas more numerous than the sands of the Ganges are 'the various phenomena.' Because of their obscuration by ignorance, they (the Arhats, Pratyeka-buddhas, and Bodhisattvas) do not know and do not awaken to them."

[28]Bodhiruci: 得有餘解脫非一切解脫。

"...they attain liberation with remaining (action to be performed) which is not liberation in its entirety."

Cf. 名有餘過解脫非離一切過解脫。
(Guṇabhadra)

[29]The two sentences which follow are not from the Chinese recensions which read as follows:
Guṇabhadra: 法無優劣故得涅槃。

"Because the phenomena are without superiority or inferiority one attains Nirvāṇa."

Bodhiruci: 於諸法中見高下者不證涅槃。

"Those who see the superior and the inferior among phenomena do not attain Nirvāṇa."

The Sanskrit fragment, quoted in the *Ratnagotravighāga* (p. 59, 11.5-8) has been selected as the clearest recension:

> *na hi bhagavan hīnapraṇītadharmāṇāṁ nirvāṇādhigamaḥ/ samadharmāṇāṁ bhagavan nirvāṇādhigamaḥ/ samajñānānāṁ samavimuktīnāṁ samavimuktijñānadarśanānāṁ bhagavan nirvāṇādhigamaḥ/ tasmād bhagavan nirvāṇadhātur ekarasaḥ samarasa ity ucyate/ yad uta vidyāvimuktir aseneti/*

[30]Bodhiruci: 便能證得過恒沙等不可思議諸仏之法。於一切法而能證得無礙神通。

> "Again one can attain the various Buddha dharmas which are inconceivable and more numerous than the sands of the Ganges. With reference to all dharmas one can manifest and attain unobstructed spiritual powers."
>
> Cf. 過恒沙等如来所得一切諸法通達無礙。 (Guṇabhadra)

[31]The "four Evil Ones" are the evils of heaven, of defilement, of the aggregates of existence (*skandhas*), and of death. The evils of heaven and of defilement cause evil effects which are the aggregates of existence and death. (Cf. *Kokuyaku-issaikyō, op. cit.*, p. 109, ft. 131).

[32]Bodhiruci: 證不思議清浄法身。

> "They manifest the unthinkable, pure Dharma-Body."
> Cf. Guṇabhadra omits "pure."

[33]Bodhiruci: 於所知地 --"in spheres of objects of knowledge."

> Cf. 於一切爾焰地 (Guṇabhadra)

[34]The ten knowledges are:

1. knowledge of correct and false conclusions
2. knowledge of consequences of all past, present, and future actions
3. knowledge of various aspirations and dispositions of different beings
4. knowledge of the true nature of the elements in the universe
5. knowledge of the higher and lower powers of beings
6. knowledge of the way that leads everywhere
7. knowledge of the defilement, purification, and origination of deliverances, concentration and ecstatic attainment
8. knowledge of all previous existences
9. knowledge of the process of life and death in all beings
10. knowledge of the destruction of his defilements

Cf. Har Dayal, *The Bodhisattva Doctrine*, *op. cit.*, p. 20.

[35]Guṇabhadra appends 不由於他。

[36]"The Dharma" is Mahāyāna which is the ultimate Dharma. Cf. *Kokuyaku-issaikyō, op. cit.*, p. 110, ft. 138.

[37]Bodhiruci:彼等於未證地不遇法故。

"...those in the stages which have not yet realized (enlightenment) do not meet the Dharma."
Cf.彼等於未證地不遇法故。 (Guṇabhadra)

The reading *yü* (愚) has been amended to *yü* (遇) in accordance with Bodhiruci's recension.

[38]Bodhiruci:能自解了 "...they can comprehend by themselves."
Cf. 亦自知得有餘地 (Guṇabhadra)

Bodhiruci adds: 我今證得有餘依地。

"I now have realized the stages with remaining (stages to be realized)."

[39]Bodhiruci: 言涅槃者即是如來清淨法身。

"Nirvāṇa is the pure Dharma-Body of the Tathāgata."
Cf. Guṇabhadra omits "pure" in accordance with the *Ratnagotravibhāga, op. cit.*, (p. 3, 1.2) which cites this passage.

[40]Cf. *Ratnagotravibhagā, op. cit.*, p. 56, 11.5-6:

nānyo bhagavaṁs tathāgato 'nyo dharmakāyah/ dharmakāya eva bhagavaṁs tathāgata iti./

"O Lord, the Tathāgata is not different from the Dharma-Body. The Tathāgata is the Dharma-Body, O Lord."

[41]Bodhiruci:究竟一乘者即離相続。

"The ultimate One Vehicle is separate from causality."
Cf. 究竟者即是無辺不斷。
(Guṇabhadra)

[42]Bodhiruci:無限誓願 --"and unlimited promises."
Cf. Guṇabhadra omits this.

[43]This sentence is omitted by Bodhiruci.

[44]Bodhiruci omits *ju-lai* (如来) (Tathāgata).

[45]Bodhiruci considers "Tathāgata" the subject of the sentence:若復說言如来是常是無盡法。

"Again, one may say that the Tathagata is the eternal, inexhaustible Dharma."

[46]Bodhiruci: 於無護世間 --"in a world without protection."
Cf. 於未度世間 (Guṇabhadra)

47 Bodhiruci omits *fa* (法) (Dharma).

48 Bodhiruci: 無說一乘道 --"there can be no path of the One Vehicle."
Cf. 無說一乘法身 (Guṇabhadra)

49 Bodhiruci: 有所作故 "because of actions to be done."
Cf. Guṇabhadra omits this.
Cf. *Ratnagotra, op. cit.*, p. 19, 11.6-7:

sa ca nityaṁ sabhayas tathāgataśaranagato niḥsaraṇa paryeṣī śaikṣaḥ sakaraṇīyaḥ pratipannakas cānuttarāyāṁ samyaksaṁbodhāv iti/

"Constantly afraid, seeking refuge in the Tathāgata and striving after salvation, the disciple, still having duties to perform, approaches the Supreme, Complete Enlightenment."

50 Bodhiruci omits: 非此二歸依 "these are not two refuges."
Instead his recension states: 是二歸依由法律潤信入歸依。如来者非法律潤信入歸依。言如来者是眞實依。此二歸依以眞實義。即名究竟歸依如来。
"As for these two refuges, due to the Dharma's permeation, they seek a refuge through faith. As for the Tathāgata, he does not seek a refuge through faith, due to the Dharma's permeation. The Tathāgata is the true refuge. These two refuges are identical with the Tathāgata, the ultimate refuge, for their true meaning.

51 The four states of fearlessness are:
1) "the supporter who is without fear" 能持無所畏。
2) "the source of knowledge which is without fear" 智根無所畏。
3) "the one who never doubts and is without fear" 決疑無所畏。
4) "the benefit who is without fear" 答報無所畏。

Cf. *Kokuyaku-issaikyō, op. cit.*, p. 11, ft. 149.

[Chapter 6 - "The unlimited noble truths"]

"O Lord, the Śrāvakas and Pratyekas first saw[1] the noble truths with their one knowledge[2] which eliminates[3] the latent stages (of defilement). With their one knowledge, one of the four wisdoms, they eliminate (the source of suffering, viz. the four latent stages of defilements), know (suffering), practice virtue (according to the path), and realize (extinction).[4] They understand these four (noble truths) very well. O Lord, they do not have the most supreme transcendental wisdom but are gradually reaching the four wisdoms and the four conditions.[5] The Dharma which is not gradually reached is the supreme transcendental wisdom.[6] O Lord, the supreme wisdom is like a diamond.

O Lord, the Śrāvakas and Pratyeka-buddhas do not eliminate the stage of beginningless ignorance. Their initial wisdom of the noble truths is (not)[7] the supreme wisdom. Lord, because they do not have the wisdom of the two kinds of noble truths, they eliminate (only) the latent stages (of defilement). O Lord, the Tathāgata, Arhat, Completely Enlightened One is not the realm of all the Śrāvakas and Pratyeka-buddhas.

The inconceivable wisdom of Emptiness eliminates the stores of all defilements. O Lord, the ultimate wisdom which destroys the stores of all defilements is called the supreme wisdom. The initial wisdom of the noble truths is not[8] the ultimate wisdom but is wisdom which is turned towards the Supreme, Complete Enlightenment.

O Lord, the meaning of 'noble' does not refer to all the Śrāvakas and Pratyeka-buddhas. Because the Śrāvakas and Pratyeka-buddhas have perfected limited merits and have perfected 'partial' merits, they are called 'noble.' The 'noble truths' are not the truths of the Śrāvakas and Pratyeka-buddhas nor are they the merits of the Śrāvakas and Pratyeka-buddhas.

O Lord, these truths are those originally known by the Tathāgata, Arhat, Completely Enlightened One. Later, on behalf of the world, which is the womb of ignorance, he appeared to extensively teach what are known as the 'noble truths'."

CHAPTER 6

NOTES

[1]Bodhiruci: 證 ; Guṇabhadra: 觀

[2]*Pao-k'u*: 一智者靈味寺諒法師及馥師悉云以一平等智斷四住地。

> "The 'one knowledge,' according to Liang-fa of Ling-mei temple and (Seng-) fu, refers to the (Buddha) knowledge of equality which eliminates the four latent stages." (p.64c)

[3]In Bodhiruci's recension the Śrāvakas and Pratyeka-buddhas do *not* sever the four latent stages: 非以一智斷諸住地。亦非一智證四遍知諸功德等。

> "They do not eliminate the latent stages with their one knowledge. They also do not attain the virtues of the four universal (i.e. noble) truths."

[4]Chi-tsang interprets this passage in Guṇabhadra's recension in the following manner: 斷者斷集，知者知苦，功德者修道。作證者證滅。

> "'Eliminate' means to eliminate the source (of suffering). 'Know' means to know suffering. 'Virtue' means to practice the path. 'Realize' means to realize extinction." (*Pao-k'u*, p. 64c)

[5]The "four conditions" refer to the four noble truths. Cf. *Kokuyaku-issaikyō, op. cit.*, p. 112, ft. 156.

[6]*Pao-k'u*: 但二乘漸見四諦，仏頓見也。

> "The two vehicles only gradually see the four noble truths whereas the Buddha immediately sees them." (p. 65b)

[7]Bodhiruci: 世尊，聲聞獨覚以於種聖諦之智斷諸住地。無有出世第一義智唯有如来応正遍知。非諸聲聞獨覚境界。

> "O Lord, the Srāvakas and Pratyekas, with their knowledge of the noble truths, eliminate the latent stages (of defilements). They do not have the supreme transcendental wisdom which only the Tathāgatas, Arhats, Completely Enlightened Ones have. This (wisdom) is not the realm of the Śrāvakas and Pratyeka-buddhas."

Guṇabhadra's recension appears to be in error, having omitted a negative.
Cf. 初聖諦智是第一義智。
See ft. 8 below.

[8]Both recensions are identical: 初聖諦智非究竟智。

[Chapter 7 - "The Tathāgatagarbha"]

"The 'noble truths' have a most profound meaning, which is extremely subtle, difficult to know,[1] and not of the cognitive and finite realms. What is known by those who have this wisdom[2] (of the noble truths' profound meaning) is unbelievable to the entire world.[3] Why? Because this (profound meaning of tbe noble truths) explains the most profound Womb (*garbha*) of the Tathāgata. The Tathāgatagarbha is the realm of the Tathāgata,[4] which is not known by all the Śravakas and Pratyekabuddhas.[5] The Tathāgatagarbha[6] explains the meaning of the noble truths. Because the Tathāgatagarbha is most profound, explaining the holy truths also is most profound, extremely subtle, difficult to know, and not of the cognitive and finite realms. What is known by those who have this wisdom is unbelievable to the entire world."[7]

CHAPTER 7

NOTES

[1]Bodhiruci: 甚深微妙難見難了不可分別。

"...extremely subtle, profound, difficult to see, difficult to comprehend, and inconceivable."

Cf. 說甚深義微細難知。 (Guṇabhadra)

[2]Bodhiruci omits 是智者所知。 --"What is known by those who have this wisdom..."

[3]Guṇabhadra omits 唯有如来応正等覚之所能知。 "Only the Tathāgata, Arhat, Completely Enlightened One can know it."

[4]Bodhiruci: 仏境界 --"the realm of the Buddha."
Cf. 如来境界 --"the realm of the Tathāgata." (Guṇabhadra)

[5]Bodhiruci: 行
Cf. Guṇabhadra: 知

[6]Bodhiruci: 如来藏
Cf. Guṇabhadra: 如来藏處。

[7]These last two sentences are repeated from above with the same deletions noted in footnotes 1-3.

[Chapter 8 - "The Dharma-Body"]

"If there are no doubts with reference to the Tathāgatagarbha which is concealed by the innumerable stores of defilement, then there also will be no doubts with reference to the Dharma-Body[1] which transcends the innumerable stores of defilement.[2] In explaining Tathāgatagarbha, one explains the Dharma-Body of the Tathāgata, the inconceivable Buddha-realms, and skillful means. The mind which attains this determination, then believes and understands the twofold noble truths.[3] Likewise, what is difficult to know and to understand is the meaning of the twofold noble truths. What is their meaning? They are referred to as the 'conditioned' noble truths and the 'unconditioned' noble truths.[5]

The 'conditioned' noble truths are the 'limited' four noble truths.[6] Why? Because one who depends on others cannot know all suffering, eliminate all sources of suffering, realize all extinctions of suffering, and practice the entire path. Therefore, O Lord, the life-death cycle is both conditioned and unconditioned; Nirvāṇa likewise is (conditioned and unconditioned), being (Nirvāṇa) with remainder (i.e. conditioned) and (Nirvāṇa) without remainder (i.e. unconditioned).[7]

The 'unconditioned noble truths are the 'unlimited'[8] four noble truths. Why? With his own power,[9] one (who knows the unlimited noble truths) can know all suffering, sever all sources of suffering, realize all extinctions of suffering, and practice the entire path.

These, then, are the eight noble truths. The Tathāgatas taught the four (conditioned) noble truths (as skillful means).[10] The meaning of the four unconditioned noble truths are the actions of the Tathāgatas-, Arhats-, Completely Enlightened Ones, who alone are ultimate. The actions of the Arhats and Pratyeka Buddhas are not ultimate. Why? Because phenomena are not inferior, mediocre, or superior, one attains Nirvāṇa.[11] Why? With reference to the meaning of the four unconditioned noble truths, the actions of the Tathāgatas-, Arhats-, Completely Enlightened Ones are ultimate. Because all the Tathāgatas-, Arhats-, Completely Enlightened Ones know all future suffering, sever all defilements as well as the sources of all virulent defilements which have been accumulated, and extinguish all the elements (*skandha*) in the mind-made bodies (of the three Vehicles), they realize the extinction of all suffering.

O Lord, the extinction of suffering is not the destruction of the Dharma. The 'extinction of suffering' signifies the Dharma-Body of the Tathāgata which is from beginningless time, uncreated,[12] non-arising, indestructible, free from destruction, eternal, inherently pure, and separate from all the stores of defilement.[13] O Lord, the Dharma-Body is not separate from, free from, or different from the inconceivable Buddha-dharmas which are more numerous than the sands of the Ganges. O Lord, the Dharma-Body of the Tathāgata is called the Tathāgata-garbha when it is inseparable from the stores of defilement."[14]

CHAPTER 8

NOTES

[1]Bodhiruci: 如来法身 --"the Dharma-Body of the Tathāgata." Cf. Guṇabhadra: 法身

[2]Cf. *Ratnagotravibhāga*, p. 79, ll. 11-13:

> *yo bhagavan sarvakleśakośakoṭigūḍhe tathāgatagarbhe niṣkāṅkṣaḥ sarvakleśakośavinirmukte tathāgatadharmakāye 'pi sa niṣkāṅkṣa iti/* (citation from *ŚDS*)
>
> "O Lord when there are no doubts with reference to the Tathāgatagarbha which is concealed by all the vast stores of defilements. There also will be no doubts with reference to the Dharma-Body of the Tathāgata, which is separate from all the stores of defilements."

[3]Bodhiruci: 若有於此如来之藏及仏法身不可思議仏秘密境。心得究竟於彼所説二聖諦義。

> "When, in this Womb of the Tathāgata, in the Dharma-Body of the Buddha, in the inconceivable profound Buddha-realms, the mind has attained the ultimate, then the meaning of the two noble truths have been explained to him."

Cf. 如来法身不思議仏境界及方便説。心得決定者此則信解説二聖諦。 (Guṇabhadra)

[4]Bodhiruci: 能信能了能生勝解.

> "One can believe, can understand and can comprehend completely (the twofold noble truths)."

Cf. 如是難知難解者謂説二聖諦義。 (Guṇabhadra)

[5]The Chinese 作 and 無作 have been equated with 有為 and 無為 "conditioned" and "unconditioned." (Cf. *Kokuyaku-issaikyō*, *op. cit.*, p. 113, ft. 163).

[6]Bodhiruci: 作聖諦者是不圓滿四聖諦義。

> "The 'conditioned' noble truths are the 'incomplete' four noble truths."

Cf. 説作聖諦義者是説有量四聖諦。 (Guṇabhadra)

[7]Bodhiruci: 是古不知有為無為及於涅槃。

> "Therefore, they (i.e. the two Vehicles who know only the 'conditioned' noble truths) do not know that the conditioned and unconditioned extend over Nirvāṇa."

Cf. 是故世尊。有有為生死無為生死。涅槃亦如是。有餘及無餘。 (Guṇabhadra)

Cf. *tasmād bhagavann asti saṁskṛto 'py asaṁskṛto 'pi saṁsāraḥ/ asti saṁskṛtam apy asaṁskṛtam api nirvāṇam iti/* (*RGV*, p. 50, ll.10-11, citation from *ŚDS*)

"Therefore, O Lord, the life-death cycle is both conditioned and unconditioned, O Lord. Nirvāṇa is both conditioned and unconditioned."

[8]Bodhiruci: 圓滿四聖諦義. --"...complete four noble truths."
Cf. 無量四聖諦義. (Guṇabhadra)

[9]Bodhiruci: 能自護 --"by self-reliance."
Cf. Guṇabhadra: 能以自力.

[10]*Gisho*: 八諦之中昔日如來為二乘七地但說有作四諦。

"Among the eight noble truths, the Tathāgata, in ancient times, taught only the four conditioned noble truths for the benefit of the two vehicles and those (Bodhisattvas) of the seventh stage (and below)." (p. 56a)

[11]Cf. *Ratnagotravibhāga* which is quoted above, ft. 29, Chapter 5 of the translation. The three Vehicles as referents for the inferior, mediocre, and superior phenomena (dharma) is another interpretation. (Cf. *Kokuyaku-issaikyō, op. cit.*, p. 114, ft. 171)

[12]The Chinese 無作 has been translated as "uncreated" in accordance with the *Ratnagotravibhāga* (*op. cit.*, p. 12, ll.10-14) which states '*kṛto* (*akṛtaḥ*) as equivalent to 無作 as an attribute of the Dharma-Body.

The entire citation from the *ŚDS* retained in the *RGV* (p. 12, ll.10-14):

na khalu bhagavan dharmavināśo duḥkhanirodhaḥ/ duḥkanirodhanāmnā bhagavann anādikāliko 'kṛto 'jāto 'nutpanno 'kṣayaḥ kṣayāpagataḥ nityo dhruvaḥ śivaḥ śāśvataḥ prakṛtipariśuddhaḥ sarvakleśakośavinirmukto gaṅgāvālikāvyativṛttair avinirbhāgair acintyair buddhadharmaiḥ samanvāgatas tathāgata-dharmakāyo deśitaḥ/ ayam eva ca bhagavaṁs tathāgata-dharmakāyo 'vinirmuktakleśakośas tathāgatagarbhaḥ sūcyate/

"O Lord, the destruction of suffering is not the destruction of the Dharma. The name 'destruction of suffering' signifies the Dharma-Body of the Tathāgata which is from beginningless time, uncreated, unborn, non-arising, indestructible, free from destruction, eternal, permanent, quiescent, perpetual, inherently pure, separate from all defilements, and accompanied by the inconceivable Buddha-dharmas which are inseparable from it, being more numerous than the sands of the Ganges. This Dharma-Body of the Tathāgata is called the Tathāgatagarbha when there is no separation from defilements"

[13]Bodhiruci: 出煩惱殼 --"transcends the covering (lit. "shell") of defilement.
Cf. 離一切煩惱藏 (Guṇabhadra)

[14]For further discussion concerning the discrepancies between Guṇabhadra's recension and Bodhiruci's, as compared with the Tibetan recensions and the Sanskrit fragments, see "Shōmangyō no Tibetto to kūshisō" by Uryūzu Ryūshin, p. 200-215, in *Shōmangyō gisho ronshu*, Nakamura Hajime (ed). (Heirakuji shoten: Kyoto, 1965).

The recensions are as follows:

Bodhiruci: 世尊、如来成就過於恒沙具解脫智不思議法。說名法身。世尊、如是法身不離煩惱名如来藏。

"O Lord, the Tathāgata is accompanied by all the inconceivable dharmas and the knowledge of liberation, more numerous than the sands of the Ganges. This is called the Dharma-Body. O Lord, similarly, the Dharma-Body, when it is inseparable from defilement, is called the Tathāgatagarbha.

Guṇabhadra: 世尊過於恒沙不離不脫不思議仏法成就說如来法身。世尊、如是如来法身不離煩惱藏。

[Chapter 9 - "The underlying truth: the meaning of Emptiness"]

"O Lord, the wisdom of Tathāgatagarbha is the Tathāgata's wisdom of Emptiness.[1] O Lord, the Tathāgatagarbha has not been seen nor attained originally by all the Arhats, Pratyeka-buddhas, and tbe powerful Bodhisattvas.[2]

O Lord, there are two kinds of wisdom of Emptiness with reference to the Tathāgatagarbha.

O Lord, 1) the Tathāgatagarbha which is Empty is separate from, free from, and different from the stores of all defilements.[3]

O Lord, 2) the Tathāgatagarbha which is not Empty is not separate from, not free from, and not different from the inconceivable Buddha-dharmas, more numerous than the sands of the Ganges.[4]

O Lord, the various great Śrāvakas can believe in the Tathāgata with reference to the two wisdoms of Emptiness. All the Arhats and Pratyeka-buddhas revolve in the realm of the four contrary[5] views because of their knowledge of Emptiness. Thus, the Arhats and Pratyeka-buddhas do not originally see nor attain (the wisdom of the Tathāgatagarbha). The extinction of all suffering is only realized by the Buddhas who destroy the stores of all defilements and practice the path which extinguishes all suffering."

CHAPTER 9

NOTES

[1]Bodhiruci: 如來藏者即是如來空性之智。

"The Tathāgatagarbha is the Tathāgata's wisdom of the nature of Emptiness."

Cf. 如來藏智是如來空智。(Guṇabhadra)

[2]Bodhiruci adds: 唯佛了知及能作證。

"Only the Buddhas can completely know and realize (this wisdom)."

[3]Bodhiruci: 謂空如來藏所謂離於不解脫智一切煩惱。

"The Emptiness of the Tathāgatagarbha is separate from knowledge which is not of liberation and from the stores of all defilement."

Cf. 空如來藏者離若脫若異一切煩惱藏。 (Guṇabhadra)

[4]The Sanskrit fragment concerning the two dimensions Empty and Not Empty are quoted in the *Ratnagotravibhāga* (p. 76, ll. 8-9):

śūnyas tathāgatagarbho vinirbhāgair muktajñaiḥ sarvakleśa-kośaiḥ/ aśūnyo gaṅgānadīvālikāvyativṛttair avinirbhāgair amuktajñair acintyair buddhadharmair iti/

"The Tathātagarbha which is Empty is due to its distinction from the stores of all defilements in which there is knowledge separable (from the Tathāgatagarbha). (The Tathāgatagarbha which is) Not Empty is due to its identity (non-distinction') with the inconceivable Buddha-dharmas."

Guṇabhadra's translation is very similar, except for the omission of the word "knowledge" (*jña/jñana*). Knowledge as the head-noun is omitted and the participle (*mukta*) simply becomes an adjective modifying Tathāgatagarbha, and dependent upon "all stores of defilement," reconstructed into Sanskrit as *śūnyas tathāgatagarbhaḥ sarvakleśakośavinirbhaktair muktaiḥ* ("The Tathāgatagarbha which is Empty is due to its being separate from and free from all stores of defilement.") Since defilement impedes knowledge of the Tathāgatagarbha, defilement may be equated with knowledge which is separate from the Tathāgatagarbha. Therefore, the Sanskrit fragment and Guṇabhadra's translation are identical in meaning.

Bodhiruci replaces "knowledge separable from the Tathāgatagarbha" (*muktajña*) (*chieh-t'o-chih*) (解脫智) with "knowledge inseparable from the Tathāgatagarbha" (*amuktajña*) (*pu chieh-t'o-chih*) (不解脫智) and reinterprets the latter as "knowledge of non-liberation" (*avimuktijñana*):

謂空如來藏所謂離於不解脫智一切煩惱。

"The Tathāgatagarbha which is Empty is separate from all defilements which are the knowledge of non-liberation."

不空如来藏具過恒沙仏解脱智不思議法。

> "The Tathāgatagarbha which is not Empty is endowed with all the inconceivable dharmas which are the knowledge of the Buddha's liberation, more numerous than the sands of the Ganges."

The Tibetan also reverses *muktajña* (*grol bas śes pa*) with *amuktajña* (*ma grol bas śes pa*) in agreement with Bodhiruci's translation. (See Uryūzū Ryūshin, "Shōmangyō no Chibettoyaku kūshisō" in *Shōmangyō gisho ronshu, op. cit.*, p. 209). Consequently the Tibetan translation by Jinamitra and Surendrabodhi and Bodhiruci's translation, both of which were translated during the eighth century and incorporated in the *Ratnakūṭa* anthology, are identical in interpretation.

The term *avinirmuktajñāna* first appeared in the *Anūnatvāpurṇatvanirdeśa* (*Pu tseng pu chien ching*) cited in the *Ratnagotravibhaga* (p. 39, 11.7-8):

> *evam eva śāriputra tathāgatanirdiṣṭo dharmakāyo 'vinirbhāgadharmāvinirmuktajñānaguṇo yad uta gaṅgānadīvālikāvyativṛttais tathāgatadharmair iti*

> "Then, Śariputra, the Dharma-Body which has the quality of knowledge inseparable and indivisible (from the Dharma-Body) has been taught by the Tathāgata, viz. the dharmas of the Tathāgata more numerous than the sands of the Ganges."

The only extant Chinese recension, translated by Bodhiruci of Northern Wei in 525, retains Gunabhadra's translation style, omitting the word "knowledge": 舍利弗、如我所説法身義者過於恒沙不離不脱不斷不異議仏法如来功德智慧。 (T.v.16, no. 668, p. 467a).

> "Śariputra, the Dharma-Body which has been taught by me is not separated, not free, not severed and not different from the inconceivable Buddha-dharmas which are the virtues and wisdom of the Buddha more numerous than the sands of the Ganges."

Unfortunately, no earlier Chinese translation of the *Anūnatvāpurṇatvanirdeśa* exists today which would furnish evidence concerning the original emphasis upon the knowledge rather than the quality of inseparability or vice versa. From the recensions now extant both the earlier Chinese recension of the *Śrīmālādevī sūtra* and Bodhiruci's *Pu tseng pu chien ching* de-emphasize knowledge for the inseparability from the Dharma-Body in contrast to the later recensions of the *ŚDS* by Bodhiruci in Chinese and Jinamitra and Surendrabodhi in Tibetan. Although the later recensions interpret the compounds *muktajña* and *amuktajña* in terms of liberation and non-liberation, the meaning of the inseparability of the Dharma-Body from the dharmas of the Buddha's wisdom is retained, identifying this inseparability with "liberation."

[5] Guṇabhadra's recension has been amended, omitting the negative (不) before "contrary" in accordance with Bodhiruci's recension which states:

如是一切聲聞獨覚空性之智於四倒境攀緣而轉.

> "Similarly, all of the Śrāvakas' and Pratyekas' knowledge with regard to Emptiness, is conditioned and revolves in the realm of the four contrary views."

Cf. 一切阿羅漢辟支仏空智於四不顛倒境界轉。
(Guṇabhadra)

Cf. *Ratnagotravibhaga, op. cit.*,

> *Sarvaśrāvakapratyekabuddhā api bhagavan śūnyatājñānenādṛṣṭapurve sarvajñajñanaviṣaye tathāgatadharmakāye viparyastāḥ.*

> "Even all the Śravakas and Pratyeka-buddhas are confused by their knowledge of Emptiness with reference to the Dharma-Body of the Tathāgata, the realm of the knowledge of all knowledges which has not previously been seen."

[Chapter 10 - "The one (noble) "truth"]

"O Lord, among these four noble truths, three are impermanent and one is permanent. Why? Because three of the noble truths are conditioned (*saṁskṛtalakṣaṇa*). What is 'conditioned' is impermanent and what is 'impermanent' is false and deceptive in nature (*mṛṣāmoṣadharmin*). What is 'false and deceptive in nature' is not true, is impermanent, and is not a refuge. Therefore, the (three) noble truths, viz. 'there is suffering,' 'there is the source of suffering,' and 'there is the path' are not the supreme truth for they are neither permanent nor a refuge."[1]

CHAPTER 10

NOTES

[1]Cf. *Ratnagotravibhāga* (*op. cit.*, p. 19, ll.1-5) which quotes the following passage, attributed to the *Śrīmālādevī-sūtra*:

> *Tatra mārgaḥ saṁskṛtalakṣaṇaparyāpannaḥ/ yat saṁskṛtalakṣaṇaparyāpannam tan mṛṣāmoṣadharmi/ yan mṛṣāmoṣadharmi tad asatyam/ yad asatyam tad anityam/ yad anityam tad aśaraṇam/ yaś ca tena mārgena nirodho 'dhigataḥ so 'pi śrāvakanayena pradīpocchedavat kleśaduḥkhābhāva-mātraprabhāvitaḥ/ na cābhāvaḥ śaraṇam aśaraṇaṁ vā bhavitum arhati/*

> "The path belongs to the conditioned. What belongs to the conditioned is false and deceptive in nature. What is false and deceptive in nature is not true. What is not true is impermanent. What is impermanent is not a refuge. The attainment of the extinction (of suffering) by that path which is the teaching of the Śrāvakas presents only the non-existence of defilements and suffering like the extinction of a lamp. And what does not exist cannot be either a refuge or a non-refuge."

[Chapter 11 - "The one refuge"]

"The one noble truth, viz. 'the extinction of suffering,' is separate from the conditioned. What is 'separate from the conditioned' is permanent. What is 'permanent' is not false and deceptive in nature. What is 'not false and deceptive in nature' is true, permanent, and a refuge. Therefore, the noble truth of the extinction (of suffering) is the supreme truth."

[Chapter 12 - "The contrary truths"]

"The noble truth of the extinction (of suffering) is inconceivable, transcending all tbe conditions[1] of the consciousness of living beings. This is also not the knowledge of the Arhats and Pratyeka-buddhas who, like those born blind, cannot see all shapes or like the week-old infant who cannot see the disc of the moon. The truth of the extinction of suffering, similarly, does not belong to the conditions of the common man's consciousness nor to the two vehicles' realm of knowledge.[2] The common man's consciousness refers to the two contrary[3] views. The wisdom of all the Arhats and Pratyeka Buddhas is pure (in comparison with that of the common man).[4]

The 'limited[5] views' refer to the common man's adherence to the misconception that there is a substantial ego within the five psychophysical elements which then causes the two views,[6] which are designated 'contrary,' viz. eternalism and nihilism. If one considers the conditioned states impermanent, this is nihilism and not the correct view. If one considers Nirvāṇa permanent, this is eternalism and not the correct view.[7] Because of misconceptions, there are such views.

In the sense organs of the body, which are discriminative in nature, some perceive the destruction of phenomena in the present moment. Unable to see phenomena in continuity, they become nihilistic in their views because of misconceptions. The ignorant, who are unable to understand or know the momentary consciousness with reference to its continuity, become eternalistic in their views because of misconceptions.[8] By this or that principle, they discriminate and maintain inadequate positions to an extreme degree. Because of foolish misconceptions they adhere to erroneous conceptions and contrary views, viz. nihilism and eternalism.[9]

O Lord, living beings have contrary ideas when they have acquired the five psychophysical constituents of the individual. The impermanent is considered the permanent, suffering is considered happiness. The non-substantiality of the ego is considered a substantial ego, the impure is considered pure.

The knowledge of all the Arhats and Pratyeka Buddhas has not originally apprehended the Dharma-Body of the Tathāgata nor the realm of His omniscience.[10] If there are living beings who believe in the Buddha's words,[11] they will have thoughts of permanence (*nitya*), of happiness (*sukha*), of ego (*atman*), and of purity (*śubha*). These are not contrary views but are correct views. Why? The Dharma-Body of the Tathāgata is the perfection of permanence, the perfection of happiness, the perfection of the substantial ego, and the perfection of purity.[12] Those who see the Dharma-Body of the Buddha in this way are said to see correctly. Those who see correctly are the true sons of the Buddha (*bhagavataḥ putrā aurasā*).[13] They arise from the Buddha's words, from the true Dharma, and from conversion to the Dharma, attaining the remaining benefits of the Dharma.[14]

O Lord, pure wisdom is the perfection of wisdom[15] which belongs to all the Arhats and Pratyeka Buddhas. This pure wisdom, although it is called pure wisdom, with reference to the (conditioned noble)[16] truth of the extinction (of suffering) is not the realm (of unconditioned wisdom). Of course, the wisdom of (those beginning to study)[17] the four basic truths (i.e. the noble truths) also (does not belong to the realm of the unconditioned wisdom). Why? The three vehicles' first actions were not ignorant of the Dharma. Because of their principles, they understood and attained (enlightenment). The Lord explained the four basic truths for their sake. O Lord, these four basic truths are the Dharma of the world. O Lord, the one refuge is all refuges. It is the transcendental and supreme refuge, viz. the truth of the extinction (of suffering)."

CHAPTER 12

NOTES

[1]Bodhiruci: 過諸有情心識境界。 "surpassing the consciousness realm of living beings."
Cf. 一切衆生心識所緣 (Guṇabhadra)

[2]Bodhiruci: 智所能及 "...the knowledge which can be attained."
Cf. 智慧境界 (Guṇabhadra)

[3]Bodhiruci: 謂二邊見 --"refers to the two limited views."
Cf. 二見顛倒 (Guṇabhadra)

The "two contrary (or limited) views" are those of nihilism (*uccheda*) and eternalism (*śāśvata*).

Strictly speaking, the limited views are nihilism and eternalism while the contrary views are permanence, substantial ego, purity, and happiness. Both categories, "limited" and "contrary" have been frequently interchanged in the two Chinese recensions.

[4]*Pao-k'u*: 淨智者對前凡夫二見及顛倒之垢故名淨智。於一切智境界者一諦理是一切智之境界及如來法身者是仏果德二乘雖有淨智本不見此二。 (p. 77c)

> "The pure wisdom (of the Arhats and Pratyeka-buddhas) is in contrast to the impurity of the contrary views and the two (limited) views held by the common man. Therefore, they are said to have pure wisdom. However, although they have pure wisdom the two vehicles cannot truly see the realm of omniscience, which is the principle of the one noble truth, nor the Dharma-Body, which are the virtues of the Buddha."

[5]Both Bodhiruci and Guṇabhadra use "limited" (邊見) here.

[6]Bodhiruci: 異分別 --"false discrimination."
Cf. Guṇabhadra: 二見

[7]Cf. *Ratnagotravibhāga*, pp. 34-35, 11.20-21, 1-2:

> *anityāḥ saṁskārā iti ced bhagavan paśyeta sāsya syād ucchedadṛṣṭih/ sāsya syān na samyagdṛṣṭiḥ/ nityaṁ nirvāṇam iti ced bhagavan paśyeta sāsya syāc chāsvatadṛṣṭiḥ/ sāsya syān na samyagdṛṣṭir iti/*

> "If someone considers 'the conditioned states are impermanent,' this is nihilism, O Lord. This is not the correct view. If someone considers 'Nirvāṇa is permanent' this is eternalism, O Lord. This is not the correct view."

[8]Bodhiruci: 於有相續刹那滅壞、愚闇不了意識界起於常見。

> "The ignorant who do not know the consciousness with reference to the momentary destruction of its continuity, become eternalistic in their views."

Cf. 於心相續愚闇不解不知。剎那間意識境界起於常見妄想見故。 (Guṇabhadra)

[9]Bodhiruci's recension has been used here because it is clearer than Guṇabhadra's. It states: 然彼彼義過諸分別及下劣見。由諸愚夫妄生異相顛倒執著謂斷謂常。
Cf. 若過若不及作異想分別若斷若常。

> "If their positions are excessive or inadequate, they maintain erroneous conceptions and discriminations, e.g. nihilism and eternalism." (Guṇabhadra)

[10]Cf. *Ratnagotravibhāga*, p. 30-31, ll.20 and 1, cited in ft. 5, Chapter 11 of the translation.

[11]Bodhiruci: 信如来 "...believe in the Tathāgata."
Cf. 信仏語 (Guṇabhadra)
Cf. *Ratnagotravibhāga* (p. 31, l.1) which cites the following:

> *Ye bhagavan sattvāḥ syur bhagavataḥ pūtrā aurasā.../*

> "If there are sentient beings who are legitimate sons of the Lord...."

[12]Cf. *Ratnagotravibhāga*, p. 34, ll.6-7:

> *tathāgatadharmakāya eva nityapāramitā sukhapāramitātmapāramitā śubhapāramitety uktam/*

> "Only the Dharma-Body of the Tathāgata is the perfection of eternity, the perfection of happiness, the perfection of self, and the perfection of purity."

[13]Cf. *Ratnagotravibhāga*, p. 31, ll.4-6:

> *ye bhagavan sattvās tathāgatadharmakāyam evaṁ paśyanti te samyak paśyanti/ ye samyak paśyanti te bhagavataḥ putrā aurasā iti vistaraḥ/*

> "O Lord, those living beings who see the Dharma-Body of the Tathāgata in this way, correctly see. Those who correctly see are the legitimate sons of the Lord, etc."

[14]Bodhiruci: 得仏法分 "attaining understanding of the Buddha and His Dharma."
Cf. 得法餘財 (Guṇabhadra)

[15]According to the *Kokuyaku-issaikyō* (*op. cit.*, p. 116, ft. 205), the perfection of wisdom refers to the four wisdoms (jñana) of the Buddha:

1) *adarśa-jñana* ("mirror-wisdom") - reflection of things as they are

2) *samatā-jñāna* ("wisdom of equality") - knowledge of the equality in nature of all things

3) *pratyavekṣanā-jñana* ("wisdom of intellectual mastery") - knowledge of dualistic thinking i.e. discrimination between subject and object

4) *kṛtyānuṣṭhāna-jñāna* ("wisdom of action") - wisdom to do what has to be done.

[16]*Pao-k'u*: 明二乘無学果智於一無作苦滅諦尚非境界。 (79b)

"This (sentence) explains that the resulting wisdom of the two vehicles who have no further studies does not belong to the realm of the one unconditioned noble truth of the extinction of suffering."

[17]*Pao-k'u*: 又擧羅漢之終果況羅漢之始因。

"Again, if this (statement) pertains to the result of Arhatship of course the beginning of Arhatship (is not of the realm of the unconditioned wisdom) also.

[Chapter 13 - "The inherently pure"]

"O Lord, the life-death cycle depends on the Tathāgatagarbha, because the Tathāgatagarbha is referred to as the (life-death cycle's) original[1] limit which is unknowable. O Lord, the 'Tathāgatagarbha' is referred to as the life-death cycle for a proper designation.[2] O Lord, the life-death cycle is the extinction of the senses and the subsequent arising of (new) inexperienced senses.[3] This is called the life-death cycle. O Lord, these two phenomena--life and death--are the Tathāgatagarbha. It is worldly convention to say 'there is life' and 'there is death.'[4] 'Death' is the extinction of one's senses. 'Life' is the arising of new senses.

The Tathāgatagarbha is neither life nor death.[5] The Tathāgatagarbha is separate from the conditioned. The Tathāgatagarbha is eternal and unchanging.[6] Therefore, the Tathāgatagarbha is the basis, the support, and foundation. O Lord, the Tathāgatagarbha is not separate, not severed, not liberated from, and not different from the inconceivable Buddha-dharmas.[7] O Lord, the basis, support, and foundation of conditioned phenomena which are severed from,[8] separate from, and different from (the Buddha-dharmas), (also) is the Tathāgatagarbha.

O Lord, if there were no Tathāgatagarbha, there would be no revulsion towards suffering, nor the aspiration to seek Nirvāṇa.[9] Why? Because the seven (mental) phenomena--the six consciousnesses and the knowledge of (accompanying) mental phenomena[10]--do not continue even momentarily and do not accept the impressions[11] of suffering, there cannot be revulsion for suffering nor the aspiration of seek Nirvāṇa.

The Tathāgatagarbha is without any prior limit, is non-arising, and is indestructible, accepting suffering, having revulsion towards suffering, and aspiring to Nirvāṇa. O Lord, the Tathāgatagarbha is not a substantial ego, nor a living being, nor 'fate,' nor a person. The Tathāgatagarbha is not a realm for living beings who have degenerated into the belief of a substantially-existent body or for those who have contrary views, or have minds which are bewildered by Emptiness.[12]

O Lord, the Tathāgatagarbha is the Womb of the dharmas, the Womb of the Dharma-Body, the transcendental Womb, and the inherently pure Womb.[13] This Tathāgatagarbha which is inherently pure is the inconceivable realm of the Tathāgata which has been contaminated by extrinsic defilements and other virulent defilements. Why? The good mind is momentary and not contaminated by defilements. The evil mind is also momentary but is not contaminated by defilements either. Defilements do not affect the mind. Then, how does the mind, which is unaffected by nature, become defiled? O Lord, there are defilements and there are defiled minds. The fact that there is defilement in a mind which is inherently pure is difficult to comprehend.[14] Only the Buddhas, the Lords, who have the eye of truth and the wisdom of truth, who are the sources of the Dharma and penetrate the Dharma, and who are the refuge of the True Dharma, can comprehend this truth."

When Queen Śrīmālā had explained the difficulties in comprehending (tbe inherently pure mind's defilement), she was questioned by the Buddha. The Buddha, with extreme joy, praised her: "Yes, it is so. The fact that there is defilement in a mind which is inherently pure is difficult to comprehend. There are two subjects which are difficult to completely comprehend. They are the mind which is inherently pure and the fact that this (same) mind has been contaminated by defilements. These two subjects can be heard by you and the Bodhisattva-Mahāsattvas who have the great Dharma. The others, viz. the Śrāvakas, can only believe through the Buddha's words."[15]

CHAPTER 13

NOTES

[1]Bodhiruci: 前際 --"prior limits."
Cf. 本際 (Guṇabhadra)

[2]Cf. *Ratnagotravibhāga* (*op. cit.*), p. 73, 1.6, which cites this quote:

> *Sati bhagavaṁs tathāgatagarbhe saṁsāra iti parikalpam asya vacanāyeti.*

> "When there is the Tathāgatagarbha, O Lord, it is discriminated as 'life-death cycle' for its name."

[3]Bodhiruci: 生死者諸受根滅無間相続未受根起。

> "The life-death cycle is the extinction of the senses in uninterrupted succession with the arising of new senses."

Cf. 生死者諸受根没次第不受根起。(Guṇabhadra)

[4]Bodhiruci: 於世俗法名為生死。"In the world the ordinary phenomena are called life and death."
Cf. 世間言説故有死有生。(Guṇabhadra)

[5]Bodhiruci adds: 不昇不墜 "...neither ascends nor descends."

[6]Bodhiruci: 常恒不壊 "...eternal and indestructible."
Cf. 常住不変 (Guṇabhadra)
Cf. *Ratnagotravibhāga*, pp. 45-46, ll. 20, 1-4:

> *lokavyavahāra eṣa bhagavan mṛta iti vā jāta iti vā/ mṛta iti bhagavann indriyoparodha eṣaḥ/ jāta iti bhagavan navānām indriyāṇāṁ prādurbhāva eṣa/ na punar bhagavaṁs tathāgatagarbho jāyate vā jīryati vā mriyate va cyavate votpadyate vā/ tat kasmād hetoḥ/ saṁskṛtalakṣaṇaviṣayavyativṛtto bhagavaṁs tathāgatagarbho nityo dhruvaḥ śivaḥ śāśvata iti/*

> "O Lord, 'what is dead' or 'what is living' are world conventions. 'What is dead' is the obstruction of the senses. 'What is living' is the appearance of new senses. However, the Tathāgatagarbha is never born, nor does it age, nor dies, nor passes away, nor arises. Why? The Tathāgatagarbha transcends the realm of the conditioned and is eternal, permanent, quiescent, and constant."

[7]Bodhiruci adds here: 與不離解脱智蔵

> "...and is not separate from the knowledge of liberation."

Cf. *Ratnagotravibhāga* (*op. cit.*, p. 73, ll.2-3) which cites this sentence:

> *Tasmād bhagavaṁs tathāgatagarbho niśraya ādhāraḥ pratiṣṭhā saṁbaddhānāṁ vinirbhāgānām amuktajñānānām asaṁskṛtānāṁ dharmāṇām/*

"Therefore, O Lord, the Tathāgatagarbha is the basis, support, and foundation for all the interconnected dharmas which are unconditioned, being the knowledge inseparable and indivisible (from the Tathāgatagarbha itself).

Saṁbaddhānām perhaps was construed by the Chinese translators as *saṁbuddhānām* since they have translated the phrase as *fo-fa* (佛法), "Buddha-dharmas" instead of "interconnected dharmas."

[8]Bodhiruci: 亦與外離不解脱智諸有為法依持建立。

"It also is the basis, support, and foundation for conditioned phenomena and is (not) separate from knowledge of non-liberation."

(Should be negative (外→不) before "separate" (離)).
Cf. 斷脱異外有為法 (Guṇabhadra)
Cf. *Ratnagotravibhāga* (*op. cit.*, p. 73, ll.3-5).

Asaṁbaddhānām api bhagavan vinirbhāgadharmāṇāṁ muktajñānānāṁ saṁskṛtānām dharmāṇām niśraya ādhāraḥ pratiṣṭhā tathāgatagarbha iti.

"The Tathāgatagarbha is also the basis, support, and foundation for all conditioned, non-interconnected dharmas which are knowledge separate and divided from (the Tathāgatagarbha itself)."

[9]Cf. *Ratnagotravibhāga*, p. 36, ll.1-2 which quotes the *Śrīmālādevī-sūtra* as follows:

Tathāgatagarbhaś ced bhagavan na syān na syād duhkhe 'pi nirvinna nirvāṇa icchā vā prārthanā vā pranidhirveti.

"If there were no Tathāgatagarbha, O Lord, there would also be no revulsion to suffering nor desire, prayer, or vow for Nirvāṇa."

[10]Guṇabhadra- 於此六識及心法智
Bodhiruci - 於此六識及以所知

The seventh mental phenomenon Guṇabhadra translates as "knowledge of mental dharmas" while Bodhiruci translates it as "mentals" (lit. "what is the object of knowledge").

Chi-tsang quotes one unidentified commentator who equates the six consciousnesses with the active consciousnesses and the seventh with mind in general when deluded and knowledge of the Dharma when enlightened. The eighth consciousness is the womb (*garbha*) consciousness or *alaya* which suggests that the Tathāgatagarbha is the eighth consciousness. 有人言六識者六是事識及心法智是第七識。迷時名心,解名法智第八名藏識是阿利耶。 (p. 83b)

Citing the *Laṅkāvatāra*, Chi-tsang gives an example of the fusion of *ālaya* with Tathāgatagarbha which had developed by his generation: 此如楞伽說六七非受苦樂。非涅槃因。藏識受苦樂是涅槃因。 (p. 83c)

> "Just as the *Laṅkāvatāra* states: 'The sixth and seventh consciousnesses do not receive (the impressions of) suffering nor are they the cause of Nirvāṇa. The womb-consciousness receives (the impressions of) suffering and is the cause for Nirvāṇa.'"

The denial of attributing the cause of defilement to the Tathāgatagarbha which nevertheless is the basis for both conditioned and unconditioned phenomena remains a paradox, inadequately explained by Chi-tsang: 若由仏性得種衆苦即是仏性令物受苦。此乃是同於魔性。何名仏性。答。此乃明有仏性衆生故得種衆苦。非是仏性令其種苦。亦明仏性衆生令其厭苦。非是仏性令其厭苦。

> "If one accepts the impressions of suffering because of the Buddha-nature, then the Buddha-nature causes things to suffer. This would be identical with the nature of the Evil One (Māra). How can one call this the Buddha-nature?"
>
> Answer: "This (sentence) illustrates that there is the acceptance of the impressions of suffering because of the living being who has the Buddha-nature. It is not true that the Buddha-nature causes the impressions of suffering. This sentence also illustrates that there is the revulsion to suffering because of the living being who has the Buddha-nature. It is not true that the Buddha-nature causes that revulsion to suffering." (p. 84a)

11 Bodhiruci: 不受衆苦 --"do not accept all suffering."
Guṇabhadra: 不種衆苦 --lit. "do not cause ('plant') suffering" which Chi-tsang glosses as 不得種衆苦 --"do not obtain the impressions of all suffering." (p. 84a)

12 Cf. *Ragnagotravibhāga*, p. 74, ll.5-6:

agocaro 'yaṁ bhagavaṁs tathāgatagarbhaḥ satkāyadṛṣṭipatitānāṁ viparyāsābhiratānāṁ śūnyatāvikṣiptacittānām iti/

"O Lord, the Tathāgatagarbha is not a realm for those who have fallen into the view of a real body, are contented with contrary views, or have minds bewildered by Emptiness."

13 Cf. *Ratnagotravibhāga*, p. 72-73, ll.16, 1:

yo 'yaṁ bhagavaṁs tathāgatagarbho lokottaragarbhaḥ prakṛtipariśuddhagarbha iti/

"O Lord, the Tathāgatagarbha is tbe transcendental Womb, the Womb which is inherently pure."

14 Cf. *Ratnagotravibhāga*, p. 15, ll.3-7:

kṣaṇikaṁ bhagavan kuśalaṁ cittam/ na kleśaiḥ saṁkliśyate/ kṣaṇikam akuśalaṁ cittam/ na saṁkliṣṭam eva taccittam kleśaiḥ/ na bhagavan kleśās taccittaṁ spraśanti/ katham atra bhagavann asparśanadharmi cittaṁ tamaḥkliṣṭaṁ bhavati/ asti ca bhagavann upakleśaḥ/ asty upakliṣṭaṁ cittam/ atha ca punar bhagavan prakṛtipariśuddhasya cittasyo 'pakleśārtho duṣprativedhyaḥ/

"O Lord, the good mind is momentary. It is not defiled by defilements. The evil mind is also momentary, and even that mind is not defiled by defilements. O Lord, defilements do not affect the mind. How then, does the mind, having an unaffected character, become defiled by mental darkness? O Lord, there is defilement and there is defiled mind. Moreover, the meaning of an inherently pure mind's defilements is difficult to comprehend."

[15]Cf. *Ratnagotravibhāga* (*op. cit.*, p. 22, ll.3-4)

Śeṣāṇāṁ devi sarvaśrāvakapratyekabuddhānāṁ tathāgataśraddhāgamaniyav evaitau dharmaviti.

"As for the others, viz. all the Śrāvakas and *Pratyekabuddhas, these two subjects will be obtained* only by faith in the Tathāgata."

[Chapter 14 - "The true sons (of the Tathāgata)"]

(The Buddha spoke:) "If my disciples comply with their (early stages of) faith and (subsequent) more fervent faith,[1] then they will attain the ultimate after completing their subsequent wisdom of the Dharma which is based upon the illumination of faith.[2] 'The subsequent wisdom of the Dharma' is the insight and fundamental investigation into the realms of sensation and consciousness,[3] insight into karmic retribution, insight into the eye of the Arhat,[4] insight into the happiness of the autonomy of mind and into the happiness of meditation (*dhyāna*), and insight into the supernatural powers[5] of the Arhats, Pratyeka-buddhas and the powerful Bodhisattvas.[6] When these five kinds of insight have been completed, even after my parinirvāṇa, in future generations, my disciples who have (the early stages of) faith, the (subsequent) more fervent faith, and the subsequent wisdom of the Dharma which is based upon the illumination of faith, will attain the ultimate even though their inherently pure minds become contaminated by defilements. The 'ultimate' is the cause for entering the path of Mahāyāna. Faith in the Tathāgata has great benefits. Do not slander my (Dharma's) profound meaning."[7]

Then Queen Śrīmālā spoke to the Buddha: "There are still remaining great benefits which I will explain, being subject to the Buddha's authority." The Buddha spoke: "Again, please explain." Queen Śrīmālā spoke to the Buddha saying: "The three kinds of good sons and daughters who, within the most profound meaning (of the Dharma), have separated themselves from injury (to the Dharma), produce great merits, entering the path of Mahāyāna. What are the three (kinds of good sons and daughters)? They are those good sons and daughters who:

1) develop their own wisdom of the most profound Dharma
2) develop the subsequent wisdom of the Dharma (which is based upon the illumination of faith), and
3) revere the Lord though they do not completely understand the most profound Dharma.

What is known only by the Buddhas is not our realm. These (above mentioned) are called the good sons and daughters who revere the Tathāgata. Only these are the good sons and daughters."

CHAPTER 14

NOTES

[1]*Pao-k'u*: "According to their (early stages of) faith" (隨信) refers to the ten stages of faith. (p. 87b).

"The (subsequent) more fervent faith" (信增上) refers to the faith produced in the ten stages of understanding. (p. 87b)

"The subsequent wisdom of the Dharma" (隨順法智) refers to the faith produced in the ten stages of practice and in the Bodhisattvabhūmi. (p. 87b)

[2]Bodhiruci omits 依明信已. However, he further modifies "the ultimate":

於此法中而得究竟 --"In this Dharma they will attain the ultimate."

[3]"The realms of sensation and consciousness" refer to the eighteen spheres (*dhātu*), viz. the six consciousnesses with their corresponding sense faculties and sense fields. (Cf. *Kokuyaku-issaikyō, op. cit.*, p. 117, #232). (*Pao-k'u*, p. 87c)

[4]"The eye of the Arhat," according to an unidentified commentator cited in Chi-tsang's *Pao-k'u* (有人), refers to the Arhat's residing in the stage of ignorance. (p. 88a)

[5]"The supernatural powers" are listed as five, six, or ten:

1. divine sight (*divya-cakṣus*)
2. divine hearing (*divya-śrotra*)
3. knowledge of others' minds (*paracitta-jñāna*)
4. knowledge and recollection of previous lives (*pūrvanivāsanusmṛti-jñāna*)
5. miraculous power (*ṛddhi*)
6. knowledge of the destruction of the passions (*āsrava-kṣaya-jñāna*)

(Cf. Har Dayal, *Bodhisattva Doctrine* (*op. cit.*, pp. 106-134)

7. manifesting many bodies or forms
8. ubiquitousness
9. power of bringing glory to one's domain
10. manifesting a body of transformation

These latter four powers are frequently subsumed under miraculous power (#5).

(Cf. Soothill, William, *A Dictionary of Chinese Buddhist Terms*, Ch'eng-wen Publishing Co. (reprint): Taipei, 1969, p. 365)

[6]Bodhiruci omits "the powerful Bodhisattvas."

[7]Bodhiruci: 汝今當知信如来者於甚深法不生誹謗

"You now should know and believe in the Tathāgata. Do not slander the most profound Dharma."

(Guṇabhadra)

[Chapter 15 - "Śrīmālā"]

(Śrīmālā spoke:) "All the remaining living beings who stubbornly cling to false teachings instead of to the most profound Dharma, turn their backs to the True Dharma, and habitually practice the corrupt ways of various heterodoxies. These corrupt ways must be subdued by the King's (i.e. Buddha's) powers and by the powers of the Divine Nāgas."

When Queen Śrīmālā and her attendants paid obeisance to the Buddha, the Buddha spoke: "Excellent, excellent, Queen Śrīmālā! In the most profound Dharma, protected by skillful means, subdue what is not the Dharma. Maintain well its correctness. You have already been very close to the 100,000,000,000 Buddhas and can explain this (Dharma's) meaning."

At that time the Lord emitted a most excellent light, radiating everywhere over the crowd. His body ascended into the sky, higher than seven Tāla trees. Walking in the sky, he returned to the kingdom of Śrāvastī. Then Queen Śrīmālā and her attendants together faced the Buddha and were transfixed by the sight of Him, not moving for even a moment. (The Buddha), having passed by their field of vision, caused them to be exalted. Each individual praised the Tathāgata's merits and was mindful of Him. The Buddha then re-entered the city. Turning towards King Mitrayaśas (Queen Śrīmālā's husband), He praised Mahāyāna. All the women of the city, seven years of age and older, were converted to Mahāyāna. King Mitrayaśas was also converted to Mahāyāna. All the men, seven years of age and older, were converted to Mahāyāna. Then all of the citizens of the state were turned towards Mahāyāna.[1]

Then the Lord entered the Jeta garden, spoke to the venerable Ananda, and called upon the king of heaven, Śakra. Śakra, along with his retinue, immediately arrived in the presence of the Buddha. Then the Lord turned towards the king of heaven, Śakra, and to the venerable Ananda and extensively explained this text (*sūtra*). Having explained it, he spoke to Lord Śakra saying: You should accept and read this sūtra, O Śakra (Kauśika). The good sons and daughters, in innumerable time periods as numerous as the sands of the Ganges, cultivate the practice of enlightenment and practice the six pāramitās. If these good sons and daughters learn and read this sūtra until its conclusion, their blessings will be immense.

How much more (advantageous) will it be for those who explain this text. Thus, O Kauśika (i.e. Śakra), you must read this sūtra on behalf of the thirty-three heavens, defining and extensively explaining it."

Then He spoke to Ananda: "You also must accept and read this sūtra. For the sake of the four orders (monks, nuns, laymen and laywomen), you must extensively explain this sūtra."

Then the king of heaven, Śakra, spoke to the Buddha saying: "O Lord, what is the name of this sūtra? How does one adhere (to its teaching)?"

The Buddha spoke to Lord Śakra. "This sūtra has immeasurable and limitless merits. All the Śrāvakas and Pratyeka Buddhas cannot, ultimately, have insight into (these merits) nor know them.[2] Kauśika, you should know all the great merits which are so subtle and profound in this sūtra. Today I shall, on your behalf, briefly explain its name. Listen well, listen well and remember this (text)."

Then, the king of heaven, Śakra, and the venerable Ananda spoke to the Buddha saying: "Excellent, O Lord! Yes, we will do as you have instructed."

The Buddha spoke: "This sūtra praises (in Chapter One) the supreme merits of the true doctrine of the Tathāgata. In this manner accept it (i.e. the *Śrīmālādevī-sūtra*). It explains (in Chapter Two) the ten inconceivable ordination vows. In this manner accept it. It explains (in Chapter Three) the great aspiration which embraces all aspirations. In this manner accept it. It explains (in Chapter Four) the inconceivable Acceptance of the True Dharma. In this manner accept it. It explains (in Chapter Five) the entrance into the One Vehicle. In this manner accept it. It explains (in Chapter Six) the unlimited noble truths. In this manner accept it. It explains (in Chapter Seven) the Tathāgatagarbha. In this manner accept it. It explains (in Chapter Eight) the Dharma-Body. In this manner accept it. It explains (in Chapter Nine) the underlying truth: the meaning of Emptiness. In this manner accept it. It explains (in Chapter Ten) the one (noble) truth. In this manner accept it. It explains (in Chapter Eleven) the one refuge which is eternal and quiescent. In this manner accept it. It explains (in Chapter Twelve) the contrary truths. In this manner accept it. It explains (in Chapter Thirteen) the inherently pure mind which is covered (by defilements). In this manner accept it. It explains (in Chapter Fourteen) the true sons of the Tathāgata. In this manner accept it. Teach the *Śrīmālādevī-siṁhanāda-sūtra*. In this manner accept it.

Again, O Kauśika, the explanations of this sūtra sever all doubts. Be steadfast in the complete meaning (of this text) and enter the path of the One Vehicle. O Kauśika, today preach the *Śrīmālādevī-siṁhanāda-sūtra*, which has been transmitted to you, until the Dharma is continued.[3] Accept, read, extensively define, and explain (this sūtra)."

Lord Śakra spoke to the Buddha saying: "Very well, O Lord, we will revere your holy teaching." Then, the king of heaven, Śakra, the venerable Ananda, and all the great assemblies of gods, Aśuras, and Gandharvas, among others, heard the Buddha's teaching and were joyful, then practicing (his teaching).[4]

The *Śrīmālādevī-siṁhanāda-mahopaya-vaipulya-sūtra*

CHAPTER 15

NOTES

[1] Bodhiruci: 國人民無不学者 --"then, the citizens of the state were not uneducated."
Cf. 向大乘 (Guṇabhadra)

[2] Bodhiruci: 一切聲聞獨覺力不能及。

"The power of all the Śrāvakas and Pratyeka Buddhas cannot compare with (the merits of this sūtra)."
Cf. 一切聲聞緣覺不能究竟觀察知見。 (Guṇabhadra)

[3] Bodhiruci adds: 於十方界開示演說 "in all directions, showing and extensively teaching (this sūtra)."

[4] Bodhiruci: 皆大歡喜信受奉行 "had great joy, believed, and practiced."
Cf. 歡喜奉行. (Guṇabhadra)

APPENDIX I
METHODOLOGY

I. Historical Investigation

There is a dearth of research on Tathāgatagarbha literature in Western languages. Until David Seyfort Ruegg's monumental work on the subject within the Indo-Tibetan tradition appeared in 1969,[1] no work on Tathāgatagarbha in its various evolutionary stages was available to the Western reader. E. Obermiller and Takasaki Jikidō, through their translations of the *Ratnagotravibhāga*,[2] also made available an important treatise on the Tathāgatagarbha doctrine in Mahāyāna Buddhism. Two Japanese scholars, Ui Hakuju and Katsumata Shunkyō, also explicated the development of Tathāgatagarbha from selected source materials, but these two works are accessible to a limited degree and only for a Japanese-reading student.

None of the above-mentioned scholars, however, attempted to hypothesize a cultural context in which the Tathāgatagarbha notion fermented. The limited resource materials available preclude any but the most tentative socio-historical analysis:

1) No Indian masters' works exist which are related to Tathagatagarbha sutras outside of the *Ratnagotravibhāga*, a work whose authorship is still in question.
2) No detailed evidence of exportation of Tathāgatagarbhan texts from India to China is available in the Chinese biographies of the major translators of these texts.
3) No accounts of translation activities of Tathāgatagarbha literature in Central Asian countries are available from the Chinese catalogues or biographies.
4) The various adaptations of the concept "the pure, luminous mind" by the eighteen sectarian Abhidharmist schools still remain almost entirely unknown.

Due to the above-mentioned deficiencies in terms of data, the geographical and historical context of Tathāgatagarbha literature was suggested from synthesizing the following evidence:

1) Delineation of all possible translations, whether extant or lost, listed in the catalogues.

2) An investigation into the biographies of the major Chinese translators, analyzing similarities in birthplace, travel routes, and dates in which translations occurred as well as the biographies of those who were alleged to have translated the specified texts but which are now lost.
3) Charting the places of origin for the transcription of manuscripts as well as the dates and social position of the scribe.
4) Reconstruction of the date of composition based upon the earliest possible translations catalogued and upon the oldest manuscript. The upper limit is then estimated by subtracting fifty to seventy-five years from the dates of translation and transcription in order to allow for the period of composition and dissemination of the text.
5) In order to estimate the lower limit for the date of composition, trace the specific key terms peculiar to the specified text in other literature through their evolutionary stages from the given period of translation back through past occurrences, noting differences in metaphors, symbolism, and emphasis in doctrine. Use indexes of major Buddhist literary works as an aid.
6) Note the first occurrences of the specific key terms within the given systematized body of literature as well as occurrences found in other literature prior to the former's systemization, if possible. This yields the lower limit for the date of composition.
7) Place these first occurrences of specific technical terms into their geographical context, if possible, from either available studies or historical accounts which demonstrate these terms were conducive to indigeneous beliefs and social conditions of the given region.
8) Trace the possible birthplaces and travel routes of major translators in order to judge congruency with the geographical location hypothesized in #7.
9) Reconstruct the social context of the text under study with relation to the hypothesized date and place of

composition based on a synthesis of the above evidence.

However, the hypothetical socio-historical context remains, at best, a tentative foundation upon which future studies may be based, especially in view of the fact that the transmission of Buddhist texts from one culture into another one presupposes the ability to limit factors peculiar to each culture, a task which is severely restricted at times due to the nature of the resource materials.

> ...the study of cultural transmissions includes the attempt to isolate factors in the result which have their parentage in the invaded culture from those whose parentage is in the invader. In the present state of our knowledge about the penetration of Buddhism into Chinese civilization, all conclusions are valuable more as hypotheses for further investigation than as factual judgments.[3]

II. Textual Investigation

Figure 4 illustrates the processes used for translation and textual analysis. With reference to the interpretation of both the technical terms and symbolic imagery of the text, a comparison of their usage with both other texts within the same trend of thought prior to its hypothesized composition and Buddhist texts prior to the theory being studied was undertaken. For practical reasons, texts outside the Buddhist tradition which may have been influential, were not utilized.

FIGURE 4 PROCESSES FOR TEXTUAL/ANALYSIS

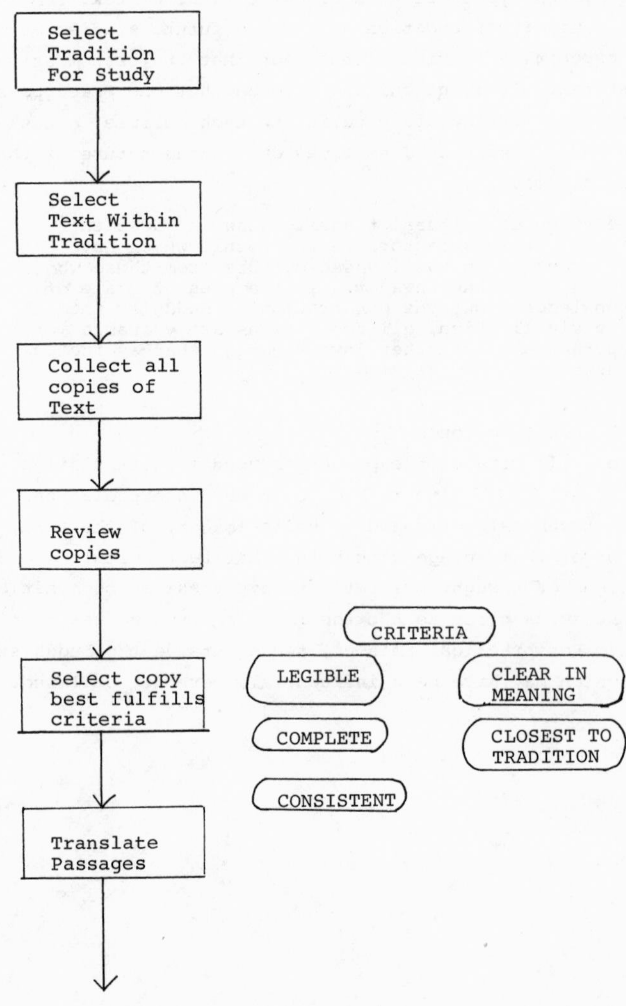

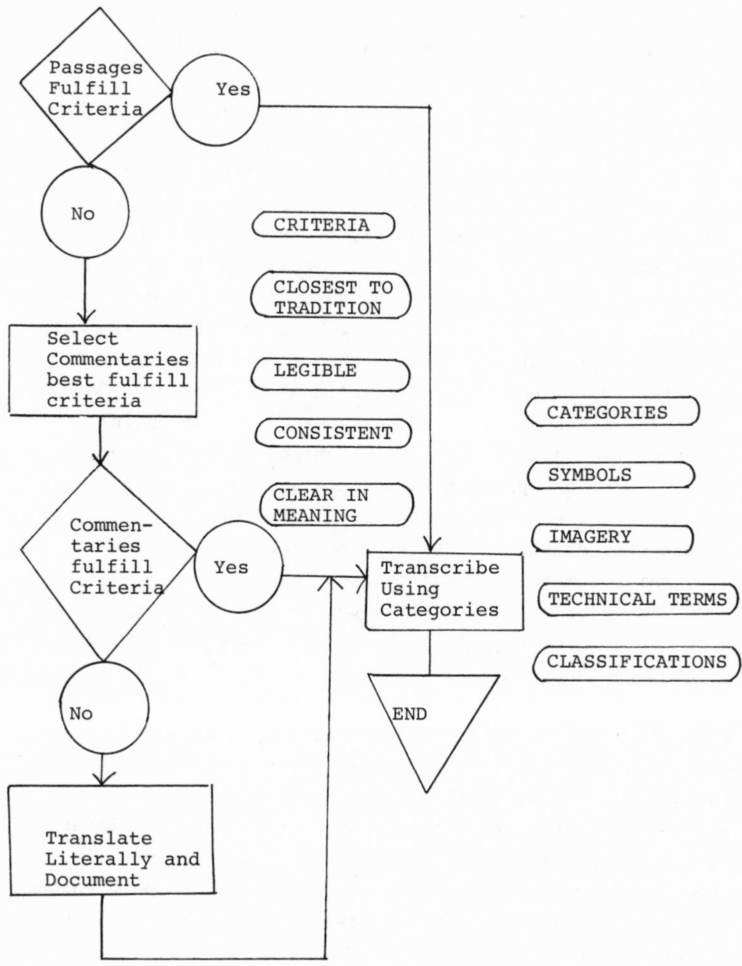
Passages Fulfill Criteria
Yes
No
CRITERIA
CLOSEST TO TRADITION
LEGIBLE
CONSISTENT
CLEAR IN MEANING
Select Commentaries best fulfill criteria
Commentaries fulfill Criteria
Yes
No
Translate Literally and Document
Transcribe Using Categories
END
CATEGORIES
SYMBOLS
IMAGERY
TECHNICAL TERMS
CLASSIFICATIONS

Technical terms were analyzed with due consideration given to two primary Chinese commentaries which enjoyed immense popularity and which are completely preserved, viz. the *Sheng-man ching pao-k'u* and the *Shōmangyō gisho* (*Sheng-man ching i-su*) with references made to the oldest extant commentary, the *Hsieh-chu sheng-man ching*. Whenever divergent interpretations occurred which were not easily reconcilable, the Sanskrit fragments would be selected only if the older Chinese recensions agreed with it, presupposing that the older Chinese recension and the Sanskrit text were, in those instances, faithful to the original text which is unfortunately no longer extant. In instances where no such agreement between the Sanskrit and older Chinese recensions occurred, the Sanskrit and both Chinese recensions were noted, either opting for the clearest recension in terms of meaning, based upon context, or, if no recension appeared to be outstandingly clear, selecting the older Chinese recension for the sake of continuity since it was used as the root text. The Tibetan recension was not used which limits the present study.

The major symbols applied to the theory under investigation were studied doctrinally in relation to their contribution to developing the principal tenets of the text and structurally as a literary unit which continued the tradition of the systemized body of literature. These symbols were investigated only with reference to prior texts within the same trend of thought which predate the investigated text's hypothetical composition. For practical reasons, there was no discussion of these symbols in relation to key texts representative of other Buddhist traditions which prefigured the incipience of Tathāgatagarbha thought nor in relation to other influential Indian philosophical texts which existed at that time.

Because of the transcultural nature of the study, selection of the culture which would be emphasized at a given time seemed at times arbitrary. However, for the purpose of hypothesizing the geographical and social context, the Indian culture was the subject of investigation since the Sanskrit text was known to have existed in China prior to the translation into Chinese. Stated otherwise, the text in question was known to have been translated from Sanskrit into Chinese and not vice versa.

For the purpose of textual investigation, Chinese sources were utilized because there are no Sanskrit commentaries extant although several allusions to a commentary by Vasubandhu are recorded. Consequently, the translation and interpretation of the text itself must be viewed within the Chinese Buddhist intellectual tradition and not from within the Indian tradition. Due to the absence of secondary references, i.e. commentaries and auto-commentaries, in Sanskrit and to the problem of methodology, no attempt was made to interpret the given text within its original Indian context.

Although the preceding discussion of the methodology used for this study is rudimentary, there is nevertheless a need for explicating and delineating the processes used for dating, placing, and analyzing Buddhist scriptures. By ignoring the need for making individual methodologies explicit, the development of a systematic and comprehensive schema for the study of Buddhism in particular and of religions in general will be hindered.

APPENDIX I

NOTES

[1]Ruegg, *La Théorie du Tathagatagarbha, op. cit.*

[2]Obermiller, *The Sublime Science, op. cit.*, and Takasaki, *A Study on the Ratnagotravibhāga, op. cit.*

[3]Robinson, Richard H., *Early Mādhyamika in India and China* (Madison: University of Wisconsin Press, 1967), p. 6.

APPENDIX II

BIBLIOGRAPHY

Abhisamayālaṁkārālokaprajñāpāramitāvyakhyā by Haribhadra, ed. by U. Wogihara (Tokyo: Toyo Bunka, 1934).

Adikaram, E. W. *Early History of Buddhism in Ceylon* (Ceylon: D. S. Puswella, 1946).

Akanuma Chizen. *Bukkyō kyōten shiron* (Nagoya: Hajinkaku shobō, 1939).

Akanuma Chizen. *The Comparative Catalogue of Chinese Āgamas and Pāli Nikāyas* (Nagoya: Hajinkaku shobō, 1929).

Bareau, André. *Les Sectes Bouddhiques du Petit Véhicule* (Saigon: École Francaise D'Extreme-Orient, 1955).

Bodhisattva-bhūmi: A Statement of Whole Course of the Bodhisattva, ed. by Unrai Wogihara (Tokyo: Sankibō Buddhist bookstore, 1971).

Bukkyō daijiten, ed. by Mochizuki Shinko (Tokyo: Sekai shoten kankō kyōkai, 1955-1960).

Bussho kaisetsu daijiten, Ono Masao (gen. ed.) (Tokyo: Daitō shuppansha, 1966).

Chaudhury, Binayendra Nath. *Buddhist Centres in Ancient India* (Calcutta: Sanskrit College, 1969).

Chen, Kenneth. *Buddhism in China: A Historical Survey* (Princeton: Princeton University Press, 1964).

Ch'eng wei-shih lun, tr. by Hsüan-tsang, T.v. 31, no. 1585, pp. 1-60.

Ch'u san-tsang chi chi, compiled by Seng-yu, T.2145, v. 55.

Cikshasamuccaya: A Compendium on Buddhist Teaching, ed. by Cecil Bendall (St. Petersburg: Imperial Academy of Sciences, 1897-1902), vol. I of Bibliotheca Buddhica, reprinted by *Indo-Iranian Journal* (The Hague: Mouton & Co., 1957).

Clark, Walter Eugene. *Two Lamaistic Pantheons* (New York: Paragon Book Reprint, 1965).

Conze, Edward. *Buddhism: Its Essence and Development* (New York: Harper Torchbooks, 1959). Reprinted from Bruno Cassirer Ltd. edition, 1951.

Conze, Edward. *Buddhist Thought in India* (London: George Allen and Unwin Ltd., 1961).

Conze, Edward (tr.). *The Perfection of Wisdom in Eight Thousand Slokas* (Calcutta: Asiatic Society, 1958).

Conze, Edward. *The Prajñāpāramitā Literature* (The Hague: Mounton & Co., 1960), Indo-Iranian Monographs, vol. VI.

Conze, Edward. *Vajracchedikā Prajñāpāramitā* (Roma: Serie Orientale Roma, 1957), v. XIII.

Daśabhūmikasūtra et Bodhisattvabhūmi, ed. by J. Rahder (Paris: Paul Guethner, 1926).

Dayal, Har. *The Bodhisattva Doctrine in Buddhist Sanskrit Literature* (Delhi: Motilal Banarsidass, 1970). Reprinted from London: Routledge & Kegan Paul Ltd., 1932.

Drekmeier, Charles. *Kingship and Community in Early India* (Stanford: Stanford University Press, 1962).

Dutt, Nalinaksha. *Aspects of Mahāyāna Buddhism and Its Relation to Hīnayāna* (London: Luzac and Co., 1930).

Edgerton, Franklin. *Buddhist Hybrid Sanskrit Grammar and Dictionary* (Delhi: Motilal Banarsidass, 1970).

Gopalachari, K. *Early History of the Andhra Country* (Madras: University of Madras, 1941).

Hsieh-chu sheng-man ching, T.v. 85, n. 2763, c. 500 A.D.; Stein no. 1649, 5858.

Jones, J. J. (tr.). *The Mahāvastu*, vol. I (London: Luzac & Co., 1949).

Kai-yüan shih chiao mo-lü, 20 ch., compiled by Chih-sheng, T.v. 55, no. 2154.

Kajiyama, Yuichi. "Hannyagyō" (Prajñā Literature) in *Nihon no Butten*, ed. by Takeuchi Yoshinori and Umehara Takeshi (Tokyo: Chūeikō ronsha, 1969).

Kao seng chuan, compiled by Hui-chao, T.v. 50, no. 2059.

The Kāśyapaparivarta: A Mahāyāna sūtra of the Ratnakūṭa Class, ed. by Baron A. von Staël-Holstein (Changhai, 1926).

Katsumata Shunkyō. *Bukkyō ni okeru shinshikisetsu no kenkyū* (Tokyo: Sankibō busshorin, 1969), (3rd. ed.)

Kegon shisō, ed. by Nakamura Hajime and Kawada Kumatarō (Tokyo: Hōzōkan, 1960).

Kokuyaku issaikyō, Ono Masao (gen. ed.) (Tokyo: Daitō shuppansha, 1958).

Lamotte, Étienne. *Histoire du Bouddhisme Indien* (Louvain: Institut Orientaliste, Université de Louvain, 1958).

Lamotte, Étienne. *La Traité de la grande vertu de sagesse* (*Mahāprajñāpāramitāśāstra*) (Louvain: Institut Orientaliste Bibliotheque de l'Université, 1966-67). v. I.

Lamotte, Étienne. *L'Enseignement de Vimalakīrti* (Louvain: Institut Orientaliste, 1962).

Laṅkāvatāra-sūtra, ed. by Nanjio Bunyiu (Kyoto: Otani University Press, 1956).

Li tai san-pao chi, 20 ch. compiled by Fei-chang, T.v.49, n. 2034.

Mahāyāna-sūtrālaṁkāra, ed. by Sylvain Lévi (Paris: 1907) (Shanghai reprint: 1940).

Majumdar, Ramesh Chandra. *Ancient India* (Delhi: Motilal Banarsidass, 1964).

Majumdar, Ramesh Chandra and Altekar, Anant Sadashiv (gen. ed.) *Vākaṭaka-Gupta Age* (Delhi: Motilal Banarsidass, 1960).

Mathews, R. H. *Mathews' Chinese-English Dictionary* (Cambridge: Harvard University Press, 1969).

Monier-Williams, Sir Monier. *A Sanskrit-English Dictionary* (Oxford: Clarendon Press, 1970).

Mūlamadhyamakakarikā, ed. by Louis de la Vallée Poussin (St. Petersburg, 1903).

Nakamura Hajime. *Shinbukkyō jiten* (Tokyo: Seishin shobō, 1972).

Nakamura Zuiryu. *Kukyō ichijō hōshōron no kenkyū* (Tokyo: Sankibō busshorin, 1972) (2nd ed.)

Nanjio Bunyiu. *A Catalogue of the Chinese Translation of the Buddhist Tripiṭaka* (Oxford: Clarendon Press, 1883) (Tokyo reprint 1930).

Nihon no Butten, ed. by Takeuchi Yoshinori and Umehara Takeshi (Tokyo: Chūeikō ronsha, 1969).

Nilakanta Śāstri, K.A. (ed.). *A Comprehensive History of India, vol. II: The Mauryas and Satavahanas* (Bombay: Orient Longmans, 1957).

Nilakanta Śāstri, K.A. *A History of South India from Prehistoric Times to the Fall of Vijayanagar* (London: Oxford University Press, 1955).

Obermiller, E. *History of Buddhism (Chos-hbyung) by Bu-ston* (Heidelberg, 1931). Reprinted by the Suzuki Research Foundation, 1965.

Obermiller, E. *The Sublime Science of the Great Vehicle to Salvation Being a Manual of Buddhist Monism* (Rome: Acta Orientalia, 1932). Shanghai reprint: 1940.

Panikkar, K. M. *A Survey of Indian History* (Bombay: Asia Publishing House, 1957). Reprinted from 3rd ed.

The Perfection of Wisdom in Eight Thousand Slokas, trans. by Edward Conze (Calcutta: Asiatic Society, 1958).

Pu tseng pu chien ching (*Anūnatvāpurṇatvanirdeśa*), T.v. 16, no. 668.

Radhakrishnan, Sarvepalli (gen. ed.). *The Cultural Heritage of India* (Calcutta: Ramakrishna Mission, Institute of Culture, 1937) (1st ed.), vol. I: *The Early Phases: Prehistoric, Vedic, and Upanisadic, Jaina and Buddhist.*

Ratnagotra-vibhāga-mahāyānottara-tantra-śāstra, ed. by E. H. Johnston (Patna: Bihar Society, 1950).

Robinson, Richard H. *Early Mādhyamika in India and China* (Madison: University of Wisconsin Press, 1967).

Robinson, Richard H. *The Buddhist Religion: A Historical Introduction* (Belmont, Calif.: Dickenson Publishing Company, Inc., 1970).

Ruegg, David Seyfort. *La Théorie du Tathāgatagarbha et du Gotra: Études sur la Sotériologie et la Gnoséologie du Boudhisme* (Paris: École Francaise D'Extreme-Orient, 1969).

Sangharakshita, Bhikshu. *A Survey of Buddhism* (Bangalore: M. Narayan, Indian Institute of World Culture, 1959) (2nd ed.).

Sanron gengi kennyū shō by Chūkan, T.v. 70, no. 2300.

Sheng-man ching i-chi by Hui-yüan, T.v. 85, no. 2761, pp. 253-261; Pelliot no. 2091 and 3308.

Sheng-man ching pao-k'u by Chi-tsang, T.v. 37, no. 1744, pp. 1-91.

Sheng-man ching shu-chi by K'uei-chi (632-682) by T'ang, *Manji zoku-zōkyō*, no. 1-30-4.

Sheng-man fu-jen hui, trans. by Bodhiruci, T.v. 11, no. 310, pp. 672-677.

Sheng-man i chi, Hui chang yun (?), T.v. 85, no. 2761; Stein no. 2660; copied in 504 (N. Wei).

Sheng-man shih-tzu-hou i-ch'eng ta-fang-pien fang-kuang ching, trans. by Guṇabhadra, T.v. 12, no. 353, pp. 217-223; Stein no. 2526, 992.

Shinbutten kaidai jiten, ed. by Nakamura Hajime and Hirakawa Akira (Tokyo: Shunjūsha, 1966).

Shōmangyō gisho, attributed to Prince Shōtoku, T.v. 56, no. 2185.

Shōmangyō shoshō genki by Gyōnen (1240-1321), *Dainihon bukkyō zensho*, no. 4.

Soothill, William. *A Dictionary of Chinese Buddhist Terms* (Taipei: Ch'eng-wen Publishing Co., reprint, 1969).

Sung kao seng chuan, 30 *ch.*, compiled by Chin-lun and Tsan-ning, T.v. 50, no. 2061.

Ta-fang-huang ju-lai-tsang ching, trans. by Amogha, T.v. 16, no. 667, pp. 460-466.

Ta-fang-teng ju-lai-tsang ching, trans. by Buddhabhadra, T.v. 16, no. 666, pp. 457-460.

Takasaki, Jikido. *A Study on the Ratnagotravibhāga (Uttaratantra): Being a Treatise on the Tathāgatagarbha Theory of Mahāyāna Buddhism* (Rome: Series Orientale Rome XXIII, 1966).

Tokiwa Daijō. *Gokan yori Sō Sei ni itaru yakkyō sōroku* (Tokyo: Tōhō bunka gakuin tōkyō kenkyūsho, 1938).

Tsukinowa Kenryū. *Shōmangyō hōgatsu dōji mombōgyō* (Kyoto: Kōkyō shoin, 1940).

Ui Hakuju. *Bukkyō jiten* (Tokyo: Daitō shuppansha, 1971).

Ui Hakuju. *Bukkyō kyōtenshi* (Tokyo: Tōsei shuppansha, 1957).

Ui Hakuju. *Hōshōron Kenkyū* (Tokyo: Iwanami shoten, 1959).

Warder, A. K. *Indian Buddhism* (Delhi: Motilal Banarsidass, 1970).

Winternitz, Maurice. *A History of Indian Literature* (Calcutta: University of Calcutta, 1933), vol. II: *Buddhist and Jaina Literature*.

Periodicals

Frauwallner, Erich. "Landmarks in the History of Indian Logic," *Wiener Zeitschrift für die Kunde Süd-und Ostaseins*, V, 1961.

Fujieda Akira. "Hokucho ni okeru Shōmangyō no tenshō," *Tōhō gakuhō* (Journal of the Institute of Humanities) (Kyoto: Jimbun kagaku kenkyūsho, 1973).

Hattori Masaaki. "Busshoron no ichi-kōsatsu," *Bukkyōshigaku*, IV, 1955.

Kagawa Takao. "Shōmangyō ni okeru bonnōsetsu no seiritsu," in Professor Etani's commemorative volume of *Jōdokyō no shisō to bunka* (Kyoto: Bukkyō University, 1973).

Kajiyama Yuichi. "Bhāvaviveka, Sthiramati, and Dharmapāla," *Beiträge zur Geistesgeschichte Indiens Festschrift für Erich Frauwallner*, XII-XIII, 1968-1969.

Koizumi Enjun. "Shōman gisho hongi," *Shōtoku taishi kenkyū*, V, 1973 (Osaka: Shitennōji Joshi Daigaku).

Nagao Gadjin, "On the Theory of the Buddha-Body (Buddha-kāya)," *Eastern Buddhist*, VI, no. 1, May 1973 (Kyoto: Otani University).

Takasaki Jikidō. "Fuzō fugengyō no Nyoraizōsetsu," *Komazawa daigaku bukkyō gakubu kenkyū kiyō*, XXIII, March 1965.

Takasaki Jikidō. "Nyoraizō shisō ni okeru shōmangyō no chii," *Shōmangyō gisho ronshu*, II, 1965 (Tokyo: Nihon bukkyō genryū kenkyū kiyō).